EAST AFRICA

An Introductory History

2nd and Revised Edition

Robert M. Maxon

West Virginia University Press
1994

Contents

iii

Maps

Preface

East Africa has a long and rich history which extends back, by most accounts, to the origins of man. This volume offers a history of the region from the Stone Age to the 1980s. Although the modern nations East Africa comprises—Kenya, Tanzania, and Uganda—did not exist in their present shape before the twentieth century, this work examines their history country by country. With the exception of the first three chapters, therefore, separate accounts are given of developments within the three mainland territories and, during the colonial period, within the offshore islands of Zanzibar and Pemba.

The book falls into two roughly equal parts. The first seven chapters deal with the pre-colonial history of East Africa, stretching from earliest times to the 1890s. Because of (among other things) a lack of written sources for most of the interior before the nineteenth century, the dates used for dividing the early chapters are necessarily arbitrary. Chapter 3 focuses exclusively on the coast and Chapters 4 and 5 focus on the interior; this approach is in line with most East African historiography, which sees the coast and the interior as having little common experience prior to the nineteenth century.

These initial chapters focus on the movement of peoples and the development of the political, economic, and social systems that came to characterize them. A major thrust of the volume is to describe how the region's major social formations, often termed "tribes" or ethnic groups, came to occupy the positions they did by the 1890s. This is a story of migration and movement of peoples and their interaction with other groups. As sketched out here, East African social formations come to reflect considerable diversity in language, culture, and economic systems. The same diversity characterizes the region's political formations. Some parts of East Africa experienced the development of centralized states ruled by monarchs. Historians have more information about these states, and relatively greater detail is provided here about their historical development than that of political formations ruled by chiefs and by councils of elders.

Beginning in the nineteenth century, East Africa experienced increasing external influences which world culminate with the European "scramble" for the region. Most important was the commercial penetration of this part of the continent by Europe. As the nineteenth century wore on, European capitalism sought sources of raw materials and markets there. These increasing trade relations, together with humanitarian motives, opened the door for the takeover of East Africa by Britain and Germany, as detailed in Chapters 6 and 7.

Chapters 8-11 constitute the second half of the book. The first three of these detail the imposition and functioning of colonial rule beginning in the 1890s. Though relatively brief, the colonial interlude has left a tremendous legacy. Patterns of political authoritarianism and economic dependency were set which have not been decisively altered by the East African states' achievement of independence.

Chapter 11 examines the history of the independent East African states from the 1960s to the 1990s.

In dealing with pre-colonial history in Chapters 4 and 5, the term Tanzania is used to refer to the mainland area of that nation. In Chapter 8 the term German East Africa reflects the fact that this nation fell under German rule from the 1890s to the end of World War I. In Chapters 9 and 10, the term Tanganyika is used since this was the name the British gave the territory when they took control. At the risk of confusion these different terms have been adopted to reflect the terminology in use at the time.

The spelling of place names and the names of peoples and languages is in accordance with current usage. For most ethnic groups, the prefix has been dropped for the sake of convenience and clarity (e.g., Ganda rather than Baganda). The classification and spelling of linguistic terms follows, for the most part, the lead of C. Ehret, D. Nurse, and G. Philipson. Spellings of ethnic names do not always match the linguistic terminology. Charts are provided in Chapters 2 and 4 to assist the reader in recognizing the relationships between various language groupings.

This narrative of East Africa's past could not have been completed without the assistance of many more individuals than can be briefly recognized here. Thanks must particularly go to John Indakwa of the University of Houston who helped convince me to undertake the project; also to E. A. Atieno Odhiambo of Nairobi University and W. R. Ochieng of Kenyatta College for sharing ideas and materials during the writing of the initial draft. John Rowe of Northwestern University and Cynthia Brantley of the University of California at Davis read the manuscript and their comments were of the greatest assistance in giving it its final shape. Maps for the volume were prepared by Ken Martis and Alison Hanham of West Virginia University. The late Robert Munn, first director of the West Virginia University Press, deserves special thanks for his encouragement and assistance.

Chapter 1

East African Geography

THE PORTION OF THE CONTINENT known as East Africa comprises the present countries of Kenya, Uganda, and Tanzania (the mainland plus the islands of Zanzibar and Pemba). This region is extremely varied in its topography, climate, and vegetation. It includes the humid coastal fringe and the snow capped peaks of Kilimanjaro and Kenya, the lush green shores of Lake Victoria and the arid northeast of Kenya, the imposing escarpments associated with the Rift Valley, and the seemingly endless sweep of the Serengeti plain. Straddling the equator, East Africa is made up of an area of almost 679,000 square miles. Its "natural" boundaries are the balmy shore of the Indian Ocean on the east, the Ruvuma River on the south, and the majestic western Rift Valley and its series of highlands on the west. The generally drier northern frontier of the region lacks a clear natural boundary.

Topography

Most of East Africa consists of a series of plateaus or plateau-like surfaces of diverse shapes and heights. These plateaus, ranging in height from about 1,200 feet above sea level to more than 10,000 feet, have been formed as a result of various processes including continental uplift, faulting, volcanic activity, and erosion. The fact that most of East Africa is clearly marked off as a highland region has an important impact on climate and vegetation patterns.

Perhaps the most effective way to gain acquaintance with East Africa's topography is to begin an imaginary sweep of the eye over the region beginning at the coast. East Africa lacks an extensive coastal plain. The plain is especially narrow from the Tana River delta in Kenya to the south of Dar es Salaam in Tanzania. To the north and south of this, the coastal plain widens somewhat.

West of the coastal plain, the plateau begins, rising gradually and imperceptibly to an elevation of about 3,000 feet above sea level. This eastern plateau is one of the lowest in the region. It is narrowest immediately to the west of Tanga on the northern Tanzanian coast, but it widens to the north and south. To the north it includes much of northern Kenya, and to the south of Morogoro it widens to include the valleys of the Great Ruaha and Kilombero rivers.

Moving further into the interior, we encounter the central plateau which differs only slightly from that further east. This plateau includes much of the interior of Uganda and Tanzania as well as Lake Victoria. It ranges in elevation from 3,000 to 4,500 feet above sea level, but is slightly higher in some places. Toward northern Uganda the plateau gradually decreases in height.

Significantly higher in elevation than the interior plateaus are the highland regions found in central Kenya, northern and southern Tanzania, and southwestern Uganda. These features, many formed as a result of volcanic activity, are clearly identifiable as they rise as high as 19,000 feet above sea level at the peak of Mount Kilimanjaro. The most extensive highlands are those of central Kenya. They are actually chopped in two by the eastern branch of the Rift Valley, leaving the Aberdare range to the east and the Mau to the west.

The eastern branch of the Rift Valley is perhaps the most distinguishable topographical feature of the entire region. The Rift Valley was formed as a result of subsidence between opposing parallel cliffs produced by an earth fracture. Characterized by remarkable variations in elevation within a few hundred miles, it stretches as a broad trough through central Kenya at a width of between twenty and forty miles. The valley floor rises from an elevation of 1,200 feet above sea level at Lake Turkana in the north to approximately 6,000 feet at Nakuru in central Kenya, only to fall under 2,000 feet near the Kenya-Tanzania border.

As one moves to the west of the region, the western branch of the Rift Valley, extending from Lake Malawi up through Lake Tanganyika to Lake Albert presents a striking picture. The valley is very deep; Lake Tanganyika is the second deepest lake in the world. The adjacent Ruwenzori mountains in Uganda form the most substantial range in all of East Africa.

The floors of both the eastern and western Rift Valleys are dotted by several extinct volcanoes and many lakes. The eastern rift is studded with saline lakes which are quite shallow. Among these are Lakes Turkana, Baringo, Nakuru, Elementeita, Naivasha, Magadi, Natron, and Eyasi. The western Rift Valley is occupied by fewer but more imposing

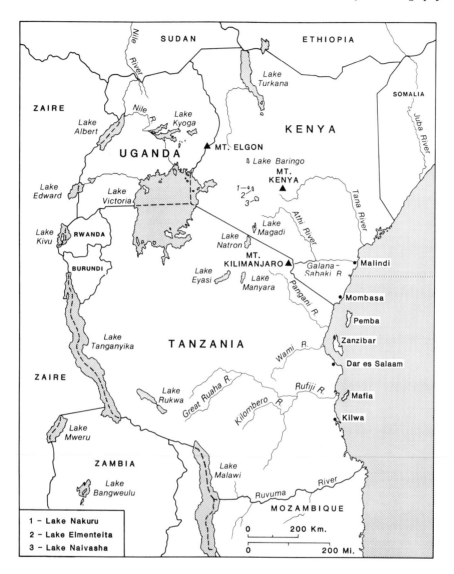

Map 1. Main Physical Features of East Africa.

lakes. Among these are Lakes Tanganyika, Albert, Kivu, and Edward.

Lake Victoria, the second largest fresh water body in the world, lies within a depression between the two branches of the Rift Valley. The lake is extremely broad, stretching as far as the eye can see. Lake Victoria seems to have been formed by earth movements which blocked an old drainage system to the west. Most lands adjacent to the lake receive more than adequate rainfall, and the area surrounding Lake Victoria, in contrast to the lake regions of the eastern Rift Valley, have historically been quite heavily populated. The area lying between Lake Victoria and Lakes Tanganyika, Kivu, Edward, and Albert to the west and Lake Kyoga to the north is often referred as the great lakes or interlacustrine region.

Lake Victoria forms one of the sources of Africa's longest river, the Nile. Winding its way north, the Nile passes through Lakes Kyoga and Albert before leaving East Africa. Most of East Africa's other major rivers flow east into the Indian Ocean. These include the Ruvuma, Rufiji, Wami, Pangani, Galana-Sabakai, and the Tana. All have well developed alluvial sections of seasonally swampy ground. The Rufiji, Wami, and Tana have large deltas in their lower courses, and the complexity of these channels has limited their use as avenues of communication. Some rivers are intersected by waterfalls and rapids as a result of the rising plateau to the west of the coast, and the estuaries of other rivers are blocked by sand bars. These factors have limited the utility of the eastward flowing rivers as highways leading from the coast to the interior.

Climate

Just as with topography and relief, the climate of East Africa is characterized by wide variations. Undoubtedly the climatic factor of greatest significance is rainfall. Rainfall patterns in East Africa tend to be uneven. Some areas, for example the coast and the great lakes region, receive plentiful rainfall, but others, such as the northeast of Kenya, receive relatively little moisture from the skies. Variations are experienced from year to year in the amount of rain and in the time that it falls. Nearly two-thirds of the region suffers an annual drought of six months or more. Less than 15 percent of Kenya, for example, receives a reliable 30 inches of rainfall per year. This means that much of the land cannot be effectively used for agriculture.

A major factor in bringing rainfall to East Africa are the so called South-East Trade Winds, or South-East Monsoon. These moisture-laden winds blow over the Indian Ocean and reach East Africa from a southeasterly direction beginning in April. The winds blow steadily, reaching peak force in July. From November to March, the main winds affecting East Africa are the North-East Trade Winds, or North-East

Monsoon. These blow from the northeast and normally consist of masses of dry air.

The alternation of these wind systems has had an important influence on travel in the Indian Ocean for many centuries. The North-East Monsoon winds facilitated travel from Arabia, the Persian Gulf, and India to the East African coast in small sailing ships (dhows). The South-East Monsoon winds, on the other hand, provided a relatively easy means of returning to those northern regions.

Within East Africa several rainfall patterns may be noted. For simplicity's sake, they may be grouped into two major types. The first is characterized by two periods of heavy rainfall, usually termed rainy seasons, separated from one another by times of very little rainfall, or dry seasons. In central Kenya north of Nairobi, for example, rainfall is normally concentrated in the March to May period and again in the months of October to December. A similar pattern is experienced in the lands around Lake Victoria and for a considerable portion of the East African coast. Such a pattern supports two growing seasons.

The second type has only a single wet and a single dry season. For much of Tanzania, rain falls in the period November to March while the rest of the year is relatively dry. Northern Uganda, however, experiences its main dry period during these months. An exception to these two major types may be seen in most of northern Kenya, which receives little rainfall at all in most years.

Inland water bodies and relief have a significant influence on the amount of rainfall received in various parts of East Africa. Highland areas are among the best watered in the region. This is particularly the case in the lands surrounding the highest peaks, Mounts Elgon, Kenya, and Kilimanjaro. The considerable surface area of Lake Victoria also has a positive effect on rainfall patterns. The areas near the lake shore are among the best watered in East Africa.

It must be emphasized, however, that the overall rainfall picture for East Africa is normally not good. In addition to the general scarcity of precipitation over the region as a whole, rainfall reliability is generally not satisfactory in terms of total amount and time of arrival. Further-more, the torrential character of the rains, normally concentrated in only a part of the day, tends to make for high loss of water through run-off. The generally high evaporation rate in East Africa further reduces the value of rainfall for farming in some areas.

Temperature is another important element of East Africa's climate. Mean annual maximum and minimum temperatures are closely con-nected to altitude. Temperatures at the coast are generally sultry and humidity is high. Mombasa's mean annual temperature, for example, is 26.3° C with little variation throughout the year. The mean diurnal range in temperature at the coast is also quite small. As one moves inland to the plateau, on the other hand, mean annual temperature drops, humidity is greatly reduced, and the dirurnal range is greater. Nairobi's mean annual temperature is 19.1° C, and higher elevations experience even lower temperatures. There, even on the equator, a temperate environment prevails.

Vegetation and Soil

Climate has a major impact on the vegetation of East Africa, and the vegetation of the region parallels the rainfall patterns. Vegetation types vary over a wide range from arid deserts to steamy rainforests and from the coastal swamps to temperate mountain peaks.

Areas of forest vegetation are relatively small in extent in East Africa in recent times if the term forest is understood as a closed stand of high trees which form a dense canopy inhibiting grass growth. Such forests, associated with heavy rainfall, may be found in some mountainous regions, particularly in Kenya, and in wetter lowland areas. Many contain evergreen trees, but a number of semi-deciduous trees also typify these regions. Tropical rainforest is absent from East Africa today except for a few remnant stands; though such heavy vegetation may have existed in the past, some 2,000 years of agricultural pursuits have led to the clearing of forest.

A more extensive vegetation type in East Africa is woodland, which consists of trees associated with a ground vegetation of grasses mixed with shrubby plants. Miombo woodlands are one of the largest vegetation types in East Africa; these correspond closely to those parts of the region which experience a single rainy season and a long dry season such as much of southwest and southeast Tanzania.

Another major vegetation type is savannah, a term used to refer to an area of tall grass mixed with trees and shrubs. Where not grazed, the grass cover normally reaches height in excess of thirty inches. The major East African type of savannah is typified by small trees associated with grasslands. This type of mixed vegetation characterizes much of Uganda, portions of western Kenya, and northwestern Tanzania. Some of these savannah regions show clear evidence of having been derived from an original forest cover as a result of human occupation.

Considerable portions of East Africa are covered by what may be termed a bushland and thicket type of vegetation. These areas are covered by small bushy trees together with lesser bushes and shrubs. The most extensive bushlands occupy semi-arid regions, and the vegetation is often thorny trees. This type of vegetation is found in northern Kenya and a smaller portion of northeastern Uganda. It forms a broad belt

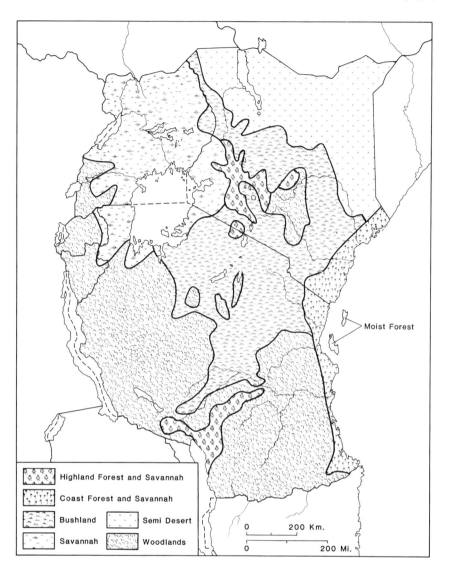

Map 2. Simplified Vegetation Patterns of East Africa.

separating the Kenya coast from the higher plateau. The Swahili name nyika (wilderness) for the belt gives a good indication of its rough, dry environment. Bushland also characterizes portions of north-central Tanzania.

With but few exceptions, semi-desert vegetation is confined to the northern portions of Kenya. In these areas the arid environment typically produces bare ground except when rainfall permits a sparse growth of tufts of grass or widely spread bushes and dwarf shrubs. Such semi-desert vegetation stretches from west of Lake Turkana to the east in a southerly arc.

At certain points on the coast, by contrast, there are zones of swamp vegetation in permanently wet or flooded areas. Often associated with these areas are mangrove trees. Although not extensive in area, these wetlands have been an important source of timber for use at and export from the coast.

Like climate and vegetation, the soils of East Africa are complex and varied. It is difficult indeed to give an accurate picture for the whole of such a large area. In general, however, East African soils are poor and fragile. Soil erosion has long been a powerful factor. The effect of heavy tropical downpours is particularly evident in the leaching process by which a great deal of water passing through the soil washes out and dissolves minerals and plant food. East African soils are often red in color because of the dominance of iron oxide, which is not leached out. Some of the best soils in East Africa, on the other hand, tend to be those formed as a result of volcanic activity.

Often as significant as the soils are the minerals found in them. In this regard, East Africa has not been as blessed with precious metals as some other parts of the African continent. Within East Africa, Kenya has major deposits of soda at Lake Magadi. Only small deposits of gold and copper have been worked, but diatomite, quartz, and limestone have been more extensively exploited. The major minerals worked in Uganda have been copper and cobalt. In Tanzania diamonds have been the most important mineral exported in recent times. Deposits of gold, silver, copper, and tin also have been worked. The existence of more than 300 million tons of coal has been proved in southern Tanzania, but because of poor communications little has yet been done to exploit this resource. Petroleum surveys have been conducted in selected areas of all three countries, but extensive oil producing strata have not been discovered.

If the richness of East Africa's natural resources is not found concentrated in huge deposits of mineral wealth, it may be discovered in the diversity and natural beauty of the region. From snow-capped peaks to verdant grasslands, from bleak deserts to the striking escarpments associated with the interior plateaus, East Africa presents an attractive and indeed breathtaking spectacle to those who have made the region their home. To the countless generations of humans who have inhabited the region over numerous millennia, East Africa has proved a challenging, yet alluring, home which has not failed to draw the keen interest of outsiders, from the Bantu-speaking farmers of the first millennium B.C. to the twentieth-century European tourists.

Chapter 2

The Peopling of East Africa to c. 1000 A.D.

THE EARLIEST HISTORY OF EAST AFRICA can only be broadly outlined here. The period of time covered by this chapter is vast; knowledge of the millennia which make up the period is sketchy and presents a challenge for the historian. Most of the information known about man's history in the region during this period, which encompasses the Stone Age and the Early Iron Age, comes from archaeology; for the Early Iron Age, linguistics also provides the historian with important insights.

During the Early Iron Age, which began slightly before the Christian era in portions of East Africa, the ancestors of many of the present day inhabitants entered the region, bringing with them a knowledge of food production and/or iron working (for some peoples the latter was adopted somewhat later than the former). The newcomers, who included Bantu-speaking and Nilotic-speaking peoples, interacted and mixed with the groups populating the regions in the final period of the Stone Age and with each other over the span of the next several centuries. This interaction went some way toward producing the social formations which would characterize East Africa in this millennium.

Archaeological research has demonstrated that East Africa was the site of widespread Stone Age hunting and gathering populations and that it was an especially important region for the evolution of man. During the past quarter century, an increasingly complete picture of early hominid fossil remains, unearthed by archaeologists in the region, has provided significant insights into the process by which hominids developed greater brain size, a bipedal mode of locomotion, and hands adapted to tool making.

By far the most important source of information about early man is the Olduvai Gorge site in northern Tanzania. Here, thanks to the pioneering and painstaking efforts of the late Dr. L. S. B. Leakey and his family, a series of five beds have been identified on the walls of a canyon which portray a geological sequence extending back more than two million years. This was a well-watered area with a lake nearby and a plain that was full of animals, among them a number of early hominids. Important hominid fossil remains have been recovered as well as some of the oldest evidence of stone tools, the pebble tools found in the lowest level—and therefore oldest—Bed 1. Since the Olduvai region has experienced volcanic eruptions, dates for archaeological finds can be obtained using the potassium argon dating technique. The pebble tools found at Olduvai have been dated to about two million years ago.

The pebbles found in Bed 1 at Olduvai, usually referred to by the type name Oldowan, represent what most scholars feel was the initial type of tool used by early hominids. Three factors support the identification of these small stones as tools. The stones exhibit a regular pattern of flaking which indicates they have been intentionally altered. They were found associated with large numbers of small animals' bones which had been fractured, evidently by the pebble tools, to extract the marrow. And finally, the lake deposits at Olduvai are comparatively stoneless, so that any significant number of stones found in the area must have been brought in to serve as tools. More recent discoveries at the Koobi Fora site, east of Lake Turkana in Kenya, indicate a pebble tool complex known as Karari dating to more than two and a half million years ago, even older than Olduvai.

Olduvai and Koubi Fora are the major sites in East Africa where evidence of Oldowan type tools have been discovered, but the larger, more complex tools known as hand axes (Acheulean tools), which first came into use in East-Africa about one million years ago, are found at archaeological sites throughout the region. Starting with these hand-sized implements, we can for convenience's sake look at the Stone Age as a sequence of three periods, Early, Middle, and Late, with divisions based on changes that occurred in the tools used by early man and in his mode of living. As might be expected, the progression is from the simple to the more complex.

Early Stone Age

Numerous hand axe sites in East and Central Africa have been investigated by archaeologists, and they permit an understanding of how the hominids who made and used them lived. The hand axe was not of course the only type of tool employed during the Early Stone Age.

Oldowan tools continued to be used well into the period, and by its end, scrapers, cleavers, knives, and- throwing stones were utilized. Wooden tools may have been used as well, but these would have decayed long ago. In this period, as in the Middle and Late Stone Ages, man obtained his food from his environment rather than by producing it himself. The makers of Acheulean tools lived by gathering wild vegetable foods, hunting wild animals (perhaps also fishing), and scavenging dead fauna. The stone tools were utilized to skin and carve up animal carcasses, break bones, and pulverize plants.

In the Early Stone Age hominids undoubtedly lived in relatively small hunting bands near bodies of water such as lakes and streams. Moving with seasonal changes, they kept their living sites in open areas. It appears that few of the hunter-gatherers of this period lived in forested or heavily wooded areas.

Middle Stone Age

The transition to the Middle Stone Age in East Africa is marked by a change in the type of tools used and in the life style practiced by early man. These changes seem to have begun in most parts of East Africa and adjacent regions at least 100,000 years ago and possibly as early as 125,000 years ago. Tools became more specialized as well as generally smaller and thinner, reflecting an increased mastery of the environment. There were tools for pounding roots and working wood as well as a large number of small stone tools that may have been used to make rope and string from animal hide. Tools from this time show considerable local variation.

Fire was systematically in use by this period, and it may well have been harnessed in the Early Stone Age. Man's control of fire made possible many dramatic improvements and alterations in the life style of the Stone Age. He could warm himself, cook, and use it in the extraction of poisons and gums. Fire enabled him to live in caves and rock shelters. Fire was of particular importance in hunting. The harnessing of fire thus had a revolutionary impact, second only to the making of tools.

Despite regional variations, two main cultural traditions can be distinguished in East Africa during the Middle Stone Age, the first clear evidence of the diversity that has characterized the region throughout its history. These two traditions are distinguished by the tool types associated with each and the different environments in which the tools were used. The Sangoan—and its successor, the Lupemban—is associated with the better-watered regions having more vegetation, such as in the areas adjacent to Lakes Tanganyika and Victoria. Sangoan tools were especially suited for wood working and related activities, and included

13

axes, chisels, and adzes.

Tool types associated with more open, less wooded regions are known as Fauresmith and Stillbay. Many of these tools are smaller and thinner than those of the Sangoan-Lupemban type, the result of having been made from stone flakes rather than from the core or original piece of stone. The flakes could be worked and refined after being struck off from the core to form scrapers, cutting tools, and spear points. Those practicing Stillbay industries undoubtedly lived more by hunting and had a less vegetarian diet than the peoples associated with the Sangoan.

Although the archaeological evidence is far from clear, it is likely that several human types co-existed in East Africa at this time. Homo sapiens evolved as the major hominid in the region during the Middle Stone Age, and by approximately 20,000 years ago modern man, or Homo sapiens sapiens, was the only human type living in East Africa.

Late Stone Age

The Late Stone Age began in eastern Africa around 15,000 years ago. Because it is more recent, we know more about the Late Stone Age than about earlier periods. Indeed, in some areas of East Africa, hunting and gathering modes of life typical of the Late Stone Age survived well into the Christian era. More in the way of skeletal remains have been discovered by archaeologists, and there is also from this period a considerable amount of rock art which depicts the way of life of the hunter-gatherers.

As a result of a process of gradual improvement in the production of stone tools, major advances in technology occurred in the Late Stone Age and more intricate techniques of production were introduced. One of the most significant advances was the development of composite tools. Previously, early man had used tools made from wood or stone but he had not combined them effectively. Although hafting and gumming techniques for joining wood and stone were in use in the Middle Stone Age, there was a more general reliance on them in the Late Stone Age, and the stone blades and points incorporated in composite tools were generally smaller and thinner than in the previous period. Undoubtedly, one of the most important innovations of the composite type was the bow and arrow. It greatly expanded man's ability as a hunter and thus increased his capacity to survive and multiply.

The Late Stone Age witnessed the continuation of different cultural traditions in differing environments. By far the-most widespread during this period were industries known collectively as Wilton, which have been found over much of East Africa. The people practicing the Wilton type tool complex inhabited open and lightly wooded areas. They lived near lakes and rivers and in caves and rock shelters. They relied extensively on hunting and fishing, and this is reflected in the tools they utilized. The remains of animal bones indicate that even the largest animals—hippopotamus and rhinoceros—were hunted, probably with the aid of poisoned arrows.

In more wooded areas early man put greater emphasis on food gathering than on hunting. The industrial complex associated with this way of life, called Tschitolian, evolved from the Sangoan-Lupemban and was found in the wooded regions in western East Africa and the Zaire basin. These people used a number of stone tools which were heavier than those found in Wilton sites. They used round, bored stones as weights for digging sticks, grindstones for preparing wild fruits and vegetables, and round-edged axes used to strip off bark.

As we have noted, the human form was now everywhere Homo sapiens sapiens, i.e., modern man. The great majority of people living in East Africa at this time undoubtedly belonged to the physical type called Bush or Bushman. Archaeologists have recovered Bush skeletal material from most parts of East Africa. Only small remnants of this once seemingly widespread physical type survive in Africa today, almost all outside our region of interest. These peoples inhabit portions of southwestern Africa in the modern era and speak languages belonging to the Khoisan family.

During the Late Stone Age what has been termed an aquatic civilization made its appearance in East Africa, just as it did in the Nile valley, the Sahara, and West Africa. This occurred some 8,000 to 10,000 years ago when the climate of Africa was extremely wet, resulting in larger and more numerous lakes and rivers. The way of-life distinctive to the aquatic civilization was associated with such bodies of water and their food resources, especially fish. Aquatic sites of this sort have been found on the west shore of Lake Edward and along the shore lines of Lakes Turkana and Nakuru in the eastern Rift Valley.

The peoples living along the lake and river shores caught fish and aquatic animals with spears or harpoons made of bone fashioned with the aid of stone tools. They practiced basket and pottery making; the pottery vessels are the most ancient in Africa. This aquatic civilization reached its height at around 7,000 B.C. With assured food supplies from lakes and rivers, the people were able to establish larger and more stable settlements than any previous populations. Available skeletal remains indicate that these people were basically Negroid.

The end of the Late Stone Age in East Africa comes with the adoption of food production and the use of iron tools. This technological revolution did not occur at the same time across the whole of the region, but for most of East Africa it took place around the dawn of the Christian Era. The transformation in technology was, most scholars agree, introduced from outside the region as a result of population movements which brought a technologically advanced people, not of Bush type, into East as well as Central and Southern Africa.

Populations and Languages of East Africa

The peoples who inhabited East Africa in the centuries between the end of the Late Stone Age and the present day belong to three main physical types, normally referred to as Negroid, Bushmanoid, and Caucasoid. The great majority in these regions today, recent twentieth-century immigrants apart, would be classified as Negroid.

Scholars generally agree that the Negroid and Bushmanoid types have an origin in sub-Saharan Africa whereas the Caucasoid type has come from outside the area. Beyond this, however, there is wide disagreement and a great disparity of view associated with racial classification. Modern prejudices and stereotypes have added confusion and misunderstanding, as in the case of the Hamitic Myth, which portrayed Negroid peoples as "backward" and the supposedly Caucasoid Hamites as bearers of "civilization." To cite another example, the Somali and Hima peoples have often been classified as Caucasoid even though their skin color and general appearance suggest they belong to the Negroid group. The classification of the peoples of East Africa by physical or racial differences is thus fraught with difficulties and tends to be vague.

Although it is common to classify the peoples of these regions according to the tribal and ethnic units which are recognized today, such classification, while useful in some ways, has serious drawbacks when applied to periods dating back several centuries. Members of a social formation such as a tribe normally possessed a common culture and language. However, as we shall see, such ethnic groups have not been hard-and-fast units, existing in the same form over several centuries. Rather they have been very fluid groupings of people, their ethnic and cultural forms at any given time the result of processes of migration and interaction among diverse groups. One cannot speak of the Kikuyu or Sukuma tribes, for example, existing one thousand or more years ago in the same cultural form that they have in the present century.

A more precise and objective way of classifying the peoples of East Africa is provided by language. The study of modern languages and of linguistic borrowing, as well as the reconstruction of parent or ancestral languages, also provide very useful information for the historian.

The most widely used system of classification is that of Joseph Greenberg, who divides African languages into four main families: Khoisan, Afro-Asiatic, Nilo-Saharan, and Niger-Kordofanian. Each of these is represented in East Africa in the present century. The Khoisan

16

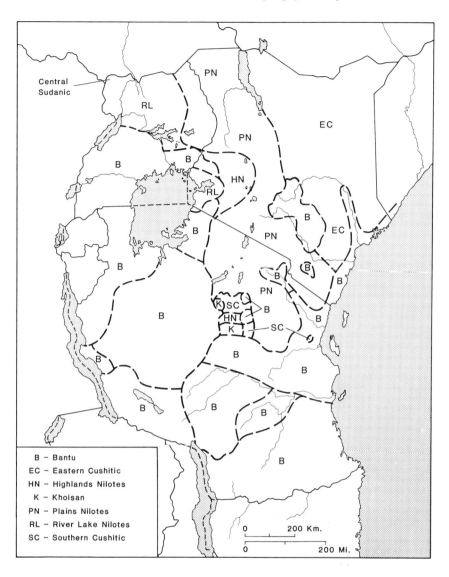

Central Sudanic

PN

RL

EC

PN

B

B

HN

RL

B

EC

B

PN

B

B

B

(B)

B

B

PN

K SC B

HN

K

B

SC

SC

B

B

B

B

B

B

B

B

B

B – Bantu
EC – Eastern Cushitic
HN – Highlands Nilotes
K – Khoisan
PN – Plains Nilotes
RL – River Lake Nilotes
SC – Southern Cushitic

0   200 Km.

0   200 Mi.

Map 3. Modern Distribution of Languages in East Africa.

and Afro-Asiatic families are spoken by the smallest numbers of people at present. Only the small Sandawe and Hadza groups of north central Tanzania are recognized as speaking a Khoisan language. It is generally agreed, however, that Khoisan languages were once—most likely during the Late Stone Age—very widely spoken in the region. Peoples speaking languages classified as Afro-Asiatic are found in greater numbers in East Africa. These languages belong to two branches of the Cushitic group spoken widely in the Horn of Africa. Most of the Cushitic languages spoken in East Africa today belong to the Eastern Cushitic division; a few peoples speak languages included in Southern Cushitic. Southern Cushitic languages, like the Khoisan languages, were once far more widely spoken in East Africa than they are in the twentieth century.

Chart 2.1

Khoisan and Afro-Asiatic Languages of East Africa

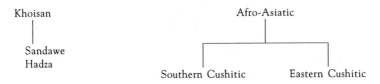

The Chari-Nile subfamily of Nilo-Saharan is represented in East Africa by the Central and Eastern Sudanic branches which are further broken down into the Moru Madi (Central Sudanic) and Nilotic (Eastern Sudanic) groups. Moru Madi speakers are found today in northeastern Zaire and northwestern Uganda, while those speaking Nilotic languages are more widespread, being located in Uganda, Kenya, Tanzania, and Zaire as well as in Sudan and Ethiopia. The Nilotic languages have been subject to a variety of terminology and some confusion, not least that which surrounds the use of the term "Nilo-Hamitic." It is proposed in this work to follow a threefold division: River-Lake (Western), Highland (Southern), and Plains (Eastern).

Chart 2.2

Chari-Nile Languages of East Africa

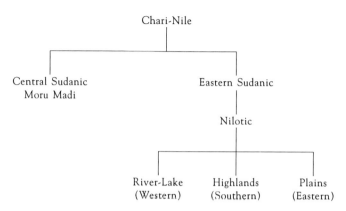

By far the greatest numbers of people in East Africa speak languages belonging to the Bantu group in the Niger-Congo subfamily of Niger-Kordofanian. The Bantu languages exhibit a remarkable degree of similarity in vocabulary and structure, a fact which has important implications for the historian. Generally speaking, the Bantu languages which are most closely related today are those which are geographically closest to one another. Following the lead of linguists Christopher Ehret and Derek Nurse, Chart 2.3 provides a simplified classification of the major groups of Bantu speakers in East Africa. Modern ethnic groups mentioned in the text are listed under each major subgroup. Map 4 portrays the modern distribution of these Bantu groups according to the number in the chart.

Chart 2.3

Bantu Languages of East Africa

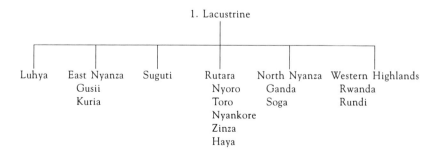

19

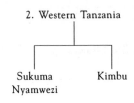

2. Western Tanzania

```
          Sukuma        Kimbu
          Nyamwezi
```

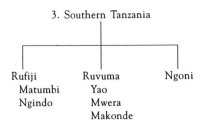

3. Southern Tanzania

```
   Rufiji        Ruvuma        Ngoni
   Matumbi       Yao
   Ngindo        Mwera
                 Makonde
```

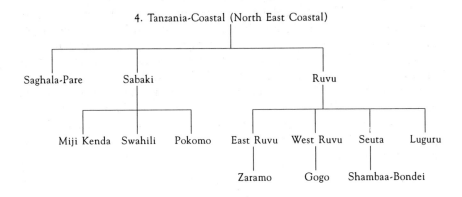

4. Tanzania-Coastal (North East Coastal)

```
Saghala-Pare   Sabaki                        Ruvu

        Miji Kenda  Swahili  Pokomo   East Ruvu  West Ruvu  Seuta  Luguru

                                         Zaramo      Gogo    Shambaa-Bondei
```

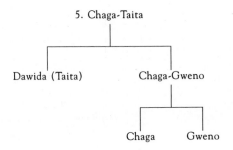

5. Chaga-Taita

```
        Dawida (Taita)        Chaga-Gweno

                               Chaga    Gweno
```

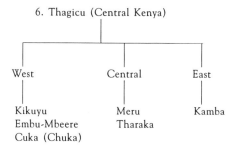

6. Thagicu (Central Kenya)

West	Central	East
Kikuyu	Meru	Kamba
Embu-Mbeere	Tharaka	
Cuka (Chuka)		

7. Kilombero

Food Production and Iron Working

There is little doubt that both iron working and food production, which so radically changed man's life-style, were introduced from outside the region. Most of the staple crops and domestic animals found in East Africa today have their origins elsewhere, and there is no evidence of a bronze or copper age in the area prior to the beginning of iron working. Over most of East Africa, food production and iron working began at approximately the same time, some 2,000 years ago. In the Rift Valley highlands of Kenya and Tanzania, archaeologists have discovered evidence of a food-producing society dating to a much earlier period, at least to the end of the second millennium B.C. Those who inhabited this area at the time are known as the Stone Bowl people because they used stone bowls, pestles, and mortars.

The Stone Bowl culture, which flourished during the first millennium B.C., combined Stone Age technology with the techniques of food production. Animal bones found in excavations clearly indicate that these people herded cattle and probably sheep and goats. No conclusive evidence of agriculture has been unearthed, but the existence of stone tools which would be useful in grinding grain strongly suggests that the Stone Bowl people cultivated grain crops such as millet and sorghum. Excavations of burial sites, such as the Njoro River Cave in Kenya, have unearthed (in addition to stone tools) pottery, basketry, and beads made of a variety of materials including semi-precious stones.

These Late Stone Age food producers likely moved south into East Africa from the Ethiopian highlands. The domestication of livestock and plants had already emerged there, and was no doubt carried south.

21

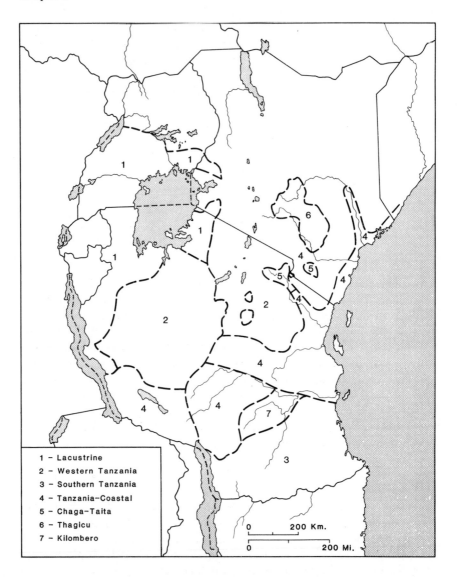

Map 4. Bantu Languages of East Africa.

1 – Lacustrine
2 – Western Tanzania
3 – Southern Tanzania
4 – Tanzania–Coastal
5 – Chaga–Taita
6 – Thagicu
7 – Kilombero

Skeletal remains from Stone Bowl burial sites show similarities to those found in the Ethiopian region as does the method of burial, the dead being placed under cairns or mounds. Cairns have been used for burial in the Ethiopian highlands down to the present. It is generally agreed that these food producers were closely linked with the Ethiopian region linguistically, speaking languages belonging to the Southern Cushitic group. As far as can be discerned at present, the Stone Bowl food producers speaking Southern Cushitic languages did not spread their influence outside the Rift Valley highlands and adjacent plains. Most of East Africa continued to be inhabited by hunter-gatherers until the coming of the Iron Age around the beginning of the first millennium A.D.

This means that a hunting-gathering way of life persisted in East Africa for a considerably longer period than, for example, in West and North Africa, where food production began several millennia earlier. Probably the most important reasons for this difference were climatic and ecological. Unlike North and West Africa, East Africa experienced no pronounced desiccation in the last 3,000 or so years B.C. There were still sufficient wild flora and fauna to support a comfortable existence by hunting and gathering.

There were also important ecological barriers to the easy transmission of food-producing techniques to East Africa. One of the most important was the tropical forest belt that stretches through Zaire. The grain crops cultivated in West Africa, for example, could not prosper in this more humid environment or in the well-watered regions adjacent to the forest and the great lakes. Nor were stone tools adequate for successful cultivation in this type of environment. Moreover, much of East Africa was infested by tsetse fly-borne forms of sleeping sickness which made it almost impossible for cattle and other large domestic animals to inhabit these regions.

When the change to food production did occur, it was principally the result of new technology being introduced by people from outside the region. That this was the case is suggested by the fact that the great majority of food crops grown in East Africa in the past two millennia are of outside origin. The cultivation of sorghum and millets probably spread from the Ethiopian highlands in the first and second millennia B.C. Plants suited to serve as staples in the wetter regions, such as bananas, rice, yams, and coconuts, reached East Africa from Southeast Asia via the Indian Ocean and, most likely, the Mozambique coast some 2,000 years ago. More recently (in the past 400 or 500 years) crops such as maize and cassava have been introduced from the Americas via the west coast of Africa. The cattle, sheep, and goats herded in East Africa appear to have come from North and West Africa, and ultimately from

Southwest Asia.

While technologies of food production came to East Africa from various sources, people in the region had to adapt the introduced animals and crops to conditions there. In this process, new varieties came into being which were better suited to the local environment. The banana provides a good example of this. Today, more varieties of banana are grown in East Africa than in all the rest of the world.

Like the techniques of food production, iron working began earlier in other regions of the continent than in East Africa. The making of tools and weapons by smelting iron ore was first practiced in northeastern Africa in the first half of the first millennium B.C. By approximately 550 B.C. the techniques of iron working had spread south along the Nile to Meroe in what is today the Sudan. At about the same time, iron working was being undertaken in West Africa, a revolution in technology that East Africa experienced slightly later.

Iron working and food production had revolutionary effects on the region. Population greatly expanded over East Africa, and people generally lived in larger and more stable groups. Food production can take place without iron tools, as it did with the Stone Bowl peoples, but iron implements enable more land to be cultivated more effectively. Without iron tools cultivators could not have coped successfully with the wetter, more heavily vegetated areas of the region. In these areas, iron tools combined with the adoption of Southeast Asian crops (such as the banana) as staples to provide the means for a much heavier population than otherwise would have been possible.

The Early Iron Age and Bantu Migrations

The period of East African history dating-from the beginning of iron working and food production down to approximately 1000 A.D. has been termed the Early Iron Age. The account provided here owes much to the work of archaeologists D. W. Phillipson and R. W. Soper. Most of our knowledge of this period comes from archaeology and is based on pottery findings associated with iron working. Although some pins, rings, arrow heads and spear heads have been found, iron implements dating to this period are very scarce. This is due largely to the relatively rapid corrosion common in the acidic soils and generally humid environment in many parts of East Africa. It is usually possible to date the pottery findings by subjecting associated organic material to radiocarbon or Carbon 14 dating techniques.

For many parts not only of East but also of Central Africa pottery making seems not to antedate the Early Iron Age. Pottery which could possibly be regarded as ancestral to that of the Early Iron Age has not been found in any part of the regions. This is but another powerful factor supporting the probability that the culture of the Early Iron Age was introduced into both regions by a rapid movement of people from outside.

The types of pottery associated with the Early Iron Age display a remarkable degree of resemblance over all of East and Central Africa. Despite the fact that such pottery has been given different names (dimple based for East Africa, channelled ware for Zambia, and stamped ware for Zimbabwe), the similarities in style and decoration leaves little doubt that the people who established the Early Iron Age in this part of Africa shared a common cultural heritage.

On the basis of pottery typology and geographic distribution, regional groupings have been divided into Eastern and Western Streams. The ceramic types differ in the use of motifs and positions. Eastern Stream jar rims, for example, are decorated with multiple facets, but the Western Stream utilizes loops and triangles and alternating blocks in the same position. Map 5 shows the distribution of the various groups (T. N. Huffman sees the pottery types of southern Malawi and Eastern Zambia as representing a Central Stream, but these will be considered here as part of the Eastern Stream). Map 6 shows the dating for the earliest manifestations of the Early Iron Age in the southern portion of Africa.

The earliest known manifestation of the Early Iron Age is in the great lakes region. It is characterized by a pottery type known as Urewe ware, after one of the earliest sites where such pottery was discovered. The people who produced this pottery appear to have settled around the western and southwestern shores of Lake Victoria by approximately 500 B.C. The earliest Urewe site dated thus far is in the west lake area of Tanzania, where Peter Schmidt's excavations have shown evidence of the manufacture of high carbon, steel-like metal centuries ahead of Europe. Later the Urewe culture spread north and then east to the eastern shore of Lake Victoria. There is no doubt that the Urewe people possessed iron-working technology, and it seems reasonable to assume that they also practiced agriculture.

From this initial manifestation in the Urewe settlements near Lake Victoria, Early Iron Age culture spread very rapidly to the east and south. The Eastern Stream is clearly derived from Urewe. It reached the coastal hinterland of present day southern Kenya and northern Tanzania by about the second century A.D. By the third century, as Map 6 shows, there had been rapid movement of Early Iron Age culture through Malawi, the eastern portions of Zambia and Zimbabwe, and south into what is now the Republic of South Africa.

The Western Stream, though not found in East Africa, is associated with ceramic types found at sites in Zaire, Zambia, western Zimbabwe,

25

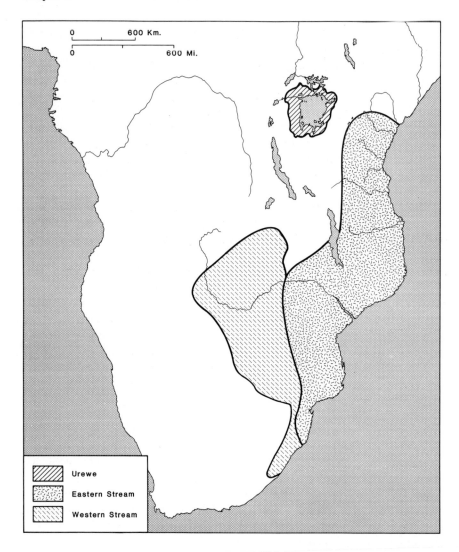

Map 5. Distribution of Early Iron Age.

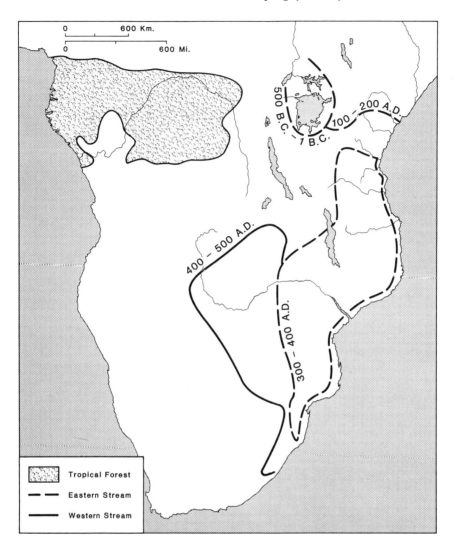

Map 6. Dating the Early Iron Age.

27

and the Transvaal. Recent interpretation of archaeological data from several of these sites has led Huffman to conclude that the Western Stream, though its origin is not precisely known, spread to the south at least as early as the Eastern Stream.

The radiocarbon dating for both the Eastern and Western Streams provides a strong indication of a very rapid movement of iron working technology throughout the southern half of Africa. From the earliest sites in the Urewe area in the first two or three centuries before the Christian era, it had spread through Central and Southern Africa by the fourth century A.D. Perhaps most important in facilitating this rapid spread was the fact that people occupying most of the areas over which the Early Iron Age spread seem to have had no knowledge of agriculture or use of iron or pottery.

There is little doubt that this spread of the Early Iron Age was accompanied by the movement of a new population group. This should not be thought of as a mass migration of large numbers of people into the region; more likely it represented small-scale movements of people over several centuries, perhaps in the form of settlements established at increasing distances from an original settlement, followed by further offshoots from these. This process would have been repeated countless times as the populations of the newcomers constantly increased through reproduction and the absorption of groups previously living in the region.

Most scholars believe that the people associated with the spread of the Early Iron Age in East Africa were ancestors of the people who occupy most of the region today, the Bantu. Bantu is a linguistic term which carries no connotation as to race or culture. Although people who speak Bantu languages are widespread in East, Central, and Southern Africa, there remains a great degree of similarity among the various dialects, probably indicating a rapid and relatively recent spread of the peoples who speak Bantu languages over the territories they now inhabit.

In attempting to reconstruct the historical migrations of Bantu-speaking peoples to East Africa, we must rely not only on archaeology but also on linguistics. Linguists have undertaken comparative analyses of present-day Bantu languages, and as a result are able to tell us a good deal about the language spoken by the original Bantu peoples (proto-Bantu) and to suggest where the Bantu-speaking peoples may have originated. (See Map 7.)

There is general agreement at present with Joseph Greenberg's identification of the southern Cameroon area of West Africa as the region from which the early Bantu-speakers began a series of movements to the south and east that would bring them to East Africa. Just how the movement to the south took place is still far from clear, but an attempt will be made, following the lead of Ehret, Nurse and Phillipson, to

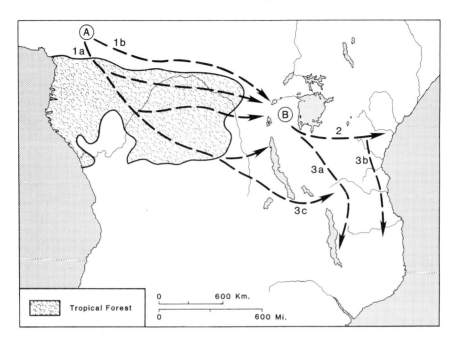

Map 7. Bantu Migrations.

From their original homeland in West Africa (A), groups of Bantu-speakers moved, during the second millennium B.C., south and east (1a) into the forest and its fringe. Several groups of Bantu eventually emerged from the eastern fringe of the forest zone and moved toward the great lakes region, probably arriving in the middle of the first millennium B.C. Here they came into contact with other Bantu-speakers whose ancestors had moved (1b) around the northern fringe of the forest and who had likely adopted techniques of iron working and cattle rearing. The earliest migrants of these groups eventually settled west of Lake Victoria, establishing the Urewe Early Iron Age culture in approximately the last five centuries B.C. (B). This became the origin of the Eastern Stream of the Early Iron Age. Further population movements saw a rapid spread of iron working, agriculture, and Bantu languages to the east (2) and south (3a), (3b), and (3c). By the fourth century A.D. Bantu-speaking peoples of the Eastern Stream were residing in Central and Southern Africa as well as East.

29

reconstruct routes of migration using available archaeological and linguistic evidence.

The area identified by linguists as the original homeland of the Bantu-speaking peoples lies in the Sudanic region, a broad belt of grassland stretching across Africa between the borders of the desert to the north and the tropical forest to the south. In this area food producing was established by the third millennium B.C., including crop agriculture and the herding of at least goats. The word for goat is clearly of Bantu origin, but words for cattle and sheep appear to have been borrowed. Sudanic pottery suggests also that it was from this region that the Bantu ancestors came. Although still imperfectly known, the Sudanic Pottery of the mid-first millennium B.C. seems to reflect the same tradition that is evident in Early Iron Age pottery in East Africa. Although iron working diffused relatively early to this part of West Africa—radiocarbon dates at Nok in the Sudanic belt of Nigeria indicate the late fifth century B.C.—historical evidence suggests that the ancestors of the Bantu-speaking peoples had already left West Africa by that time. They began their move to the south and east during the second millennium B.C., if not earlier.

In moving south, the ancestral Bantu-speaking peoples would have encountered the formidable obstacle of the tropical forest of the Zaire basin, a broad, densely vegetated, humid area. These ancestral Bantu appear to have possessed a knowledge of agriculture suited to such a wet region. Linguistic reconstructions of proto-Bantu indicate that the people who spoke the language had a knowledge of crops suited to high rainfall areas, such as the yam, which enabled them to survive in the wet forest and on its fringes, and that they had a knowledge of fishing and rivercraft. They had, on the other hand, no words for grain crops, and they herded only goats.

Over the course of several centuries the Bantu whose descendants would make their way to East Africa moved south and east through the forest belt, and during the first millennium B.C. they emerged to the south and east of the forest. They did not move as a single, coherent group. Some moved west and others moved north into the great lakes region. Here they met other Bantu, who probably possessed a knowledge of iron working and cattle keeping. The ancestors of this group had left the Cameroon area and travelled to the west.

Archaeological, if not linguistic, evidence suggests a movement of Bantu-speakers to the east along the northern fringes of the forest and then south to the great lakes region. Along the initial part of this route east of Lake Chad, pottery dating to the first millennium B.C. has been found which strongly resembles Early Iron Age wares. The route also passes adjacent to lands (southwestern Sudan and northern Uganda) in which Central Sudanic languages are spoken today. There is strong linguistic reason for thinking that the early Bantu adopted cattle and sheep keeping from peoples speaking Central Sudanic languages since the names applied to cattle and sheep in many modern Bantu languages are derived from Central Sudanic dialects. It was probably also in the course of this move along the northern fringes of the tropical forest that these Bantu ancestors acquired a knowledge of iron working. Carbon 14 dates indicate, moreover, that the area where the turn to the south was most likely made, the great lakes region, is also the earliest site of the Early Iron Age, the Urewe culture. This movement and the resulting settlements gave rise to what has been described as the Eastern Stream. These people and the Bantu who moved through the forest undoubtedly adopted grain crops more suited to the savannah region they were now entering from Southern Cushitic-speaking agricultural peoples already resident in East Africa.

Pottery representative of the Eastern Stream spread very rapidly from the Lakes region over East Africa. The Bantu peoples associated with :the spread took with them a knowledge of iron working, agriculture, and the herding of cattle, sheep, and goats. An additional basis for the expansion of these people from the Urewe area in the first half of the first millennium A.D. may have been their adoption of Southeast Asian food crops, such as bananas, well suited to the wetter regions of East Africa.

Present evidence also indicates the possibility of a movement of Bantu-speaking peoples into East Africa from the region between Lakes Tanganyika and Malawi. It is difficult to date these movements with precision, but they probably took place during the late first millennium B.C. or early first millennium A.D.

Thus, before 500 A.D. there had come into existence an Eastern Stream of Bantu-speaking peoples. It extended as far south as present-day South Africa, while at the same time a Western Stream was present in Angola and Namibia. These streams were distinguishable by differences in ceramic style and the languages the people spoke.

Early Nilotic Migrations

At about the same time (or perhaps somewhat later) that Bantu-speaking peoples were moving into East Africa, food-producing and iron-working peoples speaking Nilotic languages were moving into East Africa from the north. The term Nilotic is, like Bantu, a linguistic one, but Nilotic speakers belong to a different language family. Unlike the Bantu-speaking peoples, Nilotic speakers had an impact only on East Africa. Much less is known archaeologically of the Nilotic migrations, and most of our knowledge about the early history of these people comes from compara-

31

tive linguistic studies, particularly those of Christopher Ehret.

The early homeland of the Nilotic-speaking peoples can be identified as the relatively low and dry area west and southwest of the Ethiopian highlands. In this broad belt of territory, extending from the adjacent regions of modern Kenya and Ethiopia west to the Nile valley, the Nilotic peoples had emerged by at least the beginning of the first millenium B.C. By the end of that millenium the Nilotic speakers had divided into three groups speaking similar yet distinct languages and occupying different areas. To the west and north were the River-Lake Nilotes, in the center the Plains Nilotes, and further to the east the Highlands Nilotes.

Prior to 1000 A.D. only one of these groups had moved very deeply into East Africa. The River-Lake and Plains Nilotes seem to have largely remained on the periphery of the region throughout most of the first millenium A.D. Those speaking River-Lake languages lived in the Nile valley and vicinity in what would today be the southern part of the Sudan. The Plains Nilotes appear to have occupied the territory to the north and west of Lake Turkana. Those speaking languages ancestral to the modern Highland dialects, on the other hand, did begin to move south into the highlands region of the Rift Valley in the first millennium A.D.

As these Highland Nilotes moved south, gradually and in small groups, they brought with them a considerable Eastern Cushitic influence. This, Ehret has shown, suggests quite close contact between those speaking the ancestral Highland Nilotic languages and ancestors of the Oromo (Galla) and Somali belonging to the Eastern Cushitic language family. This contact probably took place in the first millennium B.C. Among the cultural traits adopted by the Highland Nilotes were the practice of male and female circumcision as an initiation rite, a prohibition against eating fish, and a system of cycling age sets and grades. Heavy word borrowing also points to intimate contact between the two peoples.

The ancestors of the Highland Nilotes who spread south over the Kenya highlands and what is today the border area between Kenya and Uganda appear to have combined herding of cattle and goats with the cultivation of grains such as sorghum and millet. They also had a knowledge of iron working. After the middle of the first millennium A.D. these Highland Nilotes differentiated or split into several groups, only two of which, Kalenjin and Tatoga (Dadog), have survived to the present century. These Highlands Nilote groups probably were confined largely to what is today western Kenya by 1000 A.D.

Population Interaction and Absorption

In addition to the movements of the Bantu and Nilodc peoples into East Africa, a very important theme of this period of history, as later, is the interaction of peoples speaking different languages, often adhering to different ways of life, and the absorption of one group by another. As the Bantu and Nilotes entered the region, they did not come into a vacuum. Peoples speaking Khoisan languages and practicing hunting and gathering economies with stone tools were widespread. In the Rift Valley food-producing communities speaking Southern Cushitic languages flourished, and in Northern Uganda, if not further south, there lived peoples speaking Central Sudanic languages.

Although it is all too easy to oversimplify and generalize about this process, it is fairly clear that in the first millennium A.D. the Bantu and Nilotes began the absorption of the earlier populations resident in East Africa. This was a gradual process which was not even completed during the second millennium, but in general it was these two newcomers, with their superior technology, who would dominate East Africa. Not all of the earlier populations would be absorbed. A few would be pushed into areas unfavorable for supporting large populations of food producers, such as the high altitude forests of Kenya and the dry plains of Tanzania. There they maintained an essentially hunting and gathering way of life down to the late nineteenth century.

With Bantu-speaking and Nilotic-speaking peoples moving into East Africa in the first millennium A.D., the stage was set for the next millennium, in which the descendants of these groups would play so dominant a role. They would continue to adapt themselves to the environment of the region, its previous inhabitants, and each other. The next 1,000 years would witness continued movement and change among the peoples of East Africa and the further development of their distinctive social, economic, and political formations.

Suggestions for Further Reading

Clark, J. D. *The Prehistory of Africa* (London, 1970).

Ehret, Christopher. *Southern Nilotic History* (Evanston, 1971)

Ehret, Christopher, and Posnansky, Merrick, eds. *The Archaeological and Linguistic Reconstruction of African History* (Berkeley, 1982).

Huffman, Thomas N. "Archaeology and Ethnohistory of the African Iron Age," *Annual Review of Anthropology*, XI (1982).

Ki-Zerbo, J., ed. *General History of Africa*, Vol. 1 (Berkeley, 1981).

Leakey, Richard, and Lewin, Roget. *Origins* (New York, 1977).

Nurse, Derrick, and Philipson, Gerard. "The Bantu Languages of East Africa: A Lexicostatistical Survey," in Polome, Edgar C., and Hill, C. P., eds. *Language in Tanzania* (Oxford, 1982).

Ogot, B. A., ed. *Zamani* (Nairobi, 1974).

Oliver, Roland, and Fagan, Brian. *Africa in the Iron Age* (Cambridge, 1975).

Phillipson, D. W. *The Later Prehistory of Eastern and Southern Africa* (New Yotk, 1978).

Soper, R. "A General Review of the Early Iron Age of the Southern Half of Africa," *Azania*, VI (1971).

Spear, Thomas. *Kenya's Past* (London, 1981).

Chapter 3

The East African Coast to 1800

It is useful for historians to consider the East African coast and interior as separate entities with divergent historical experiences. This is not because there was no contact between the relatively narrow coastal belt and the interior, nor because the people who resided at the coast were different from those of the interior, but because the coast was far more influenced by the Indian Ocean than the interior. The East African coast was part of the Indian Ocean world commercially, culturally, and even at times politically and much more is known about it.

Indian Ocean influences had much less impact on the interior, probably because contact between the coast and the interior was never easy. As one moves toward the interior, the narrow coastal region gives way to a belt of very dry land (nyika) characterized by bush or semi-desert vegetation. This was not an area which could support a substantial agricultural population, and it served as a barrier, though by no means a complete one, to intercourse between the coast and regions further inland. Moreover, few if any of the rivers which flow to the coast provide satisfactory natural highways to the interior. In contrast, contact with lands adjacent to the Indian Ocean has been much easier to accomplish and more far reaching in its impact.

It would be wrong to suggest that there was no contact between the East African coast and interior since items of trade did pass to and from the latter. This trade, however, must not have been on a substantial scale. Unlike the situation further south, there is little evidence of the presence of coast traders in the interior or of any coastal cultural influences before the latter part of the eighteenth century.

The Coastal Plain

The coastal plain of Kenya and Tanzania, though narrow, is made up largely of relatively fertile, sandy soil with fresh water available in most places. It is thus very suitable for settled agriculture. It enjoys a rainfall reliable and substantial enough to support crops, such as coconuts and rice, associated with a humid environment.

The coastline itself is a significant factor influencing life in the region and encouraging contact with other lands touched by the Indian Ocean. The shore is provided considerable protection from ocean waves by the coral reefs which line it. Moreover, the shallow off-shore waters are the habitat of large numbers of small fish, and these have long formed an important part of the diet of coast inhabitants. The configuration of the shore also makes it well suited for use by small boats. They can sail in at high tide and anchor a distance from the shore. When the low tide sets in, the boat comes to rest on the gently sloping lower section of the shore and can be easily unloaded by hand. As a result, any part of the coastline which is protected by coral reefs and free from mangrove swamps can serve as a suitable harbor.

The most important harbors of the coast provide even better protection for boats. A number of deep inlets have been formed from old estuaries which are now submerged by the sea. Good examples of this type are the harbors of Mombasa and Dar es Salaam. Some of these inlets have islands within or associated with them, as is the case with Mombasa, the Lamu group, and Kilwa. Close to—but protected by water from—the mainland, such islands early became the sites of important towns.

The larger offshore islands of Zanzibar, Pemba, and Mafia are part of the coastal region as well. Their soil and climate are very similar to those of areas along the coast, but these islands normally receive more rainfall. These and the smaller coastal islands attracted settlers and fostered the establishment of towns from an early period, but almost all of these were established on the west or landward side since the eastern side is exposed to ocean storms.

The modern Somali coast, which historically and culturally is part of the East African coastal region, enjoys an environment quite different from that just described. It lacks the plentiful rainfall found further south, and the coastal belt, especially in the north, tends to be rather arid with sand dunes often extending right down to the shore. In this type of environment, only a pastoral type of existence is possible, and agriculture on any scale has been practiced only in the valleys of the Shebelle and Juba rivers. Also in contrast to the coast further south, there are few good harbors on the Somali coast.

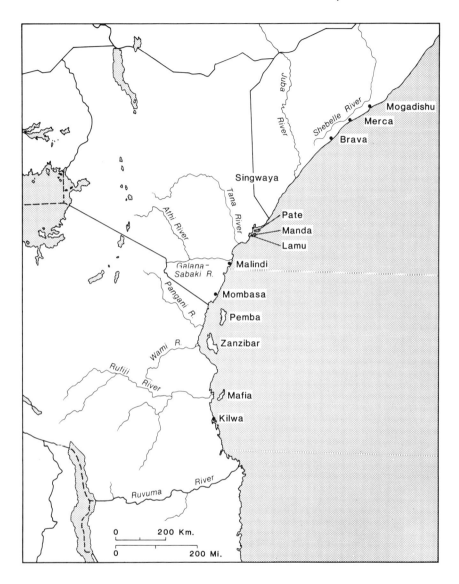

Map 8. East African Coast.

Azania: the Coast to 1000 A.D.

For the earliest period of coast history there are few sources for the historian to draw on. Archaeologists have discovered little substantial in the way of settlements along the coast dating to the period before the eleventh century. Oral tradition is also of little help, and written sources are sketchy, their references to East Africa being unclear until after the dawn of the Christian era. The most important source of useful information about the coast is the Periplus of the Erythrean Sea, a Greek merchant-sailors' guide to the Red Sea and Indian Ocean which was written in the first century A.D.

The guide book shows that the East African coast was already linked by commercial ties to other parts of the Indian Ocean and indeed to the wider world. The East African coast was known to the writer of the Periplus as Azania. From his account of Azania's trade it appears that voyages were made, especially to the Somali coast, to obtain the aromatic gum resins widely valued by the ancient world, frankincense and myrrh. Further south the major item of export was ivory, which was shipped not only to the Mediterranean world but also to India and China, where craftsmen found it far more suitable for ornamental carving than Asian ivory. Slaves were mentioned as exports from the region of the Horn but not further south; virtually no mention is made of what later would be a major item of export from the coast, gold. Weapons and implements of iron as well as glass vessels are given by the Periplus as the major imports of Azania.

It is quite probable that by this time commercial contact with the East Coast had been facilitated by a knowledge of the monsoon winds. These winds blow from a northerly direction toward East Africa for approximately half the year, and from the southwest for the other half. Aided by these winds, sailing ships, especially those from Arabia, the Persian Gulf, and northwest India, found it relatively easy to reach Azania.

These commercial contacts undoubtedly fostered cultural and political influence from other parts of the Indian Ocean. Indeed, the Periplus states that Azania was subject to the ruler of Himyar in southwest Arabia. Men from Arabia regularly visited the coast and some knew the local language as they had married and taken up residence in Azania. However, it would certainly be wrong to look at this as representing a sizable stream of immigration; rather it represented only a trickle.

Valuable as it is, the Priplus provides us with very little information which does not deal with commerce, and even some of this is unclear and confusing. The chief town of Azania is referred to as Rhapta, but its site has not been definitely identified. It perhaps was situated near the mouth of the Rufiji River. Little is said about the people of the coast; they are described as tall and pirates. This paucity of detail has led to much speculation and argument among scholars as to whether or not the inhabitants of Azania were Negroid Bantu speakers.

The lack of details of the Periplus notwithstanding, Bantu-speaking peoples must have begun to settle along the coast near the dawn of the Christian era. The rapid spread of iron working techniques during the Early Iron Age suggests that Bantu-speaking peoples were resident at the coast by the first half of the first millennium A.D. By the middle of the first millennium A.D. Bantu-speaking farmers had become the dominant element in the population both at the coast and in the hinterland. Particularly important concentrations lived along the coast stretching north of the Tana River. These were the ancestors of peoples who speak languages belonging to the East Coast subdivision of the Coastal-Tanzania group of Bantu speakers.

By the second half of the first millennium A.D. the proto-Sabaki had separated from other languages of the group, and proto-Sabaki had divided as shown in Chart 3.1. By this time the Mijikenda and Pokomo ancestors were likely settled along the Shebele and Juba river valleys in what is today the Somali Republic. The proto-Swahili lived further south in the regions stretching north from the Tana River to the modern Somali-Kenya border.

Chart 3.1

Sabaki-Speaking Peoples

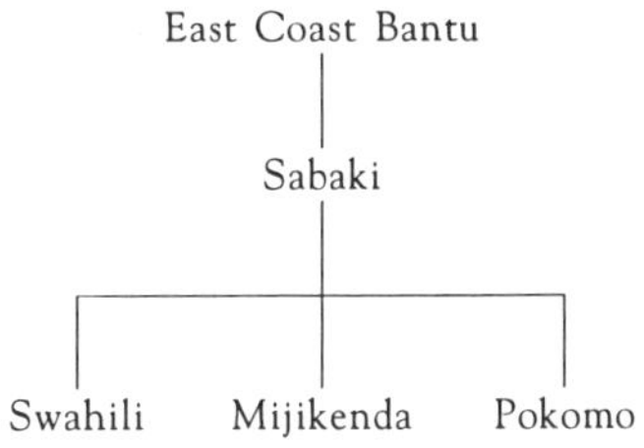

East Coast Bantu
|
Sabaki
|
┌───────────┼───────────┐
| | |
Swahili   Mijikenda   Pokomo

From the time of the Periplus until the tenth century, there are, aside from Ptolemy's geography dating from perhaps the fifth century, few reliable written sources of information about the east coast. While trade probably continued to link it to lands bordering the Indian Ocean, this cannot be stated with anything approaching certainty.

The Swahili Period: 1000-1500

The first half of the second millennium A.D. witnessed the development of trading towns along the East African coast which were peopled by Swahili-speakers. Some of the towns grew, through involvement in the Indian Ocean trade, into city-states. Mogadishu, Kilwa, and Mombasa, to name just three, grew to prominence through commercial success.

In any discussion of the coastal towns, the origin of the Swahili themselves is quite significant. It has been common for historians to view the Swahili as representing a fusion of Shirazi (Persian and Arabian) traders and immigrants with Sabaki-speaking peoples. This was thought to have occurred just prior to the ninth century in the region known as Singwaya (Shungwaya) along the southern Somali coast. Derek Nurse and Thomas Spear recently produced an impressive and provocative alternative account of the origins of the Swahili and the coastal culture associated with them. Their reconstruction of coastal history is relied upon here.

By the ninth century Swahili-speakers had taken up residence at the coast, with the earliest settlements at Manda, Pate, and Shanga in the Lamu archipelago. They founded Mombasa around 1000 A.D., and by 1100 were resident at Brava, Merka, and Mogadishu. With these movements, the language spoken in the northern towns began to split into what would become the dialects of modern Northern Swahili. Some Swahili-speakers moved further south during this period, establishing themselves initially at Kilwa, perhaps as early as the ninth century. Subsequently, towns took shape along the coast of Tanzania and Mozambique and on Zanzibar, Pemba, and Mafia islands, where dialects of what became modern Southern Swahili developed. By 1200 Swahili-speaking towns were scattered along the coast of East Africa, each evolving its own dialect and history but all linked by a common language and culture and by mutual involvement in the world of the Indian Ocean. It was this involvement which would separate them from other Sabaki-speaking groups.

The involvement with the Indian Ocean world not only produced commercial contacts with Arabia, the Persian Gulf, India, Indonesia, and China but also opened coastal East Africa to the cultural impact of Islam. From the descriptions of Arabic writers and travellers, it appears that the population of the towns was largely non-Muslim until the thirteenth century, when increasing commercial contact with the Muslim world led to the wide acceptance of Islam by inhabitants of the Swahili towns.

It seems unlikely that Islam was spread in any substantial way by Shirazi immigrants from the Persian Gulf and Arabia. Although practically every Swahili town has traditions claiming for it a Shirazi origin,

Nurse and Spear argue that these claims cannot be given credence in view of the sparse evidence of a Persian or Arabic linguistic influence on Swahili before 1100. Swahili history, in their view, was characterized by considerable movement of people among the coastal towns, largely because of economic forces. The so called Shirazi migrations were thus "proto-typical of recurring processes of movement, interaction and integration" along the coast. The name Shirazi reflects not the impact of Islamic settlers on the coast but attempts by Swahili families to provide a prestigious origin for themselves. This was especially the case after 1100 as social stratification began to emerge in the coastal towns, and the wealthy merchant classes sought to entrench their position through appeals to prestigious origins, in this case Shiraz, since many of the Arab traders with whom they dealt came from that region.

The increasing wealth and expansion of the Swahili towns in the twelfth and thirteenth centuries is indicated by the use of coral for building, the first appearance of mosques, and increasing quantities of Islamic and Chinese pottery and imported glass beads. Evidence of this comes from archaeological excavations at several sites along the coast. The period after approximately 1150 is marked by the rapid rise of Mogadishu as the most important and prosperous town on the coast. Arabic accounts dating from the thirteenth century as well as traditions from the coast itself, later written in the form of chronicles, show that Mogadishu was wealthy. The town derived its wealth from control of the gold trade with the land known as Sofala (the present-day coast of Mozambique).

Similar sources point to Kilwa as the coast's major trading town approximately a century later. The beginning of what is termed the Shirazi dynasty at Kilwa is marked by the appearance of coins bearing the name Ali bin al-Hasan, who is identified by the Kilwa Chronicle, one of the oldest and most important of the chronicles encompassing the history of the coast, as the initial Shirazi ruler. He "bought" rather than conquered Kilwa island. It was some time later that Kilwa's rise to prominence began. From the middle of the thirteenth century, the commerce of Kilwa expanded. This is attested to by the increased importation of goods such as the Chinese porcelain and Indian glass beads found in excavations on Kilwa.

In the fourteenth century, Kilwa came to surpass Mogadishu as the most prosperous town on the East African coast. Control of the gold trade was probably linked to the change in dynasty which took place at Kilwa toward the end of the thirteenth century. Kilwa had by this time developed a political system which centralized power in the hands of a ruling family. The new rulers were from the Mahdali family. The Kilwa Chronicle identifies the first ruler of this dynasty as al Hasan bin Talut;

he seized control of the island by force and expelled the previous dynasty. During the reign of al-Hasan's grandson, the Shirazi dynasty's attempts to reassert control from Mafia were finally defeated, and soon after this Kilwa came to surpass Mogadishu in importance. From about 1330 Kilwa was able to channel her trade directly to Arabia and the Persian Gulf rather than through Mogadishu. The first decades of the fourteenth century saw the kings of Kilwa obtain control of the gold trade which originated in what is today Zimbabwe; gold was exported through Sofala on the Mozambique coast. Kilwa's position was thus that of middle man rather than producer, but it was one which provided considerable wealth.

The prosperity that this brought to Kilwa is clearly evident from the archaeological excavations on the island. Buildings of coral and stone, a sure sign of increasing wealth, grew markedly more numerous in the early fourteenth century. A new architectural style made its appearance at this time, exemplified by the construction of larger buildings such as the extension to the Great Mosque and the great palace which seems to have doubled as a commercial establishment known as Husuni Kubwa. About a mile from the center of Kilwa town, this imposing edifice covers two acres of ground with space for more than one hundred rooms.

Although this prosperity seems to have declined somewhat in the last part of the fourteenth century, Kilwa was without doubt at the peak of her wealth and power from about 1350 to 1450. In addition to the Sofala region and its gold trade, Kilwa also controlled the coast in the immediate vicinity of the island. As Kilwa itself was not large enough to provide sufficient fields to support the population resident there, the mainland was used for purposes of cultivation. The picture of wealth associated with Kilwa or the significance of overseas trade should not, however, be overemphasized. The stone houses of the wealthy merchants were outnumbered by mud and wattle houses where most people lived. Most pottery at Kilwa during the fourteenth century was locally made rather than imported. Though wealthy merchants controlled plantations on the mainland, most farmers worked small holdings.

During this prosperous period Kilwa was strong enough, at times, to extend its influence over Mafia and also the larger island of Zanzibar further north. In general, nevertheless, the commercial prosperity of Kilwa did not produce any sort of extensive political hegemony over the East African coast.

The second half of the fifteenth century was a time of decline for Kilwa. A series of disputes over the throne had a weakening effect. The dissension and almost constant intrigue caused Kilwa's hold over her southern possessions to weaken and her trade from these lands to fall. By the arrival of the Portuguese at the turn of the sixteenth century, Sofala had become virtually independent of Kilwa.

While Kilwa was by far the most prosperous and powerful of the East African coastal city-states, others also enjoyed varying degrees of prosperity in the fourteenth and especially the fifteenth centuries. By that time the spread of Islam had made all of them Muslim. Each of the communities, with the exception of those subject at times to Kilwa's dominance, was independent of the others. Thus, the term city-state is a useful descriptive label. The most important cities north of Zanzibar were Mombasa, Malindi, Lamu, and Pate.

By the last half of the fifteenth century Mombasa was the most important of these northern cities. Like many of the other coastal towns, Mombasa has traditions of a Shirazi dynasty inaugurating the period of Islamic dominance, but much less is known of the history of Mombasa during this period than, for example, of Kilwa. As late as the middle of the fourteenth century Mombasa was less prosperous than Kilwa or Mogadishu. By the end of the fifteenth century, however, Mombasa seems to have cornered a great deal of trade, with ivory a prominent part of her exports.

Although they had early developed as oligarchies, most of the southern and northern city-states had become monarchies by the fifteenth century. An increasingly wealthy merchant class developed that was able to monopolize political power; normally one family came to dominate as the city's ruler or sultan. In most cases such a ruler was assisted and advised by a council of elders. The ruler normally appointed certain officials such as a qadi (judge) or an amir to assist him in the tasks of administration. Most rulers remained very interested in trade and appear to have obtained most of their revenue from trade and taxes on commerce.

From the fourteenth century, gold from the Sofala region was the most important item exported from the East African coast. Ivory was next in importance as an export, and frankincense and myrrh continued to be the chief exports of the Somali coast. Timber and iron also were items of trade in demand in other parts of the Indian Ocean. Contrary to past estimates, present evidence suggests that slaves were not an important article of export from East Africa before 1500. Indeed, there is little to indicate the shipment of human beings from other than the region north of Mogadishu. In addition to raw materials, the towns produced cotton cloth, pottery, and beads for sale overseas, in other coastal towns, and in the interior. These, together with porcelain, were also imported from abroad for trade along the coast and in the interior.

The coastal city-states appear to have developed effective working relations with the African peoples inhabiting the coastal belt, but their influence further in the interior of East Africa was negligible. Amicable relations with the Bantu-speaking peoples are suggested by some of the chronicles, most notably the Book of the Zanj for the southern Somali coast, by the obvious fact that trade was carried on without great difficulty, and by the absence of defensive fortifications from most of the cities on the mainland prior to the sixteenth century. Yet with the exception of the Zambezi River valley, there was no significant Muslim penetration of the interior. Trade was obviously carried on without traders from the coastal towns journeying into the interior. The coastal towns were, in fact, much more closely tied to the world of the Indian Ocean than to the African hinterland.

The Coming of Portuguese Dominance: 1500-1600

The arrival of the Portuguese in the Indian Ocean at the turn of the sixteenth century produced substantial changes in the political and economic life of the East African coastal city-states. Although the Portuguese established no permanent presence north of Mozambique prior to the end of the century, their dominance of the Indian Ocean had a disastrous effect on trade. Portuguese fleets from time to time unleashed brutal and destructive attacks on various of the coastal cities as they sought to force them into tributary relationships. For their part, the city-states strove as best they could to maintain the independence and trade they had enjoyed before 1500.

Portuguese ships came to the East African coast not as an end in itself but on their way to the more attractive opportunities for trade in India and the East Indies. East Africa would be important to the Portuguese as a stopping point on voyages further east, but only the gold of the Sofala region attracted them sufficiently to establish a permanent presence. The first Portuguese captain to visit the coast was Vasco da Gama, who arrived in 1498. The prevailing winds carried him past Kilwa, but he did stop at Mombasa. The ruler of Mombasa, having heard of the force and brutality which had marked da Gama's stay in Mozambique, did not prove friendly, and da Gama sailed north to Malindi, where he and his crew were given a warm reception. From the ruler of Malindi, da Gama obtained a pilot to guide him to India.

This would mark the beginning of a long alliance between Malindi and the Portuguese. The ruler of Malindi was aware that the strength of Mombasa, his major rival, was superior to his own. He therefore sought an alliance with the Portuguese as a means of improving his position vis-a-vis his rival. For the Portuguese, Malindi hereafter presented a friendly outpost on an otherwise hostile coast, a spot where supplies could be obtained for their ships as well as military aid in their sorties against Mombasa.

In the first decades of the sixteenth century, a number of Portuguese captains attacked the coastal city-states. The aim of such violent action was to seize as much wealth of the towns as they could and to force the rulers to recognize the overlordship of Portugal through the payment of tribute. They also often seized Muslim trading vessels along the coast. Shrinking from neither piracy nor brutality, the Portuguese justified their actions on grounds of religion and the strategic necessity to dominate the western shore of the Indian Ocean. This Portuguese action caused much property damage and loss of life, and it disrupted the trade of the city states. It thus severely weakened them and reduced the prosperity of the previous century.

Though fewer in numbers, the Portuguese had great superiority in weapons and tactics. Their cannon and firearms gave them an advantage over the Swahili towns. These first European invaders of East Africa also successfully employed the time-honored imperialist policy of divide and conquer. The coastal city-states were never able to combine against them effectively, and the Europeans were able to attack and defeat them, sometimes in alliance with other of the towns. At other times they were able to play off rival factions within the cities against each other to their own advantage.

Kilwa suffered perhaps more than any of the other city-states from Portuguese attacks. Returning to the coast with a much larger fleet in 1502, Vasco da Gama forced Kilwa to accept Portuguese overlordship and extracted a promise of tribute in gold from Kilwa's ruler. Three years later Francisco de Almeida, Portugal's first viceroy in India, attacked the city. He had already initiated measures in Mozambique which would finally end Kilwa's involvement with the gold trade there. Taking advantage of the factionalism and struggles for power in Kilwa, the Portuguese drove away the ruler and placed a man friendly to them on the throne. A garrison of Portuguese troops was left behind by Almeida, but Kilwa was abandoned within ten years because it had ceased, by the second decade of the sixteenth century, to be the leading commercial city-state of the East African coast. Loss of the gold trade together with the heavy handed destruction and loss of life caused by the Portuguese attacks thus reduced Kilwa's status to relative unimportance.

Mombasa was another city which suffered heavily from repeated Portuguese attacks. After dealing with Kilwa in 1505, Almeida attacked the northern city, and despite a brave defense by the Mombasans, the Portuguese fleet destroyed and looted much of Mombasa. Unlike Kilwa, however, Mombasa quickly recovered and continued to play an important role in coast affairs. Despite the brutal Portuguese conquests, Mombasa continued to demonstrate, through periodic rebellions, her dislike of the foreigners and their attempts to assert their control along the coast.

For most of the sixteenth century the Portuguese were content to attempt to control trade and exact tribute while launching sporadic military expeditions against recalcitrant cities. While the Portuguese were never able to completely control trade in the western part of the Indian Ocean, their actions altered patterns of trade in the area and reduced the level of trade, with a resultant decline in the prosperity of the coastal communities.

This caused continued hostility toward Portugal and a desire to be free of Portuguese influence, demonstrated clearly by the support given to the Turkish adventurer, Amir Ali Bey. Claiming to represent the Sultan of Turkey, he came to the east coast in a single vessel in 1585, and he called upon the cities to join him, a fellow Muslim, against the Portuguese. He was well received all along the coast. Mombasa, in particular, gave him a warm welcome, and Amir Ali Bey left the Indian Ocean the following year laden with loot and gifts. When Portuguese officials in Goa heard of this, they sent a strong fleet to punish the coastal cities that had shown sympathy and support for the Turkish pirate. In spite of the brutal punishments meted out on Pate, Lamu, and Mombasa, the coastal cities once again rose to Amir Ali Bey's support when he returned to the coast with a larger expedition in 1588. The Portuguese were still powerful enough, however, to overcome Amir Ali Bey and his coastal allies.

In 1589 the Portuguese despatched a large fleet to East Africa from Goa. It came face to face with Amir Ali Bey at Mombasa, the city which gave the Turkish adventurer his strongest backing. The Portuguese were not the only threat faced by Mombasa at this time. The Zimba, a warlike people who had cut a violent swath from Central Africa to the coast, now appeared on the mainland opposite the city. Widely feared for their ferocity and reputed cannibalism, the Zimba had sacked Kilwa in 1587. The Portuguese attacked from the sea, cooperating with the Zimba, who crossed from the mainland, in taking Mombasa. Many, including Amir Ali Bey, fled from the Zimba to the captivity of the Portuguese. Having punished Mombasa and captured Amir Ali Bey, the Portuguese extracted heavy vengeance on Lamu and Pate before sailing back to Goa.

For the Zimba the capture of Mombasa seems to have been their last success. They proceeded north along the coast, possibly intending to attack Malindi. Before reaching that city, however, they were wiped out in a battle with the Segeju, a Bantu-speaking group which had recently moved to this region of the coastal hinterland from an area further north.

The Decline of Portuguese Control: 1600-1700

The rebellions of Mombasa and other cities, coupled with further conflict between Mombasa and Malindi two years later, seem to have convinced Portuguese officials that a change in policy was necessary with regard to the East African coast. After a century without any fixed presence on the coast, the Portuguese now decided upon Mombasa as the site for a permanent strong point in East Africa. In 1593 they placed Malindi's ruler in control of Mombasa and began construction of a fort, named Fort Jesus, overlooking the entrance to Mombasa harbor.

By the turn of the seventeenth century, therefore, Portugal had established a garrison in Mombasa and made that city its headquarters on the coast. This change of policy, however, did not lead to a strengthening of Portuguese control because the Portuguese position in the Indian Ocean steadily weakened throughout the seventeenth century and English and Dutch commercial competition grew more and more intense. By the second half of the century the Portuguese had lost much of their trade as well as control of many areas of strategic and economic importance (for example, the East Indies). This erosion of Portuguese dominance in the Indian Ocean was accompanied by rebellions and revolts against the Portuguese by the coastal cities.

Despite the fact that Fort Jesus was the main Portuguese stronghold in East Africa, Mombasa, as before, played a leading role in resistance to foreign domination. The best example of such resistance is provided by the reign of Yusuf bin Hasan as ruler of Mombasa in the 1630s. Yusuf, whose father had been killed by the Portuguese, was sent as a child to Goa to be raised as a Portuguese. Having accepted baptism and taken a Portuguese name (Dom Jeronimo Chingulia), Yusuf returned to Mombasa in 1630. The Portuguese captain at Fort Jesus treated Yusuf very poorly, and Yusuf gradually came to feel an identity with the Muslim population as he was allowed to exercise little authority. Falling on the Portuguese in the fort by surprise, he seized control of Mombasa in August 1631, immediately proclaimed his adherence to Islam, and reverted to his Muslim name. A Portuguese fleet sent from Goa to deal with the rebellion was unable to defeat Yusuf, despite a lengthy siege of Fort Jesus. He left Mombasa shortly thereafter and continued to harass the Portuguese in the western Indian Ocean. Although they failed to capture Yusuf, the Portuguese did later regain control of Fort Jesus and Mombasa.

During the decades after 1650, the Portuguese position in the Indian Ocean continued to weaken, and her hold on the coast became more difficult to maintain. At this time the coastal cities received increasing help from Oman (in southeast Arabia) in their revolts against the Portuguese. With the accession of the Yarubi dynasty in the 1620s, Oman had emerged as an influential sea power. The Omanis drove the Portuguese from the Persian Gulf, and after 1650 attacked them in East Africa. Pate played a significant role in encouraging Omani interest in the east coast as its ruler took the lead in seeking their assistance in rebellions against the Portuguese. Mutual hostility against the Portuguese and religious solidarity only partly explain Omani interest in the East African coast; trade and potential economic advantages were probably more important. In the 1690s Mombasa, the last bastion of Portuguese power on the coast, was taken from them with the aid of the Omani Arabs. The Portuguese at Mombasa, together with their supporters in the coast population, put up a brave resistance in the face of a long siege, but they finally lost control of Fort Jesus at the end of 1698.

The capture of Fort Jesus effectively brought an end to the Portuguese period on the East African coast. Although they briefly resumed control of Fort Jesus in 1728-29, the era when Portugal was powerful enough to hold any influence over the coastal city-states was past. From 200 years of Portuguese presence, surprisingly little in the way of lasting influence has remained. Portuguese traders, officials, and religious functionaries lived in a number of places along the coast as well as Mombasa, but other than a few customs and Portuguese words in Swahili, their legacy is almost nil. Especially significant is the fact that Christianity did not survive north of Mozambique once the Portuguese were driven away.

In addition to marking the end of Portuguese influence at the coast, the seventeenth century was a period when very important events were occurring on the mainland of the northern coast. Most of the Bantu-speaking ethnic groups which today inhabit the Kenya coast moved into the region—generally from the north—in the sixteenth and seventeenth centuries. The most important in this regard were the Mijikenda (literally "nine towns") peoples who settled at this time in the hinterland adjacent to Mombasa. They were part of the Sabaki-speaking peoples who in earlier centuries had been resident in the Juba and Shebelle river regions of the Somali coast. When the Eastern Cushitic-speaking, pastoralist Oromo (Galla) moved into the lower Juba and Shebelle region around the middle of the sixteenth century, they touched off a series of migrations over the next one hundred years or so by which the Mijikenda moved south from the area (which their traditions refer to as Singwaya) to very near the ones they inhabit today. The Mijikenda cultivated millet and sorghum in their hilltop kayas, or villages. They did not have chiefs, but decisions were made and disputes settled by wealthy male elders.

The Pokomo were another Sabaki-speaking group displaced by the Oromo. At approximately the same time the Mijikenda were moving to their new homeland, the Pokomo moved south to take up residence in the Tana River valley. There the Pokomo adopted agricultural practices well suited to the riverine environment; they grew rice, bananas, and coconuts close to the river and millet and sorghum further away from the river in the flood plain. The Pokomo did not have chiefs; clan alliances functioned as territorial political groups, and decisions were made by a council of elders drawn from the wealthiest men of the various clans making up the alliance.

The sixteenth and seventeenth centuries were thus a time of change and insecurity on the mainland, marked by raids and movements of peoples, and this same atmosphere had an effect on the coastal cities themselves. The inhabitants of the Swahili towns and cities of the north coast also moved south, seeking refuge in the larger, better established, and more wealthy cities such as Mombasa. Many of the twelve tribes which make up the modern Swahili population of Mombasa were drawn there during the seventeenth century.

The Omani Period at the Coast: 1700-1800

While Oman now replaced Portugal as the dominant outside force on the coast after 1700, the Yarubi rulers of Oman were unable to exert anything more than very loose control. Early in the eighteenth century, Oman established military garrisons at certain points along the coast, such as Pemba, Kilwa, and Mombasa. Liwalis, or governors, were also sent to the most important coastal cities by the Omani rulers. Omani attempts to control the coast, however, were undermined by problems at home, including attacks on the country by neighboring states and severe succession disputes which eventually culminated in the overthrow of the Yarubi dynasty. Beset by these domestic problems, Omani rulers could not give a great deal of attention or utilize much wealth and manpower to establish and enforce their rule along the East African coast.

Another reason the Omanis were unable to establish effective control over the coast was the hostility of the city-states to any such overlordship. While accepting Oman's assistance in their struggles against Portuguese domination, the Swahili peoples of the coast were no more willing to accept Omani overlordship—despite religious ties—than that of the Europeans. This stance was demonstrated very clearly in the 1720s when several of the coastal cities actually allied with Portugal in an attempt to get rid of the Omanis. As a result, the Portuguese regained control of Fort Jesus in 1728-29, but they lacked the resources to assert their hold for more than a very brief period. The Swahili city-states thus were left largely alone to consolidate their independent position.

Although Oman never gained effective control of the coast, Omani influence was important there, particularly in the area of trade, as prosperity now returned for many of the city-states. An increasing Arabic impact on the coast can also be noted in changes in architectural styles during the eighteenth and nineteenth centuries, in alterations in coastal Islam, and in the markedly increased number of Arabic loan words which entered Swahili at this time. Immigration from Oman occurred, and some immigrants, like the Mazrui family at Mombasa, sent out in the service of the Omani rulers, took up permanent residence on the coast.

The most significant city on the coast continued to be Mombasa. Until late in the eighteenth century it was certainly one of the most prosperous coastal states, thanks largely to the close relations which were established with the Mijikenda peoples on the mainland and to links with the northern city-states. Mombasa was relatively free from succession disputes and other internal political problems after the middle of the century, and this helped to establish the city as a continued spot of safe refuge on the northern portion of the coast.

The economic strength and political stability of Mombasa was due in considerable measure to the Mazrui. These Omani Arabs, who had initially come to East Africa as governors serving the ruler of Oman, established themselves as the hereditary rulers of Mombasa by the 1750s. This was no small accomplishment, as the Swahili tribes were divided into two antagonistic groupings. The Thelatha Taifa (three tribes) and the Tisa Taifa (nine tribes) not only were hostile but openly quarrelled from time to time. A series of outstanding Mazrui liwalis were able to bring an end to such open hostilities and provide a stabilizing influence.

Under the Mazrui, Mombasa reached considerable heights of wealth and power in the second half of the eighteenth century. Closer ties with the Mijikenda peoples brought benefit in the shape of increased trade being channelled through Mombasa, including commerce in livestock, ivory, and wild rubber. Each Mijikenda people allied with a specific Mombasa community. The coast from Tanga north to Pate was largely subject to or dependent on Mombasa. Thus, Mombasa was by 1800 a major power on the East African coast. The Omanis might claim sovereignty but they were unable to exercise control.

For much of the eighteenth century the coast was free from foreign domination and control, a situation no doubt pleasing to the majority of city-states, which had struggled against Portuguese dominance for some 200 years. The future, however, would witness a renewal of foreign domination. Indeed, the nineteenth century would bring renewed attempts by powers outside East Africa to gain control of the coast, and they would be far more successful than in any previous era.

Suggestions for Further Reading

Alpers, Edward A., and Ehret, Christopher. "Eastern Africa," in Gray, Richard, ed. Cambridge History of Africa, IV (Cambridge, 1977).

Chittick, Neville. "The East Coast, Madagascar, and the Indian Ocean, "in Oliver, Roland, ed. Cambridge History of Africa, III (Cambridge, 1977).

Freeman-Grenville, G. S. P. *The East African Coast: Select Documents . . .* (Oxford, 1962).

Kirkman, J. S. *Men and Monuments on the East African Coast* (London, 1964).

Nurse, Derrick, and Spear, Thomas. *The Swahili* (Philadelphia, 1985).

Ogot, B. A., ed. *Zamani* (Nairobi, 1974).

Spear, Thomas. *Kenya's Past* (London, 1981).

Strandes, J. *The Portuguese Period in East Africa* (Nairobi, 1961).

Chapter 4

The East African Interior: c. 1000 to 1650

DURING THE SIX AND HALF CENTURIES after 1000 A.D., the various population groups, speaking different languages and practicing varied cultures, which had made a place for themselves in the region continued to adapt to conditions in East Africa through settlement, migration, and interaction. As a result of this interaction, several distinctive linguistic and cultural formations, sometimes called tribes, came into being. Moreover, as in earlier centuries, peoples from outside East Africa moved into the region to make their homes and in the process intermingled with other population groups. In some parts of East Africa, especially portions of Uganda and Tanzania, these years witnessed the growth of a centralized form of political system characterized by institutional leadership through chiefs and kings.

Uganda

As in the other East African countries, the physical environment of Uganda had a considerable impact on its history. In particular, settlement patterns and modes of life were influenced by rainfall and vegetation patterns. In general, the area north of the Nile River and Lake Kyoga is relatively dry, with a single rainy season. The northeast is extremely dry and capable of supporting only a pastoral existence at best. The south typically receives more rainfall, concentrated in two rainy seasons over most of the area. For the period under review the south experienced a larger and more concentrated population than the north.

The population of southern Uganda during the period was almost exclusively Bantu-speaking. The peoples of the region spoke languages ancestral to the Lacustrine subgroup, one of the major divisions of the East African Bantu languages. Most Bantu speakers combined agriculture with cattle raising, but in west-central Uganda groups known as Hima herded cattle exclusively. Near Lake Victoria, agriculture, rather than herding, was of most significance. The north of Uganda was by 1650 inhabited by peoples speaking Nilotic and Sudanic languages, most practicing an economy based on herding and grain cultivation. Two historical movements outweighed all others in importance for the greater part of what is today Uganda: the evolution of centralized kingdoms in the west-central portion of the country, and the movement of River-Lake Nilotes speaking Lwoo languages into the northern and eastern areas. Both developments were gradual, taking place over a number of years, but by 1650 they had left a deep impact on the political, social, and economic pattern of Uganda.

The Rise of the Interlacustrine Kingdoms: Bunyoro-Kitara

By the fifteenth century centralized states ruled by kings had emerged in west-central Uganda. The earliest of these was the kingdom and empire of Bunyoro-Kitara. The origin of the kingdom cannot be identified with certainty. In the past the origin of Bunyoro-Kitara and other interlacustrine states was clouded by the so-called Hamitic myth, which claimed that centralized states originated as the result of the invasion of superior caucasoid Hamites who came as a conquering pastoral aristocracy to dominate the Bantu-speaking agriculturalists. However, this simplistic and racist explanation is no longer credited by scholars.

Undoubtedly, the western portion of Uganda was an area of interaction between pastoral, cattle-keeping peoples and agriculturalists. It is quite probable, moreover, that such interaction and the need to organize defences against invaders, to divide pasture land, and to settle disputes helped to provide the impetus for the formation of a centralized state. Military, political, and economic factors probably combined to facilitate the emergence of Bunyoro-Kitara.

The earliest rulers of the kingdom identified by oral tradition are the Tembuzi. The information relating to them is largely in the form of myths and legends. While the period of the Tembuzi is commonly referred as the reign of the gods, stories relating to this dynasty undoubtedly contain some elements of truth; and as they have become part of the culture of the people, they tell us much about the society and how its people perceive their origins and explain their customs and practices. The legends, moreover, may well indicate the existence of large political formations among the Bantu-speaking groups resident in the area. In the several complications of Bunyoro-Kitara oral tradition, anywhere from nine to twenty Tembuzi rulers are recognized.

The next ruling dynasty, the Chwezi, was clearly not mythical. Oral tradition provides an interesting, though rather unlikely, connection between the two dynasties. According to this account, Isaza, the last Tembuzi mukama (king), married the daughter of the king of the underworld. She returned to the underworld and gave birth to a son named Isimbwa. Soon after this, Isaza went to the underworld never to return, leaving his gatekeeper, Bukuku, as ruler of the kingdom.

Bukuku's rule was neither strong nor lasting. He was not widely recognized, and the kingdom broke up, with power being divided among various chiefs who refused to recognize Bukuku. Many years before, Bukuku had been told by diviners that he would have cause to fear any child that his daughter NyinamwIru might bear. He did not kill her, but he placed her under a strong guard and sought to reduce her attractiveness to suitors by putting out an eye and lopping off an ear and a breast. Despite these precautions, Isimbwa made his way to NyinamwIru on one of his frequent hunting trips which took him from the underworld to earth. In due course she gave birth to a son. This young man, who became known as Ndahura, the first Chwezi king, miraculously survived Bukuku's attempts to murder him. Ndahura eventually killed his grandfather, claimed the throne, and reunited the empire. Thus the legends provide a link between the Tembuzi and Chwezi dynasties, a mythical connection probably encouraged by the Chwezi so as to legitimize their rule.

Although the origins of the Chwezi are far from clear, traditions suggest the Chwezi pastoralists came, with herds of long horned cattle, to western Uganda and imposed themselves as a ruling aristocracy on the agricultural population. It is also possible that the Chwezi were local rulers who emerged as powerful figures as a result of economic and demographic change. These new rulers of Bunyoro-Kitara introduced a number of administrative innovations. It appears that they established a systematic administrative structure which was hierarchically organized. At the apex were the mukama and his palace officials, with chiefs appointed by him ruling over other parts of the empire. To help safeguard their cattle, the Chwezi rulers appear to have constructed substantial earthworks fortifications, the most famous of which was excavated by archaeologists at Bigo near the Katonga River. The ditches surrounding the earthen walls, more than six miles in extent, clearly reinforce the assertions of oral tradition that a substantial and powerful kingdom existed in this part of Uganda. These were likely built sometime during the period 1350 to 1500 which most scholars identify as roughly the period of Chwezi rule.

The oral traditions of Bunyoro-Kitara credit the Chwezi with other important innovations. They introduced much of the regalia of kingship (e.g., drums, clothes, and stools) and such new technology as the making of barkcloth and the cultivation of coffee. They built and lived in reed palaces.

At its height the territory controlled by the Chwezi rulers must have included a great deal of west-central and southwestern Uganda. The center of Chwezi rule lay between the Kafu and Katonga rivers, and included what would today be western and southern Bunyoro, eastern Toro, and western Buganda. Though this included substantial territory, the political structure ruled by the Chwezi was a loose confederation rather than a highly centralized state.

Chwezi rule was not lengthy. There were only two Chwezi kings, Ndahura and Wamara. It has been suggested that Ndahura abdicated in favor of the latter before proceeding to the west. Wamara built his capital on the southern bank of the Katonga river, but in the course of his reign things began to deteriorate. There were disputes among the Chwezi themselves, threats of invasion by outsiders, infiltration by Hima and Lwoo immigrants, rebellions against their rule, and cattle disease which severely reduced their herds. According to the traditions, disastrous omens eventually convinced Wamara and the Chwezi to depart the country. Leaving behind only the regalia of kingship, the Chwezi "vanished" and their state collapsed.

The Bito replaced the Chwezi as the ruling dynasty of Bunyoro-Kitara. They were part of the Lwoo migrations of River-Lake Nilotes from further north in the Nile valley. The Bito took over as rulers around the turn of the fifteenth century. Although oral traditions indicate that the Bito succeeded the Chwezi peacefully and were even linked to them by ties of marriage, many scholars believe that the Lwoo-speaking Bito conquered the kingdom by force, killing many of the ruling group and driving others away.

Led by their first king, Isingoma Mpuga Rukidi, the Bito adopted much of the Bunyoro culture. They adopted Bantu speech, and Rukidi took over much of the royal regalia and style of the Chwezi, though he and his successors added innovations of their own.

Thus established, the Bito, in the form of twenty-six mukamas, would rule Bunyoro-Kitara for the next several centuries. Moreover, the coming of the Bito had a significant effect on areas well beyond the boundaries of Bunyoro-Kitara itself. Bito dynasties were later set up in Toro and in parts of Busoga. Dynasties also were established in Nkore and Karagwe further south as well as in Rwanda and Burundi by Hima pastoralists and Chwezi survivors. The Hima were able to move into those regions and

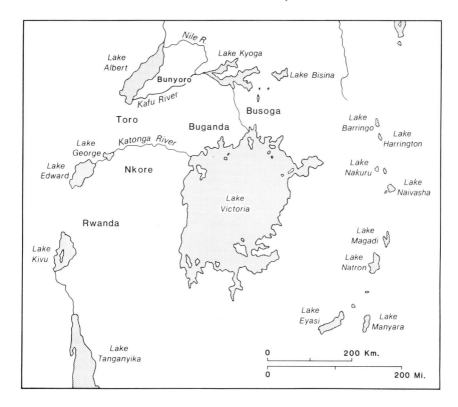

Map 9. West-Central Uganda

assume political influence as a result of the conditions created by the Chwezi downfall.

Origin of the Kingdom of Nkore

Prior to the disappearance of the Chwezi rulers and their replacement by the Bito, much of the southwestern portion of Uganda which came to be within the kingdom of Nkore or Ankole was part of the empire of Bunyoro-Kitara. With the end of Chwezi rule, however, control of this region lapsed, and into the power vacuum stepped the Hinda clan under their leader, Ruhinda. Nkore traditions claim that Ruhinda was descended from the Chwezi rulers; he is said to have been a son of Wamara. Other accounts make him a Hima leader who had been appointed chief herdsman of Bunyoro-Kitara by Wamara. It is probable that his move south and west to establish hegemony and rule in that area forms part of the story of the retreat of the Chwezi in the face of the Lwoo Bito, or the traditions may merely reflect an attempt of the Bahinda dynasty to establish a connection to the famous Chwezi. Whatever his origin, Ruhinda was apparently the leader of a group of cattle-herding peoples who moved to the southwest; taking advantage of the unsettled conditions brought about by the Lwoo invasion, he made himself the first mugabe (king) of Nkore.

Ruhinda started his kingdom in a small area known as Isingiro, and his rule had probably not been well established by the time of his death, for Nkore traditions speak of revolts against his son and successor, Nkube. Ruhinda was responsible for the start not only of Nkore; he also established several of the Haya states, most notably Karagwe, further south in what is today Tanzania.

As it developed, the kingdom came to consist of two different groups. Hima pastoralists were the ruling group. They herded large numbers of long horned cattle on the open plains which made Nkore attractive cattle country. The Iru made up the agricultural population. Politically, and to some extent socially, they did not enjoy a very privileged status.

Buganda Origins

In the area south and east of Bunyoro-Kitara, another kingdom rose to prominence after the fall of the Chwezi. This was the kingdom of Buganda. Buganda occupied a rather different ecological zone than that of Bunyoro-Kitara and Nkore; the former was in a wetter region, less suitable for cattle but well-suited to intensive agriculture, especially banana cultivation.

Buganda traditions suggest that the kingdom developed gradually over a considerable period of time. The peoples who made up the state came to occupy the region as a result of numerous migrations from several directions. Some clans, though they were certainly not the first, came from the northeast with Kintu, recognized in Buganda traditions as the founder of the kingdom. Others seem to have come with Kimera, who according to Bunyoro-Kitara traditions was the brother of Isingoma Mpuga Rukidi. The question of whether this means that the Buganda dynasty was of Bito origin after Kimera's time (most kinglists place him as the fourth ruler of Buganda) has been much debated by historians, and despite these Bunyoro-Kitara traditions, there is certainly no strong reason for assuming that Buganda was a Bito-ruled state.

In the fourteenth and fifteenth centuries Buganda remained a very minor state. She expanded, as time passed, from a small nucleus. Moreover, attempts to expand the territory controlled by Buganda were thwarted by the more powerful Bunyoro-Kitara. Down to the middle of the seventeenth century, Bunyoro-Kitara was militarily far stronger than Buganda and quite able to place limits on the territorial ambitions of the latter.

Nor was the power of the early kabakas (kings) overwhelming. They were little more than first among equals. The heads of the various Buganda clans, the bataka, were very influential, and this served to limit the power of the ruler.

Lwoo Migrations into Uganda

While kingdoms were developing in west-central and southwestern Uganda, the northern and eastern portions of the country were greatly influenced by the coming of River-Lake Nilotes speaking Lwoo languages in the period down to 1650. The homeland of the Lwoo-speaking groups probably lay somewhat to the south of the Nuer and Dinka in what is today the southern Sudan. Their way of life was shaped by the environment, which was marked by pronounced wet and dry seasons. In these conditions the Lwoo undoubtedly practiced transhumance, moving to the river valley for water for their herds in the dry season, and moving to ridges and hills away from the river when the wet season rains produced flooding.

Sometime in the fourteenth century the Lwoo began to move away from this area. It has been suggested that overpopulation, cattle too numerous for the land to support, and external threats were among the most likely factors bringing about the move. The movement itself was a very complex process, and although it can be simplified for purposes of explanation, it should not be assumed that large populations were moving quickly and rapidly to the south. Probably small groups were involved, moving at intervals sometimes as much as fifty or one hundred years apart.

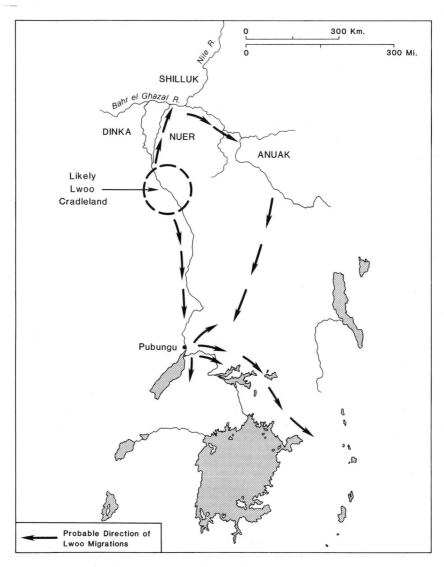

Map 10. Lwoo Migrations to East Africa.

Two broad views are represented in Lwoo traditions as to how this movement took place. One sees the migrations as going first north as far as the region of the junction of the Bahr el Ghazal River with the Nile; there, after disputes among the leadership, some groups stayed behind, but most continued on east and south, finally reaching Pubungu (Pakwach) on the Nile near Lake Albert. The other sees the move as initially south to northern Uganda. There a division occurred, and a group moved back to the north to the Bahr el Ghazal-Nile junction where another split took place, some Lwoo speakers staying behind while others moved to the east and west. Whichever version one accepts, it is certain that a number of Lwoo speakers arrived in northern Uganda in the fourteenth and fifteenth centuries. Lwoo speakers also established the Shilluk kingdom in the area north of the junction of the Bahr el Ghazal and the Nile, and to the southeast, the Anuak, another Lwoo-speaking group, settled.

The Lwoo-speaking migrants seem to have been highly adaptable, adjusting with ease to new situations. Indeed, the flexibility of the Lwoo has been a striking feature of their history. The Lwoo migrants borrowed much in the way of culture, ideas, and language from the people they encountered, and those people in turn were influenced by the Lwoo. One of the striking facts of the history of northern and eastern Uganda is that many of those who came to speak a Lwoo language and to adapt the Lwoo culture and ideas were peoples who originally spoke Bantu, Sudanic, or Plains Nilotic languages.

Although the Lwoo speakers were generally cattle-keeping peoples, they did adopt intensive agricultural techniques. It would appear that chiefs were a part of Lwoo society prior to the migrations from the Sudan, and in some areas (e.g., Shilluk) highly centralized kingdoms developed.

Lwoo Migrations Within East Africa

For East Africa the groups which came to Pubungu made a considerable imprint. One group moved across the Nile into an area inhabited by people speaking Sudanic languages. These peoples do not seem to have been organized into chieftaincies or to have had any degree of political centralization. The followers and descendants of the Lwoo established chieftaincies in the area, and gradually the earlier inhabitants, who became known as the Alur, gave up their language for Lwoo. A change of almost revolutionary proportions had been set in motion in northwestern Uganda.

As has already been described, another Lwoo group moved south across the Nile into Bunyoro-Kitara. They drove out the Chwezi, founded

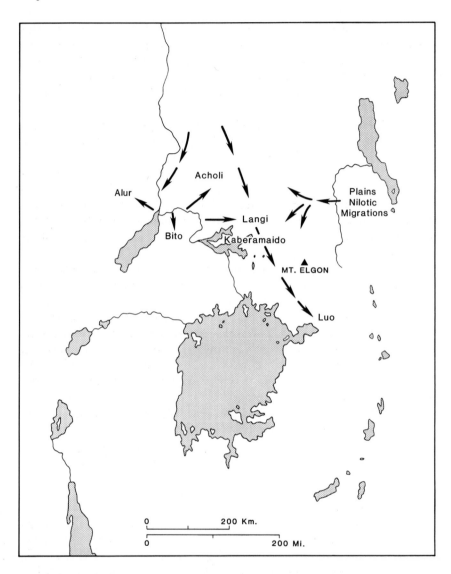

Map 11. Lwoo Migrations within East Africa.

the Bito dynasty, and remained the rulers of the kingdom until the second half of the twentieth century.

Another group remained longer at Pubungu, and then they gradually migrated to the north and east into the country of the Acholi, the Langi, and the Padhola. Descendants of this group would even make their way to western Kenya. The group which moved north-northeast to Acholi country were known as the Patiko. In this region lived Plains Nilotic-speaking cultivators known as the Iseera and also agriculturalists speaking Sudanic languages. A very complex process of interaction occurred, lasting many decades. Out of this there developed by the end of the seventeenth century a society known as the Acholi. Fuelled by a continuing stream of migrants from the north and assisted by their ability to absorb and adapt, the Lwoo speakers came to dominate the area. Their language became the language of all the people, and after the seventeenth century a number of small, centralized states under Lwoo rulers emerged.

In the Langi country a somewhat similar development took place. A new society emerged from a process of complex interaction between Lwoo speakers and Plains Nilotic cultivators. This occurred through fusion rather than by simple domination. Lwoo speakers also came into the area from the north. Their language triumphed, but the Langi people retained the clan structure that had existed among the Plains Nilotic-speaking peoples (Ateker). Clan leaders were often referred to by a form of the Lwoo word for chief, but they do not appear to have been as powerful as the chiefs among the Alur and the Acholi.

Some Lwoo speakers continued on to the east and south through Acholi and Langi country. A portion of the group which passed to Bunyoro-Kitara returned north and moved into Acholiland, Lango, and further east and south. These were joined by others who had migrated from the north. People from these groups came to make up the Padhola of eastern Uganda and the Luo of western Kenya. Thus, Lwoo speakers were moving into eastern Uganda from several directions by the seventeenth century. They stayed for a time in the Kaberamaido peninsula jutting into Lake Kyoga. Then they seem to have moved further east. These movements were still going on by 1650, and the Padhola had not yet settled into the territory they now inhabit. Neither had the major movements of Lwoo-speaking peoples into what is today Nyanza Province of Kenya been completed. These will be detailed in the section on Kenya.

Kenya

In the period under review, Kenya experienced a continuous movement of peoples of varied languages and cultures. Highlands, Plains, and River-Lake Nilotes established themselves in the territory while Bantu-speaking groups continued their movement toward settlement of the coast, the eastern highlands, the northeastern shores of Lake Victoria, and the slopes of Mt. Elgon. These were the regions of Kenya most suited to settled agricultural pursuits. Here adequate rainfall and soil fertility allowed for effective settlement. The northern portions of Kenya, on the other hand, have for long been characterized by an extremely dry environment, with portions of the northeast approaching desert conditions. In the north, and in portions of the central and southern Rift Valley, only a pastoral way of life was possible.

No centralized states or kingdoms developed in Kenya as they did in Uganda. It will therefore be useful to start with descriptions of the movements of the various language groups.

Highlands Nilotes

The homeland of the Highlands Nilotes was the southwestern area of Ethiopia. The culture and language of this group, before it moved into East Africa proper, were considerably influenced by the Eastern Cushitic speakers (age sets, circumcision as an initiation rite, etc.). As they spread into western Kenya, the Highlands Nilotes came into contact with and absorbed many Southern Cushitic-speaking peoples who had formed food-producing communities in the highlands.

During the first millennium A.D. the Highlands Nilotes differentiated into a number of distinctive groups, diverging from one another principally in language and culture. Most occupied portions of what is now Kenya, but the ancestors of one group, the Tatoga (Dadog), settled in northern Tanzania. These Highlands Nilotes expanded beyond Lake Natron, interacting and coexisting with Southern Cushites, Bantu, and possibly Khoisan speaking groups in this region. Since about 1600 the areas occupied by the Tatoga have been reduced as a result of the advance of Bantu-speaking peoples into the north-central part of Tanzania.

The other Highlands Nilotes groups occupied portions of northwest Kenya stretching roughly form Mount Elgon to Mount Kenya. They practiced an economy which combined livestock herding (cattle, sheep, and goats) with cultivation of sorghum and millets.

By far the most important of the Highland Nilotic groups is the Kalenjin. They occupied territory in the western Kenya highlands which was largely free from external pressures, and by the first half of this

64

millennium they had differentiated into several distinct communities, as shown by Chart 4.1.

Chart 4.1

Modern Highlands Nilote Languages

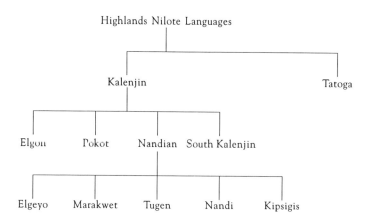

Only one of these communities experienced any significant expansion prior to 1650, and this was the South Kalenjin. Sometime before 1500 they spread their language and culture southward, covering an area as far south as the modern Gogo country of Tanzania. By perhaps 1600 this expansion was over, and in the next two centuries the Plains Nilotic-speaking Maasai would move into the region, imposing their language on the descendants of the South Kalenjin.

Prior to 1650 the other Kalenjin groups, while expanding only gradually, continued to move further apart from each other. The Elgon group proceeded west from the Rift Valley highlands and eventually settled around Mt. Elgon. The Pokot separated from the other Kalenjin groups by about 1500 and had moved off to the north, where they came into contact with Plains Nilotes speaking Karamojong-Teso languages who were in the process of replacing earlier Highlands Nilotes living there. With contact the Pokot began to adopt the Karamojong-Teso traits which differentiate them from other Kalenjin peoples.

At the beginning of the sixteenth century, the Nandian group was still largely concentrated on the western slopes of the Rift Valley to the east of Mount Elgon. They then moved east to the territory between Mt. Elgon and the Cheranganyi Hills. Here a division appears to have taken

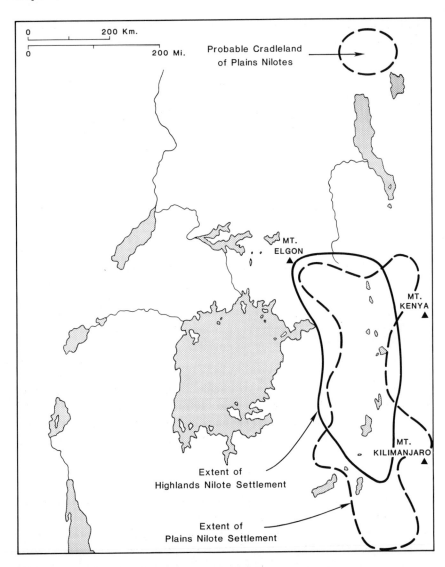

0

200 Km.

0

200 Mi.

Probable Cradleland
of Plains Nilotes

MT.
ELGON

MT.
KENYA

MT.
KILIMANJARO

Extent of
Highlands Nilote Settlement

Extent of
Plains Nilote Settlement

Map 12. Highlands and Plains Nilotes Before 1800.

place with the ancestors of the Elgeyo, Marakwet, and Tugen moving east and those of the Nandi and Kipsigis to the southwest.

Plains Nilotes

As has already been indicated in dealing with the history of the Highlands Nilote groups, a new and powerful force entered East Africa during the second millennium A.D. in the form of the Plains Nilotes. Unlike the Highlands Nilotes who combined stock raising with agriculture, the Plains group were primarily pastoralists who thus occupied the open grasslands of the Rift Valley. Moreover, their herds' need for fresh pastures and water kept them frequently on the move, often coming into contact with other peoples, and Highlands Nilotes and Bantu groups had to give attention to the problems of dealing with Plains people.

In the first millennium A.D. the Plains Nilotes were divided into two branches. The Bari speakers moved into the Sudan, and they have had little impact on East Africa. The other, the Teso-Maasai branch, is far more important in East African history. By about 1000 A.D. this branch had split up to form three major communities speaking similar yet distinct languages: the Lotuko, Karamojong-Teso, and Maasai. From a dispersal point possibly located in the Lake Turkana area, the Lotuko eventually moved west to settle in the Sudan. The Karamojong-Teso moved west and south toward Mt. Elgon, and the Maasai spread gradually to the southeast towards Mt. Kenya.

Chart 4.2

Plains Nilotic Languages

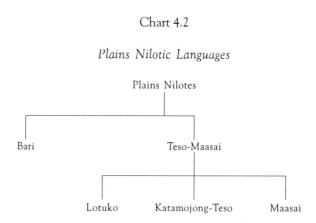

The spread and impact of the Maasai group of Plains Nilotes is by far the most important. They moved first southeast to the country east of the Rift Valley, perhaps settling in the areas between Mounts Kenya, Kilimanjaro, and the Taita Hills. There they strongly influenced, through trade and intermarriage, the Bantu-speaking peoples resident in the region, the ancestors, among others, of the Kikuyu, Kamba and Chagga. The Maasai were also considerably influenced by this contact borrowing a number of words from Bantu languages. The Maasai also came into contact with Highland Nilotes during the course of these movements. From them it appears the Maasai groups adopted their oval shaped shields and other elements of armament as well as ideas of circumcision.

The Karamojong-Teso group moved to an area stretching roughly from the north and east slopes of Mt. Elgon to northern Uganda. In this region they displaced the Highlands Nilote peoples resident there, and they began lengthy contacts (trade, marriage, raids for cattle, etc.) with the Pokot. The major period of Karamojong-Teso expansion, however, lies largely in the period after 1650.

Bantu and River-Lake Nilotes of Western Kenya: the Luhya and Luo

The major population groups resident along the eastern and northeastern shores of Lake Victoria in modern times, the Luhya and the Luo began to evolve as distinct linguistic and cultural entities during the period under review. The story of this process in each case is exceedingly complex, involving migration into the area by peoples from Uganda who stamped their languages on the highlands and lake shore and interaction between peoples speaking Southern Cushitic, Bantu, Plains, Highlands, and River-Lake Nilote languages.

The evolution of the Bantu-speaking Luhya of western Kenya represents just such a complicated process of interaction and integration between peoples. The Luhya are, to use Gideon Were's phrase, a "hybrid community." The highland regions north and east of Lake Victoria that the Luhya came to occupy in the second millennium A.D. were also inhabited by Highlands Nilotes in the north and by Bantu populations whose settlement in the south of the present Luhya area dated from early in the first millennium A.D. The Bantu were significantly influenced by contact with Highlands Nilotic and likely also by Southern Cushitic peoples resident in the western Kenya highlands. Through several centuries' interaction and acculturation the Bantu-speakers came to practice male circumcision as an initiation rite. These Bantu communities also seem to have been organized, like the Highlands Nilotic and Southern Cushitic peoples, into small clan or lineage units without chiefs.

However, at about the dawn of the seventeenth century, large migrations of Bantu clans from eastern Uganda and Buganda began. The causes of these migrations are unclear, but they probably included clan and dynastic disputes, overcrowding, and disease in eastern Uganda. These movements of people lasted until about the middle of the eighteenth century. The ancestors of most of the southern Luhya people seem to have arrived at this time. They settled not only in what is the southern Luhya region today, but also along the shores of Lake Victoria, where they would be supplanted by Lwoo-speaking River-Lake Nilotes.

The Bantu migrants from eastern Uganda placed their stamp linguistically and, to a lesser extent, culturally on the region they moved into. Many Highlands Nilotes were effected. Several groups of Kalenjin and other Highlands Nilotes residing near Mt. Elgon were absorbed and Bantuized, though a few retained their language and culture. Some clans retained their corporate structure while adopting the Bantu language. From these Highlands Nilotes and the earlier Bantu people, the Bantu migrants adopted some cultural practices, notably the practice of male circumcision, which are not followed in Busoga and Buganda, the areas from which they came.

The picture of cultural interaction is even more complex than this, however. Between the first quarter of the sixteenth century and the middle of the seventeenth century, Plains Nilotes of the Maasai group settled in the southwest of the Luhya region. These immigrants were also absorbed as individuals and clans, and their descendants lived scattered over the southern Luhya settlement area. The emergence of the Luhya thus represents a very complex process of interaction among groups of varied origins and cultures.

The neighbors of the Luhya in recent centuries, the Luo of Nyanza Province, represent the final stage of the migration of the Lwoo speakers from the southern Sudan. Generally speaking, the arriving Nilotes found Bantu-speaking peoples occupying the shores of Lake Victoria, but they were able to push the ancestors of the Luhya and the Gusii to higher ground or absorb them in the incoming Luo groups.

Luo traditions indicate four distinct waves of migration into the region east of Lake Victoria, beginning in the sixteenth century. The migrating Lwoo-speaking peoples came from several directions. Some came directly from the southern Sudan, others were offshots of the Lwoo migrants who had made their way to Pubungu, and still others broke away from the Padhola in Uganda to move east. The initial movements into western Kenya were relatively peaceful. Although the Lwoo speakers came as a largely pastoral people, they appear to have shifted to a primarily agricultural existence. The reasons for this important shift are not known with certainty, but perhaps endemic cattle disease and interaction with the agricultural Bantu may have had an effect.

The real conquest of Nyanza by the Luo comes with the second and third waves of migration. Arriving in the last half of the sixteenth and first quarter of the seventeenth century, the Lwoo speakers clashed heavily with the Bantu. As a result, Bantu peoples were pushed away

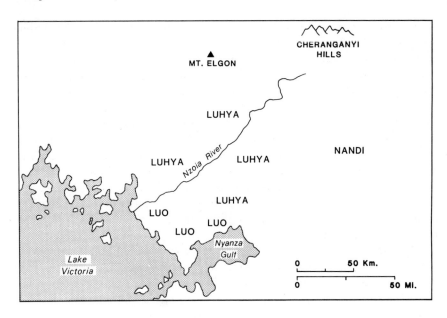

Map 13. Western Kenya.

from the lake shore, and a period of extensive interaction with Luhya groups began. The last of the migrations recognized by the Luo had not concluded by 1650. This movement included many non-Luo who eventually adopted Luo speech and customs through contact with the Luo of Kenya in the area south of Nyanza Gulf.

The Thagicu Peoples

The Bantu languages spoken in the southeastern and central highlands of Kenya have been classified as part of the Thagicu subgroup of East African Bantu. Linguistic comparison indicates that its origin as a distinct subgroup dates to the early second millennium A.D. The proto-Thagicu speakers eventually differentiated into four subdivisions, three of which came to inhabit the region around Mt. Kenya. Chart 4.3 illustrates the main divisions.

Chart 4.3

Thagial Languages

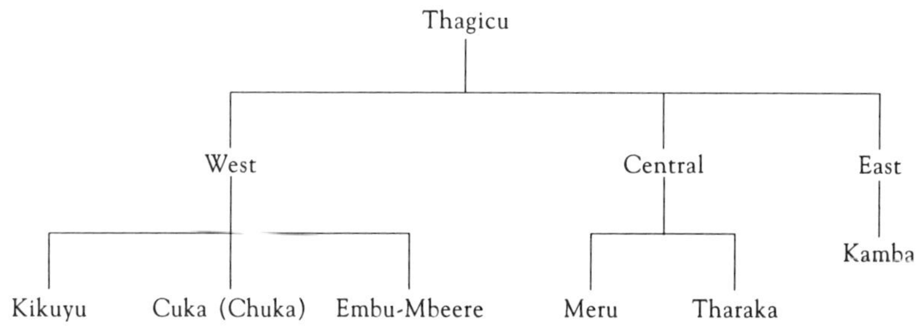

```
                          Thagicu
                             |
        _____
        |                       |                 |
       West                  Central            East
        |                       |                 |
   _____       _____         Kamba
   |      |        |       |          |
Kikuyu  Cuka    Embu-Mbeere  Meru   Tharaka
       (Chuka)
```

The Thagicu moved into a region which appears to have been inhabited by Southern Cushites, and as the former came into contact with these Cushites, they absorbed them into Bantu-speaking communities. The West and Central Thagicu, in particular, adopted many Cushitic customs such as circumcision and age sets and grades. Since 1500 contact with the Eastern Cushitic-speaking Oromo people has set northern limits to the regions settled by the Thagicu. It will also be recalled that contact with the pastoral Maasai affected these groups of Bantu in the region east of Mt. Kenya. In addition to contact with other languages and culture groups, the climate and geography of Eastern Kenya played a part in shaping the people's way of life. This region was generally drier than the western highlands, and for this reason these

Bantu speakers tended to form small, self-sufficient communities, often moving from place to place.

The western and central Thagicu gave rise to the groups collectively known as the Mt. Kenya peoples. These include the present-day Meru, Embu, Chuka, Tharaka, and Kikuyu. An examination of the traditions of these peoples suggests a multi-stage colonization of the Mt. Kenya region.

The initial inhabitants of this region were apparently Bantu-speaking peoples who moved into the area during the Early Iron Age in the first millennium A.D. The Mt. Kenya peoples' traditions suggest they moved initially from the region north of Mt. Kenya, but by the twelfth century they seem to have inhabited a broad region south and east of Mt. Kenya with Southern Cushitic communities as neighbors.

The second stage of migration and settlement of the Mt. Kenya peoples began about the middle of the fifteenth century. The migration in this case was initially to the south. It has been suggested that the reasons for this included the fact that the regions further west were wetter and better suited for cultivation; also, population pressure, Oromo threats, and internal family quarrels played a part. The movements helped to shape a complex process of divergence that would lead the Embu and Mbeere to the east of Mt. Kenya, the Chuka and Tharaka to the north, and the Kikuyu to the south and east of Kenya's highest peak.

Another important movement into the Mt. Kenya highlands brought the ancestors of the Meru peoples. Their traditions suggest they lived for some time at the Kenya coast. At the end of the seventeenth century they migrated from there across the dry lands until they came to the present Tharaka and Mbeere regions. From this area they would continue their penetration north and west.

The present-day eastern neighbors of the Mt. Kenya peoples, the Kamba, present a complex picture of population interaction and movement. Thagicu-speaking peoples interacted with Bantu speakers from the coast to produce a social formation which was Thagicu in language but culturally similar to the coastal Bantu speakers. Unlike the Mt. Kenya peoples, for example, the Kamba ancestors demonstrate little impact of the age set principle on their political or social organization. Kamba traditions indicate that their ancestors moved from the Mt. Kilimanjaro region. There the Kamba community was resident from the end of the fifteenth century until the dawn of the seventeenth. At this time the Kamba were little more than migrating groups, frequently shifting location on the dry plains bordering the mountain and its adjacent highlands.

In the last decades of the sixteenth century the Kamba began to abandon the Kilimanjaro plains. Initially this was a slow movement, but it soon grew into a widespread resettlement of people. Part of the reason

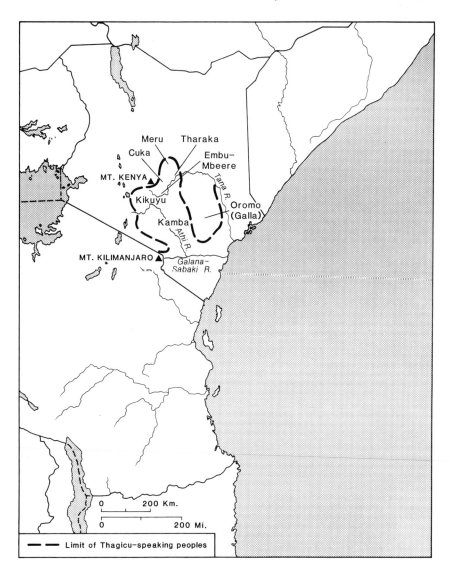

Map 14. Modern Distribution of Thagicu-Speaking Peoples.

for the movement was encroachment of the region by Maasai; overpopulation and a desire to find better grazing also help to explain the move. The Kamba moved first to the north, into the southern portion of present-day Ukamba, but did not put down roots there. About the middle of the seventeenth century, they moved northwest through relatively dry plains, finally reaching the Mbooni hills. Here in the well-watered highland forests, much different and more secure than the plains they had left, the Kamba established settlements from which the further occupation of Ukamba could be launched.

Mainland Tanzania

The history of Tanzania in the first half of the second millennium A.D., in contrast to Uganda and Kenya, is almost exclusively the history of Bantu-speaking peoples. With the exception of the movement of the Tatoga and Kalenjin into Tanzania from the north and some Southern Cushitic and Khoisan-speaking populations resident there, Bantu speakers formed the bulk of the population, and by 1650 almost all portions of the country were occupied by Bantu speakers. The heaviest concentrations of such peoples were in the well-watered areas to the west and south of Lake Victoria and in the highlands near Mt. Kilimanjaro. These areas, especially the latter, were characterized by good volcanic soils. In both regions relatively large, settled populations were in place by 1650, and political centralization had gone far enough to produce a number of chieftaincies or centralized states. In a broad area of west-central Tanzania characterized by smaller and less reliable amounts of rainfall, populations were not so concentrated. Hence a type of political organization distinguished by smaller-scale chieftaincies evolved.

West Lake Region: the Haya States

The history of the Haya states west of Lake Victoria is usually linked with that of kingdoms further north in Uganda, particularly Nkore. In this region Hinda rulers under Ruhinda, who also established the kingdom of Nkore in the fifteenth century, established control. Ruhinda and his pastoral followers founded seven new Hinda sub-dynasties under the rule of his sons; among these were Ukerewe, Busiza, Gisaka, Kyamtwarea, and Busiba.

When Ruhinda died, the "empire" he had forged did not survive. It broke up into small, independent kingdoms, each retaining its Hinda rulers. They were acceptable to the local people because of their military power, their association with important royal symbols and regalia which seem to have been brought from the north, and their reputation for justice.

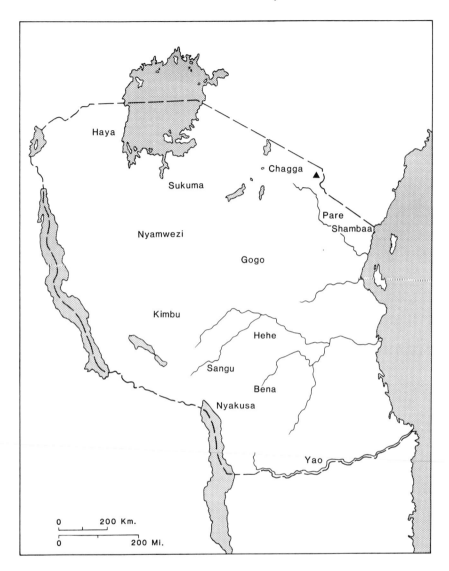

Map 15. Mainland Tanzania.

In these kingdoms, as in Nkore, a society with two distinct classes came into existence, the Hima pastoralists and the Iru cultivators. The considerable prestige and power associated with cattle ownership helped make the Hima the dominant group. Nevertheless, the two classes were dependent on each other, as in Nkore, and the efficient functioning of the state and economy depended upon cooperation between the groups.

West Central Tanzania: the Ntemi Chieftaincies

The people of this part of Tanzania during the period under review spoke languages belonging to the Western Tanzania Bantu group. After 1000 A.D. divisions took place into at least three subgroups, including the ancestors of the Kimbu and also the Nyamwezi-Sukuma. The homeland of the latter probably lay in the general region of what is today Sukumaland. Down to 1650 these peoples continued to spread and differentiate.

As in other parts of East Africa, climate and other ecological factors played an important part in determining settlement patterns and political development. West-central Tanzania consists of a broad plateau which is quite open; dry grasslands and woodlands predominate. Rainfall is not plentiful and is often unpredictable; there are, moreover, few major rivers in this region. This type of area could not sustain large, permanent concentrations of people, and the Bantu-speaking peoples living here tended to establish and maintain small, independent villages. These were normally self-sufficient communities, but as time passed, villages combined to form larger political units. These were headed by a chief, and such chieftaincies came to be known as Ntemi.

Ntemi chiefs came, over time, to hold political, social, and religious powers. They took the lead in group decision making, in settling disputes, and in religious rituals associated with the welfare of the people. A chief was seen as the link between the people and their ancestors. His own personal well being was intimately connected with the welfare of the country. In most cases Ntemi chieftaincies became hereditary, with the position remaining in a single family. Such chiefs were normally not authoritarian rulers; they were assisted and advised by a number of officials and councilors.

An Ntemi chieftaincy was not normally large. There were many reasons for this, but probably the most important was a continued process of division: a leader and followers could always break away and establish a new Ntemi unit. This would normally occur with a growth of population and/or shortage of resources. Thus, by an ongoing process of migration, settlement, and contact between groups, the system of Ntemi chiefs spread over a broad area of Tanzania. By the end of the fourteenth century this system was in use among the Sukuma and Nyamwezi south of Lake Victoria. Over the next several centuries rule by Ntemi chiefs spread to the south and east. By the nineteenth century more than 200 such units were in existence.

In south-central Tanzania, near the north end of Lake Malawi, lived the ancestors of such peoples as the Hehe, Bena, and Sangu in the period between the eleventh and seventeenth centuries. To the southwest of them lived the ancestors of the Nyakusa. Most of the peoples of this broad region seem to have been organized politically in small, relatively unstable chieftaincies.

Eastern Tanzania

The Bantu who inhabited this region spoke languages which were part of the Tanzania-Coastal and Chaga-Taita groups. Proto-Chaga-Taita had already differentiated into several divisions by 1100. The ancestors of the Chagga were probably settled on the southeastern slopes of Mt. Kilimanjaro. The Gweno, on the other hand, seem to have emerged as a distinct group in the north Pare highlands.

Chart 4.4

Chaga-Taita Languages

The Tanzania-Coastal speakers who lived in northern and northeastern Tanzania are identified in Chart 4.5. Linguistic comparison suggests that the likeliest homeland for this group is the Tanzania-Kenya border region near the coast.

These Bantu speakers moved into areas where peoples speaking Southern Cushitic languages lived. Eventually, though the process was not complete by 1650, the Bantu absorbed Southern Cushitic speakers. Ehret suggests that one reason the Bantu were able to do so may well have been their development of an intensive highland agriculture based on bananas which in turn helped produce an expanding population.

Chart 4.5

Tanszania-Coastal Bantu (Tanzania Groups)

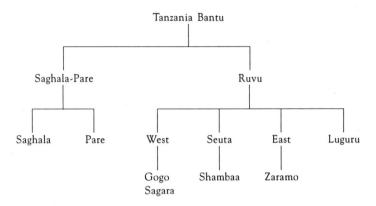

The Usambara and Pare highlands were fertile and well-watered regions, well suited for cultivation. By 1650 the population density of these areas and of the southern slopes of Mt. Kilimanjaro, with their rich volcanic soils, was increasing. As a result of this population growth and other factors, political centralization would take place leading to the formation of chieftaincies and kingdoms in the eighteenth and nineteenth centuries.

In the southeastern corner of Tanzania lived peoples speaking languages ancestral to the group, which have been termed Rufiji-Ruvuma because they lived in the lowland region between the Rufiji and Ruvuma rivers, and Kilombero. They seem, unlike peoples living further north, to have had little contact with Southern Cushites. Cattle did not play an important part in their economies, and most of the individual ethnic groups were not characterized by political units ruled by chiefs before 1650.

Between approximately 1000 A.D. and 1650, the East African interior thus underwent a variety of historical experiences. These developments were in some ways similar in many areas, involving the migration of peoples, the subsequent interaction between groups that resulted, and the absorption of one group by another. The interactions among peoples of the Nilotic-, Cushitic-, and Bantu-speaking groups were shaping the complex linguistic and cultural patterns of East Africa by the mid-seventeenth century.

East African political history during this period was characterized by striking differences in political developments and structures. In western

Uganda and Tanzania, highly structured, centralized states emerged under kings. In western and central Tanzania, Ntemi chiefs developed as a focus for political activity. In most of Kenya, on the other hand, there were neither kingdoms nor societies ruled by hereditary chiefs with judicial and political influence.

Reasons for these differences cannot be established with certainty, but the environment and the settlement patterns of the various regions was probably of considerable influence. Kenya is, on the whole, less open than, for example, western Uganda. The plateau is intersected by high hills and valleys, and there was not a great deal of open country which could be controlled without having to surmount natural barriers. Moreover, Kenya was in these centuries much more characterized by the movement and interaction of peoples of varied cultures and languages. Western Uganda, on the other hand, had been the earliest scene of Bantu settlement in East Africa, and large population concentrations had developed there before 1500, in contrast to the more fluid situation in most of Kenya and southeastern Tanzania.

Suggestions for Further Reading

Dunbar, A. R. A *History of Bunyoro-Kitara* (Nairobi, 1965).

Ehret, C. "Between the Coast and the Great Lakes," in Niane, D. T., ed. *General History of Africa,* IV (Berkeley, 1984).

Ehret, C. *Southern Nilotic History* (Evanston, 1971).

Ehret, C., and Posnansky, Merrick, eds. *The Archaeological and Linguistic Reconstruction of African History* (Berkeley, 1982).

Karugire, S. R. A *History of the Kingdom of Nkore in Western Uganda to 1896* (Oxford, 1971).

Kiwanuka, M. S. A *History of Buganda From the Foundation of the Kingdom to 1900* (New York, 1972).

Ogot, B. A. "The Great Lakes Region," in Niane, D. T., ed. *General History of Africa,* IV (Berkeley, 1984).

Ogot, B. A., ed. *Kenya Before 1900* (Nairobi, 1976).

Ogot, B. A., ed. *Zamani* (Nairobi, 1974).

Roberts, A., ed. *Tanzania Before 1900* (Nairobi, 1968).

Spear, Thomas. *Kenya's Past* (London, 1981).

Chapter 5

The East African Interior from the Mid-Seventeenth to Mid-Nineteenth Centuries

THE PERIOD STRETCHING FROM THE middle of the seventeenth to the middle of the nineteenth centuries was a time of continued movement and interaction among East Africa's peoples. These years witnessed some substantial movements of peoples within the region and from outside. By the end of the period the ethnic and linguistic groups of East Africa had largely assumed the form they have in the present century. In addition, these years witnessed a development of political centralization in areas outside western Uganda, most notably in eastern and central Tanzania. There such political developments typically were the result of changes in economic structure which led to growth in surplus production and trade. However, it would be wrong to assume that the growth of chieftaincies and states was a phenomenon experienced by all peoples of the interior; in fact, diversity characterized the economic and political formations of East Africa.

Uganda

Between 1650 and 1850 an important characteristic of the territory which would become Uganda was the diversity which developed between north and south. In some considerable measure, this was the result of the different ecological regions noted in Chapter 4. The north provided a more difficult environment; droughts were common and population was normally not densely concentrated. Cultivation of cereals utilizing, shifting patterns of land use within a communal mode of production centered on the household, combined with stock raising was typical of the Acholi and Langi, while pastoralism was practiced by the Karamojong. The small division of labor that existed in such societies was gender-based, with mutual assistance between households fairly common. There was little surplus production other than for local exchange.

Until the eighteenth century most northern societies were character-ized by small-scale political formations without kings. After that time, however, most Acholi and Langi societies experienced a growth of centralized political organization which was distinguished by increasing emphasis on territorial (as opposed to ethnically based) formations, the growth in power of hereditary chiefs or kings, and the organization of war bands, especially among the Langi. At the same time, the important and extremely complex social transformation of much of northern Uganda, begun prior to 1650, was continuing. Lwoo-speaking communities would predominate by the middle of the nineteenth century.

In the south of Uganda, Bantu-speaking peoples predominated. Better watered and more fertile than the north, the southern portion was more heavily populated. Here surplus production of agricultural produce (both grain and bananas) was possible on a larger scale. Such surpluses were—at least before the end of the nineteenth century—for consumption rather than profit. Trade links existed, such as those joining the Hima and the Iru, but these were more complementary than competitive. While distinctions based upon wealth and political influence had emerged in the southern kingdoms by the middle of the nineteenth century, it would be incorrect to see in this a developing capitalism. The surplus production of the south, still largely the result of household and communal labor methods, was not directed toward the world market. Those who benefited from it were the monarchs and chiefs of the southern kingdoms who claimed such produce as tribute.

The centralized states of the south thus continued to exist after 1650; the kingdoms themselves, however, underwent dramatic changes. Buganda now emerged as the most powerful state in the region, supplanting Bunyoro-Kitara. As the political, economic, and military power of Buganda expanded, so did the territory she controlled, and the political system of the kingdom was altered. A centralization of power within Buganda made the position of the kabaka virtually all powerful by the middle of the nineteenth century.

Bunyoro-Kitara

For some time after the accession of the Bito rulers, Bunyoro, as the kingdom was now known, remained the largest and most powerful state in the interlacustrine region. In a series of conflicts Bunyoro rulers beat back attempts of Buganda to expand at its expense. Bito rulers waged successful wars of expansion to the north and west and also south into Nkore. The borders of the empire were expanded and great numbers of cattle were captured.

Bunyoro power began to shrink at the beginning of the eighteenth century and that of Buganda began to increase. Two events in the eighteenth century may be cited as examples of this power shift. Around the beginning of the century, Mukama Chwa I invaded Nkore with large forces. His aim was to capture cattle to replace Bunyoro herds killed by an epidemic disease. He was successful in Nkore, but continued on to raid the kingdom of Rwanda further south. There he was killed, and his leaderless army was defeated on their retreat by the mugabe of Nkore. Later, during the reign of the seventeenth Bito ruler, Duhaga I, war began with Buganda. Unlike in previous conflicts, the war that now started over land and tribute areas saw Buganda gain the upper hand. Buganda expanded her control over territories which had been within the empire of Bunyoro-Kitara or had owed tribute to the mukama. Thus while the size of Buganda dramatically enlarged during the eighteenth and nineteenth centuries, that of Bunyoro shrank. Not only was territory lost to Buganda but other areas on the borders of Bunyoro, such as Toro, broke away to forge an independent existence.

There are several reasons for the decline of Bunyoro, and particularly for her weakness in comparison to Buganda. First, the Bunyoro system of government was not as centralized as that of Buganda; the empire continued to be governed as a loose federation. Provincial chiefs could raise their own armies, and this could always provide a potential threat to a mukama. It is also apparent that Bunyoro-Kitara experienced a great deal of political instability in the eighteenth and nineteenth centuries, exemplified by the increasing numbers of succession wars between claimants for the throne after the reign of Duhaga I. Such wars must have weakened the capacity of the kingdom to halt the advance of Buganda. Moreover, Buganda was able to take advantage of her larger population and, in the nineteenth century particularly, her control of trade with the East African coast to maintain the upper hand over Bunyoro.

Although the position of Bunyoro weakened relative to Buganda, the mukama remained the center of government. He was head of the administration as well as judicial and ritual leader. At his capital the mukama was surrounded by various officials and advisers who made up a well-defined bureaucracy. These included officials charged with looking after the royal drums and other regalia of kingship, those who served as chief herdsmen, craftsmen, and a group of informal advisers and retainers.

The mukama maintained no standing army. In time of war, chiefs were expected to provide men to fight for the mukama. This meant that chiefs could, and often did, raise armies on their own. Nevertheless, in normal circumstances the mukama's power was supreme.

The territorial administration was also organized under the control of the mukama. He appointed chiefs to rule the various provinces and districts within the kingdom on his behalf. The chiefs were directly responsible to the mukama and owed their control over territories to him. There were a limited number of great chiefs, or bakungu, who ruled territories that could be termed provinces. Below this rank of chief were the more numerous batangole who ruled smaller areas and had more limited powers. The chiefs administered the kingdom, settled disputes, collected tribute, and raised armies on behalf of the mukama. Although in theory the ability of the mukama to control his chiefs—through removal from office, the use of religious sanctions, and the requirement that they spend much time at his court—was substantial, this control weakened in the context of succession wars and unsuccessful military campaigns against Buganda in the eighteenth and nineteenth centuries.

Kaberega and the Rejuvenation of Bunyoro

The decline of the kingdom was checked in the middle of the nineteenth century by the resolute leadership and brilliant tactics of Mukama Kabarega. Coming to the throne at the end of the 1860s, he created a standing army, the abarusura, which was divided into ten divisions, each under its own commander. These were sent to the outlying regions of the empire to guard against invasions and discourage any royal princes or chiefs who might challenge the mukama's power. He was also able to strengthen his army by obtaining firearms from the north. Kabarega's military strength is shown by the fact that he was able to reestablish Bunyoro's control over Toro, which broke away at the beginning of the nineteenth century, and to turn back attempts by Egypt to establish dominance over northern Uganda in the 1870s.

It is possible that without European intervention Kabarega might have reestablished a great Bunyoro empire. However, in the 1880s and 1890s he was drawn into Buganda affairs. Conflict with Buganda led to hostilities with Britain. This checked Kabarega; Toro was lost to him, and his own territory was invaded. Although Kabarega carried on a skillful guerilla campaign against British forces for seven years, he was eventually defeated; his kingdom suffered loss of land and other humiliations at the hands of the British and Buganda.

Buganda: Territorial Expansion

One of the main features of Buganda history after 1650 was the great increase in territorial extent that she experienced. As has been pointed out, this coincided in large measure with the decline of Bunyoro and was achieved, to a considerable extent, at the latter's expense. Still, this expansion was both remarkable and significant. At the beginning of the sixteenth century Buganda was only a small principality, but by the middle of the nineteenth century it was unquestionably the largest and most powerful kingdom in East Africa.

Several of the reasons for Buganda's expansion have been noted previously. Lying on the well-watered shores of Lake Victoria, Buganda was favored with fertile soil and great agricultural potential. Extensive cultivation, especially of bananas, made food plentiful throughout the year, and Buganda's population grew rapidly. During the same time as expansion was proceeding, and indeed partly as a result of it, Buganda developed a highly centralized and efficient government, centered on the kabaka. In the eighteenth and nineteenth centuries, Buganda was able to control trade with the east coast. This furthered her strength, most notably through the acquisition of firearms in the nineteenth century.

In the seventeenth century, most notably during the reign of the warlike Kabaka Kateregga, Buganda began to expand into areas that had been lost to Bunyoro in previous decades of fighting. Kateregga then took his armies into lands that had never been under Buganda's control. Ultimately, he doubled the size of Buganda, and these gains were consolidated by his successor, Mutebi.

A new era of expansion began with the reign of Kabaka Mawanda around the beginning of the eighteenth century. A highly popular ruler, Mawanda launched a campaign of deliberate territorial expansion. He began in the northwest and annexed a large area around Lake Wamala after defeating Bunyoro. He then invaded the lands just to the west of the Nile and overran much of it. From that springboard, Mawanda sent his armies to Busoga, across the Nile, where they mercilessly plundered the local population. Finally, Mawanda succeeded in pushing his control to the northeast.

After a breathing space of two or three reigns, expansion once again occurred toward the end of the eighteenth century under Kabaka Junju. He warred against Bunyoro and other neighbors, and as a result pushed the boundaries of Buganda further outward. He conquered Buddu to the south, and his armies overran the region as far south as Karagwe in what is today Tanzania. The major expansion after 1800 occurred under

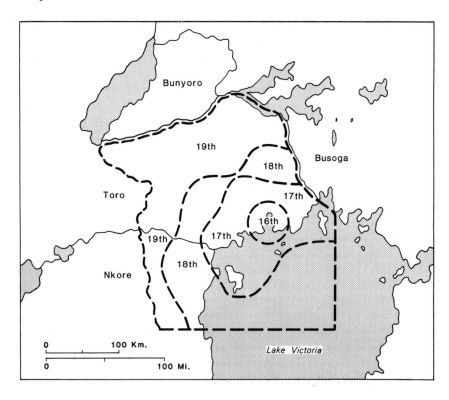

Map 16. Buganda Expansion, Sixteenth Through Nineteenth Centuries.

Kamanya who defeated Bunyoro and annexed territory to the north of Buganda.

From the 1820s to the 1890s Buganda undertook no major campaigns of expansion. Rather, she used her military power to raid, plunder, and establish tributary states or spheres of influence over a broad area. Buganda armies ranged successfully over a vast expanse of territory from Bunyoro to Nyamwezi territory to the south and to western Kenya. However, these campaigns were not followed up by annexation. One of the major areas to suffer from Buganda attacks and exploitation was Busoga. A number of small states and principalities existed there, but they were not strong enough to withstand the military might of Buganda. To her large armies Buganda had added a very effective navy on Lake Victoria. The numerous boats and canoes that could be called upon by the kabaka added the dimension of sea power to the strong land forces Buganda possessed. Thus, despite a slowing of expansion by Buganda in the middle of the nineteenth century, she remained the most powerful and wealthy state in Uganda.

Centralization and Strengthening of the Monarchy in Buganda

A prominent theme in Buganda history down to the middle of the nineteenth century was the increasing centralization of power in the hands of the kabaka. This was a gradual process, the result of several factors. One of the most important, it appears, was the series of wars with Bunyoro and the capture of territory which resulted. As noted earlier, kabakas before the seventeenth century were little more than "first among equals." Those who administered the various territorial divisions were usually the hereditary clan heads, the bataka. However, success in war gave the kabakas a chance to increase their power by using the spoils of conquest, especially new lands, to reward their loyal followers. The kabaka could thus make loyal men chiefs in the newly occupied territories.

According to Buganda tradition, Kabaka Mutebi was the first ruler to do this. His attempts to install his own men as chiefs were opposed, however, by the bataka. It was left to Mawanda in the eighteenth century to do this on a considerable scale, and his successors followed suit. The most important saza (county) chiefs came to be "king's men" who owed their appointment and loyalty to the kabaka. By the middle of the nineteenth century practically all the major chiefs of Buganda were "king's men" rather than hereditary chiefs.

Another factor which played a part in the strengthening of the position of the monarch was the absence of a royal clan. This limited succession wars. Although disputes over the throne were initially fairly common, by the beginning of the nineteenth century the succession issue had largely been settled. Control of trade by the kabaka must also have strengthened his hand. By the middle of the nineteenth century the powers of the kabaka were considerable and his control of affairs was far reaching.

The Buganda government was hierarchically organized. The kabaka appointed chiefs loyal to him to administer county and sub-county units. A number of officials were selected to undertake special duties at court. Among the most important were the katikiro, or chief minister, and the omuwanika, or treasurer. Leading families from each clan were encouraged to send some of their sons to court where, serving as pages, they were trained and then appointed to offices. An advisory council, the Lukiko, also existed, but in the middle of the nineteenth century it does not seem to have had great influence over kabakas such as Suna or Mutesa I.

Internally, Buganda society had developed a remarkable dynamism. No one was excluded from high office by birth or origin. Anyone who served the kabaka well could expect to get ahead. The growing wealth of the kingdom and its ruler thus fueled a patronage system which emphasized achievement and was marked by fierce competition at all social levels. This competition helped produce a spirit of acquisitiveness and farsightedness practically unequalled in East Africa. The Ganda were thus quick to take up new ideas and techniques, and this openness would be particularly significant in the latter half of the nineteenth century when new influences, notably Islam and Christianity, would find rapid acceptance among the population of Buganda.

The Kingdom of Nkore

For most of the seventeenth century, the kingdom of Nkore was largely on the defensive against more powerful neighbors, most notably Bunyoro, and she experienced little change in her borders. At the beginning of the eighteenth century, as we have noted, an invading force from Bunyoro forced the mugabe, Ntare IV, to flee, but the Nkore forces won a great victory, routing the Bunyoro army on its return from Rwanda. After defeating these invaders, Ntare strengthened the position of the monarchy through reforms that tied the various clans in the kingdom more closely to the king. He also reorganized and improved the army, and this innovation strengthened the monarchy. Nkore could now counter forays from outside and gain territory at the expense of her neighbors; Ntare extended the boundaries of his kingdom north to the Katonga river.

Nkore's borders gradually expanded in the eighteenth and nineteenth centuries, despite the more frequent occurrence of succession disputes in the kingdom itself. Perhaps the greatest period of expansion came during the reign of Mugabe Mutambuka in the nineteenth century. He expanded to the northwest and launched raids on neighboring states to the south and north. By the end of the third quarter of the nineteenth century, Nkore was at its peak of power, but disasters soon overtook both the human and animal populations (e.g., smallpox and rinderpest). At the time of the colonial intervention of the 1890s, Nkore was not in a very strong position to resist the British.

Like the Haya states and Rwanda further south, Nkore society consisted of two distinct communities—the Hima, who were pastoralists, and the Iru, who were agriculturalists. To the Hima, cattle were all-important. Cattle were the center of their lives, and they had social importance for their owners. The greater prestige of the cattle owners tended to give the Hima the position of a separate and ruling class.

This should not, however, be overemphasized. There were important mutual links between the two groups which encouraged cooperation and meant in practice that one group could not easily do without the other. The Hima supplied milk, meat, hides, and manure, while the Iru provided agricultural produce and iron goods needed by the Hima. The Iru provided a steady food supply, while the Hima provided the fighting forces to protect the kingdom.

Although the Hima assumed the position of a ruling class, Iru were not excluded from the political process. Not all of the bakungu (chiefs) who ruled the various administrative divisions of the kingdom under the mugabe were Hima. Moreover, any cultivator who particularly distinguished himself could be given cattle by the king and thereby become a part of the Hima. Thus, while important distinctions existed between the two groups, the social gulf was not unbridgeable.

The Kingdom of Toro

The kingdom of Toro was established in the nineteenth century by the Bito prince Kaboyo. Realizing he would not inherit the Bunyoro throne, Kaboyo broke away and established the kingdom of Toro southwest of Bunyoro. Unhappy with Bunyoro overrule, the people of the region welcomed Kaboyo's creation of an independent state with a government similar to that of Bunyoro. Moreover, the new mukama was able to fight off the forces his father sent against him.

Independence was maintained during the lifetime of Kaboyo and for a time after it. His death was followed by succession wars that lasted from the 1850s to the 1870s. Finally, Nyaika I emerged as ruler, but he saw his kingdom invaded and captured by Kabarega of Bunyoro. Kabarega's military power was sufficient to keep much of the kingdom under his control until Captain Frederick Lugard, then in the service of the Imperial British East Africa Company, intervened to establish Toro's independence of Bunyoro by placing Kasagama on the throne as the 1890s opened.

Lwoo-Speaking Communities

It will be recalled that northern Uganda was an area into which Lwoo-speaking River-Lake Nilotes had moved by 1650. In both the Acholi and Langi regions, a complex process of ethnic interaction produced peoples speaking Lwoo languages who were in fact of very mixed origins.

By the eighteenth century the Lwoo-speaking element among the Acholi had come to dominate the area through the formation of many small kingdoms. Such Acholi states were typically based on the close linkage of several clans to the rwot (king) and his family. Many of the rwots developed an elaborate regalia of kingship. To help administer the kingdoms the rwots appointed jago (village chiefs). These jago collected taxes and tribute for the rwot. The ruler's authority was also fortified by his association with religious sanctions. Thus, by the middle of the nineteenth century there were a number of small Acholi kingdoms in northern Uganda.

In what is today Lango, similarly, the Langi people emerged as a Lwoo-speaking group by the beginning of the eighteenth century. However, small centralized states did not develop here. War became an important feature of Langi society as a source of glory and wealth. The Langi raided and fought neighbors on all sides with success. Warfare demanded specialized organization, and in the nineteenth century war leaders known as witong emerged. These witong played an important role in coordinating and organizing military activity in a society that lacked centralized rule and was not organized as a single political unit. Langi soldiers also fought as mercenaries for neighboring rulers, notably with Kabarega's abarusura.

Prior to 1650 the Lwoo-speaking peoples who would form the core of the Padhola were still moving in eastern Uganda, and they had not settled in their present homeland as yet. By about 1700 they had set down roots in eastern Uganda in a relatively empty region. They had to fight off Maasai pressure from the east, and this appears to have forced them west into an area of thick forest. Here more clans and families of both Lwoo and Bantu origin arrived and joined the original group. The need for cooperation in defense and in clearing the forest helped to forge a new community. As time passed, a Lwoo-speaking population emerged from a people of diverse origins in an environment much different from that of the southern Sudan.

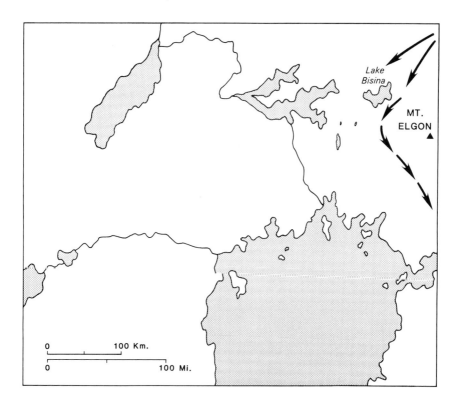

Map 17. Teso Movements.

Karamojong-Teso Movements

The period after 1650 likewise witnessed important movements of the Plains Nilotic peoples belonging to the Karamojong-Teso group. Prior to this time, these pastoral peoples appear to have lived in the dry country north and east of Mt. Elgon. In the seventeenth and eighteenth centuries they began to move to the west into present day Uganda, pushing aside some peoples and absorbing others as they went. The Karamojong followed a northerly course and eventually came to occupy northeastern Uganda adjacent to the modern Kenya border where they continued their pastoral pursuits.

The Teso, on the other hand, followed a more southerly route of migration into eastern Uganda. They moved into the region between Mt. Napak and Lake Bisina by the beginning of the nineteenth century. Later in the same century, they moved round the slopes of Mt. Elgon, and some migrated further southeast into what is today Kenya, splitting several Luhya groups and pushing others into new homes in the process. In the course of these movements to the west of Mt. Elgon and toward Lake Victoria, they moved among a population consisting largely of Bantu-speaking agriculturalists. As a result of interaction with these people, the Teso adopted an agricultural way of life while maintaining their customs and language. With cultivation came a growing population, and this, it would appear, necessitated changes in political and social organization to cope with the large numbers. By the end of the nineteenth century this had not resulted in the formation of centralized chieftaincies, though military leaders were able to mobilize support in portions of the area settled by the Teso.

Kenya

Kenya experienced no economic or political changes on the scale of those that occurred in Uganda and Tanzania in the nineteenth century. Trade with the east coast certainly increased, but difficulties with terrain and potentially hostile peoples discouraged the development of long-distance trade until the latter portion of the century. Correspondingly, the period under review witnessed, with perhaps one exception, the emergence of no centralized states in Kenya. With few exceptions, the Kenya interior was characterized by political formations lacking institutionalized political roles, often classified as "stateless societies."

There was, on the other hand, no absence of significant movements of peoples in this period. Many of the ancestors of Kenya's present day ethnic units moved towards the areas they would come to occupy at the end of the nineteenth century. The Nandi, the Gusii, and the Kikuyu provide some examples. A contrasting example is presented by the Maasai-speaking peoples. They swept south through the Rift Valley during the early part of this period, bringing a large area directly or indirectly under their sway. By the end of the nineteenth century, however, these Plains Nilotes would no longer be able to dominate such a far-flung region.

Even at the height of the their power, the Maasai were not involved in extensive networks of exchange. The Maasai economy, like those of most of Kenya's peoples in this period, did not produce large surpluses. Many peoples living in Kenya practiced stock raising in combination with cultivation; the degree to which one or the other predominated was normally determined by the environment. Most of these groups were characterized by a gender-based division of labor within extended family units, with little specialization in production except in cases where blacksmithing was concentrated in a particular clan. Men cleared the land for planting, women planted, weeded, and harvested, boys herded cattle, and young men defended stock. In most cases there was little incentive to produce a large surplus of annual cereals, and cattle were normally retained by families and clans as insurance against possible food shortage. Unpaid cooperative labor was provided by neighboring kinfolk in most Kenya societies.

Highlands Nilotes

In the previous chapter the movements of the Kalenjin in the Rift Valley highlands have been noted. By 1650 a division had already occurred between the Pokot and Nandian groups. A further division was accentuated by the Uasingishu Maasai, who penetrated south into the highlands. This helped to finally divide the Nandian group into separate entities (Nandi, Elgeyo, Tugen, etc.). It is possible also that this Maasai penetration and raids forced the Kalenjin to reduce their herds and turn more toward agriculture. It may also have led the Nandi, having parted company from their close relatives the Kipsigis, to push north and west toward their present homeland.

By the eighteenth century the Nandi were taking shape as a separate Kalenjin community. In the course of their movement to the north and west, they absorbed other Kalenjin groups. Like other Kalenjin peoples, the Nandi had no chiefs. Political and judicial decisions were taken in councils which were representative of men living within a local semi-autonomous unit, the pororiet. Prominent and wealthy individuals could play an influential role in these councils, but decision making was essentially democratic. An important unifying element among the Nandi, as well as other Kalenjin peoples, was the existence of cycling age sets to which every man belonged.

The Nandi political and social organization, unlike that of some other Kalenjin groups, did undergo important changes in the nineteenth century, most significantly through the adoption of a new centralized leadership position, the orkoiyot. This new institution came about as the result of an Uasingishu Maasai named Barsabotwo settling among the Nandi. He advised and coordinated Nandi military efforts against the Luhya-speaking Bukusu and the Uasingishu Maasai. As these ended successfully, the prestige and influence of Barsabotwo was greatly increased. As orkoiyot, he became a central authority for all Nandi pororiet to consult in affairs concerning war, planting, circumcision, and the transfer of power from one set to another. Even after his death, the Nandi continued to recognize the importance of the orkoiyot, but such officials never held a position really analogous to a chief or king.

The nineteenth century was also a time of increasing Nandi strength. As the military power of the Uasingishu Maasai waned, that of the Nandi increased, helped more than a little by the guidance and coordination of the orkoiyot. The Nandi expanded north and west, which brought them into contact and conflict with the Luhya and Luo in the second half of the century. There can be little doubt that the Nandi were the most powerful people in western Kenya in the 1890s. Moreover, they put up a more sustained and fiercer resistance to colonial conquest than any other Kenya group.

Plains Nilotes

The period from the middle of the seventeenth century until approximately 1800 was marked by substantial Maasai power and expansion. Though not great in numbers, this primarily pastoral people swept down through the Rift Valley and dominated many of the grazing lands formerly held by the Kalenjin. Not only the Kalenjin were affected by this movement; almost every major population group was touched by Maasai stock raiding and the practice of Maasai warriors hiring themselves out to other peoples as mercenaries (e.g., in Wanga). The Maasai, moving periodically with their herds, thus dominated large areas of territory, stretching from the Uasin Gishu plateau in northwestern Kenya to the Laikipia plateau, and from the central Rift Valley all the way to central Tanzania.

The Maasai were not a single, united entry. Several Maasai groups emerged during the course of this expansion, differing somewhat in way of life and the areas in which they lived. An important distinction among groups was that which separated the pastoralists, the IlMaasai, and those who practiced agriculture as well as herding, the Iloikop. The IlMaasai lived only off their herds and disdained vegetable foods or the meat of wild game. Iloikop groups grew crops, and some, such as the

Arusha of Tanzania and Njemps of Kenya, developed intensive agriculture.

Like the Kalenjin, the Maasai developed no centralized political system. Unity was maintained and leadership exercised through a system of age sets. Administration and decision making lay in the hands of the elders while the moran, or warrior age grades, provided the fighting men. By the end of the eighteenth century, a central religious and ritual figure, the olaiboni, had emerged among the pastoral IlMaasai. As the nineteenth century wore on, secular power was added to the religious power of the olaiboni.

By the second half of the nineteenth century, Maasai power had begun to decline. Among the prime reasons for this was a series of "civil wars" fought between Maasai groups in the course of the century, often over grazing land and water. Several conflicts pitted IlMaasai groups against Iloikop, as in the conflict between the Purko and the Laikipiak in the 1870s. Some of these conflicts were devastating enough to significantly alter settlement patterns and population. In the second half of the century, moreover, a series of natural disasters broke down over the Maasai, including rinderpest epidemics which wiped out herds and a smallpox pestilence which took the lives of many people. By the 1890s the power that Maasai groups had been able to wield a century or more earlier was largely a thing of the past.

Western Kenya: the Luhya, Luo, and Gusii

In the highlands northeast of Lake Victoria, the complex interaction among Luo, Kalenjin, Maasai, and the dominant Bantu groups from Uganda continued after 1650. As a result of this process, the eighteen sub-tribes of the Luhya had taken shape by the end of the nineteenth century. Migration from Uganda continued in this period, and so did conflict, trade, and intermarriage with the Luo to the south. The most important change in the Luhya region during these centuries was the arrival of the Plains Nilotic-speaking Teso in the eighteenth and nineteenth centuries. The Teso had considerable impact on the settlement patterns of the northern Luhya people.

By the beginning of the seventeenth century, the Bukusu, largest of the northern Luhya groups, as well as other groups were settled in the Gishu and Tororo areas of what is today Uganda. In the first eighty years of the eighteenth century the Teso moved southeast into these regions. They displaced the Bantu of the area, many of whom moved north to become part of the Gishu people. Other Bantu scattered further south. The Bukusu withdrew south near the modern border of Kenya and Uganda. At the end of the eighteenth century and extending into the first decades of the nineteenth, the Teso moved further south into this

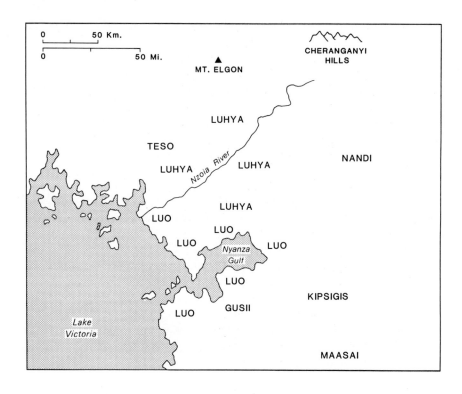

Map 18. Western Kenya in the Nineteenth Century.

area. The Bukusu were forced northeast into their present homelands, while other Luhya groups, such as the Bunyala, were pushed further to the south.

With one exception, no centralized political authority developed amongst the Luhya peoples. In fact, as was suggested in the previous chapter, there were few, if any, political links binding all the sub-tribes into a single entity. Political decision making usually took place at the level of the sub-tribe or, more commonly, the level of the clans which made up the sub-tribes. Such decisions were normally made by councils of elders representing the major sub-clans or lineages. While there was no institutionalized chieftaincy, there was normally a wise and influential elder who took a leading part in affairs. This individual, known as the omwami, helped settle disputes and provided leadership in times of crisis, but he ordinarily did not act separately from a council representing the principal elders of the clan.

The exception to the pattern of decentralized political control which developed among most Luhya peoples was the kingdom of Wanga. By about the beginning of the seventeenth century the Abashitetse dynasty had established itself in the southwestern portion of the Luhya area. Their initial ruler was a man named Wanga, after whom the kingdom was named. They built up a monarchy and consolidated their position in the face of hostile neighbors. In the middle of the eighteenth century expansion and centralization was increased under Nabongo (king) Wamukoya Netya. He used Uasingishu Maasai in his wars, but in the end disputes with these mercenaries led to his death. His successor, Osundwa (1787-1814), called back the Maasai to help against hostile neighbors. Perhaps the most significant period for Wanga before the coming of colonial rule was the reign of Shiundu in the second half of the nineteenth century. He extended Wanga influence to the south, becoming deeply involved in hostilities with the Luo of the region in the process. Shiundu's reign was also important as it marked the first appearance of Swahili and Arab traders and European adventurers in this part of East Africa. The Wanga kingdom would profit from such contacts in the final years of the century.

The period after 1650 was marked for the Luo of Nyanza (as for the Luhya) by what may be termed "the birth of a new people." There had been little or no unity in the four major streams of migration which brought the Lwoo speakers to western Kenya. After their arrival, however, several factors helped promote unity. Among these were the conflict with the Maasai, Luhya, Nandi, and Gusii; the arrival of the Teso in eastern Uganda and western Kenya, which cut off ties with the Padhola and ended further major migrations; common religious practices; and extensive intermarriage among Luo groups and with non-Luo. As a result of such factors, from very diverse origins a new people came into being by the end of the nineteenth century.

A distinctive kind of political organization gradually emerged among the Luo, combining traditional values of the Lwoo-speaking peoples with innovations arising from local conditions. The pattern of political organization which thus emerged was based on a unit which was larger than a clan and which is sometimes referred to as a sub-tribe. By the middle of the nineteenth century more than a dozen such sub-tribes existed among the Luo. Each was headed by a ruoth, or chief, who normally was drawn from a clan within the sub-tribe on the basis of its wealth and manpower. Though standing at the top of the political organization, the ruoth was not an absolute ruler. In disputes, for example, he was an arbiter rather than a judge or law giver.

The experience of the other major ethnic group of western Kenya, the Bantu-speaking Gusii of the southwestern highlands, was somewhat different. Oral tradition suggests that they did not emerge as a distinct group occupying their present home until well after 1650. Together with other Bantu-speaking peoples of western Kenya, the ancestors of the Gusii seem, according to their traditions, to have settled on the northeastern shores of Lake Victoria by the first half of the sixteenth century. They were eventually pushed from this area by incoming Luo migrants in the first half of the seventeenth century. Moving with the Luhya group most closely related to them in language and traditions, the Logoli (Maragoli), they put down roots in the low-lying Kano plains east of Nyanza Gulf. Settling along the lake shore and in the river valleys, these Gusii ancestors practised an economy in which cattle keeping and fishing were more important than cultivation. They stayed in Kano for slightly more than a century (c 1640-1755), and during this period Gusii society expanded and developed a number of "corporate" clans which later developed into sub-tribes. The Gusii occupation of Kano ended as a result of the pressure of Luo peoples who moved south into this area; their presence and raids on Gusii cattle caused most of the Bantu speakers to move from the plains to the higher elevations to the southeast.

It is important to recognize that the Gusii did not move directly to the highlands they inhabit today, nor did they travel as a single group. Nevertheless, the movements of the major Gusii divisions can be sketched briefly. They first stopped in what would later be part of Gusii country, but moved on to the east as a result of continued Luo pressure. They eventually settled in the present-day Kericho district where they came into contact first with Maasai and then Kipsigis. As a result of conflict with these peoples, the Gusii moved back west and south. By the end of the eighteenth century Gusii settlements appear to have spread south and east of Kericho district. Some groups moved from here into the present-day Gusii highlands, but most moved south to the region near the Migori river. Here they came into conflict with another group of Maasai, who inflicted a devastating defeat on the Gusii in the battle of Migori early in the nineteenth century.

From the battle, the Gusii were routed to the north and west in two main groups. The people who came to occupy the higher elevations of the Gusii highlands (the Masaba) moved to those regions directly; the sub-tribes who came to occupy the lower regions of present Gusii country (the Chache) took refuge with the Luo peoples in South Nyanza, and only in about 1850 did they move into the Gusii highlands.

Thus, the Gusii have occupied their present homeland only since the first half of the nineteenth century. In a gradual process, the people adopted agriculture as more suited to the cool, hilly environment than the keeping of large herds of cattle. The Gusii population did not develop a centralized political system. By the end of the nineteenth century, however, several distinct sub-tribes had emerged as a major focus of political and social organization.

The Thagicu Peoples: Kikuyu and Kamba

The Kikuyu form part of the Mt. Kenya group of Thagicu-speaking peoples. In this chapter, we shall restrict ourselves to their settlement in their present homelands, which involved movements to the north, west, and south beginning in the first part of the eighteenth century. These did not, of course, occur in a vacuum. The migrations brought the Kikuyu into contact with various groups, and the lands into which they moved often were inhabited by others. The Kikuyu interacted with and absorbed these peoples, including Maasai. The language and culture of modern Kikuyu peoples are thus a product of these interactions.

Some of the Kikuyu moved slowly north to what is now Nyeri district and others moved northeast. Some moved west to present-day Nyandarua, arriving in the region about the middle of the nineteenth century; still others advanced south towards present Kiambu district. Expansion into these areas was an ongoing process which continued to the end of the nineteenth century. During the course of these movements, an important change took place in the Kikuyu way of life. The ancestors of the Kikuyu had put a high premium on hunting and herding cattle. Now, moving into a highland region which was forested and well watered, the Kikuyu turned increasingly to an agricultural way of life in which cultivation of crops was of primary importance.

Kikuyu society was largely molded by the pattern of their settlement. Migration was undertaken either by individuals or by small groups of relatives. Because of the topography of the region they were entering, the pioneers settled on ridges separated from others by rivers or valleys, and each group formed an independent and self-contained unit. These settlements, known as mbari (sub-clans), did not have chiefs in the sense of hereditary, institutionalized leadership; administration normally was headed by the muramati (guardian) and a council of elders.

Land belonged to the mbari as a whole. Any member had a right to land as long as he made first claim and informed the muramati. Land could be sold so long as the sale had the prior approval of the mbari. Non-clan members, such as the ahoi (tenants-at-will) were also given rights to land by the muramati on condition of good behavior. Land considerations and the condition of tenure would be the source of considerable debate and controversy in the twentieth century.

The other major Thagicu-speaking group to be discussed here is the Kamba. By about 1650 the Kamba had settled in the wet and forested Mbooni hills, where they were to remain for approximately 125 years. The forests were cleared and agriculture gradually became more important than herding. Initially, shifting cultivation was practiced, but in the eighteenth century the Mbooni Kamba adopted a new system of terrace cultivation involving irrigation. Streams were dammed, and furrows and ditches were built to transport water. The years during which the Kamba were living in the Mbooni hills were a time of recovery after the insecurity of the migrations and a time of population growth.

The rising population led to movements out of the hills. Beginning in the second decade of the eighteenth century, Kamba settlers began to move to the east across the Athi river into Kitui, a movement followed by larger migrations between 1740 and 1780. Movements to the north, west, and south from Mbooni also took place during the same century. In most cases, the migrating Kamba moved into lands drier and agriculturally more marginal as they got further from Mbooni.

In the late eighteenth and early nineteenth centuries, increasing numbers of Kamba became involved in long-distance trade. At first, a network of trading links grew up among Kamba communities in Ukamba. In time, the trade proceeded further afield as the Kamba traded with the Kikuyu, Embu, and Meru regions. Later, trade links were developed with the coast. Initially, ivory and agricultural products were the most important items of trade, the Kamba serving as middlemen between the coast and peoples as far away as Lakes Baringo and Victoria; at mid-century the Kamba were also involved in the trade in slaves. By the 1860s, however, Arab and Swahili traders who had previously shown little interest in trade routes through Kenya now came into commerce with the Kenya interior in a much greater way. As a result, Kamba control of the trade progressively weakened in the latter half of the nineteenth century.

Despite considerable involvement in trade, Kamba society remained largely untouched by political centralization. Kamba communities normally were not ruled by chiefs, rather homesteads and villages were governed by groups of prominent elders.

Mainland Tanzania

In northwest Tanzania the Haya states continued to exist, and in the west-central portions of the interior Ntemi chieftainships expanded in number and area. Until the end of the nineteenth century, moreover, the majority of Tanzanian peoples were characterized, as before, by small-scale economies which produced little in the way of surplus. Communal modes of production typified by a gender-based division of labor were the rule.

In the eighteenth century the political and economic situation began to change in some parts of Tanzania, notably the northeastern highlands, and in the nineteenth century a large portion, though certainly not all, of the country was dramatically affected by economic and political change. In the northeastern highlands, political centralization developed among the Shambaa and Pare. This was the result of chiefs' ability to take advantage of surplus production of food crops, their control of such specialized skills as blacksmithing, and later their ability to take advantage of opportunities offered by long-distance trade.

The nineteenth century witnessed a dramatic increase in long-distance trade with the coast. The impact of trade may be seen in changing economic formations characterized by new forms of labor organization and production for export, to cite just two examples. The great upsurge in long-distance trade also had immense political impact. It provided an impetus for the increase in power of many rulers and for the emergence of larger, more complex political units. Nineteenth century long distance trade, which involved an increasing emphasis on slave exports, produced many destructive social and political influences as well. The same can be said for the movement of the Ngoni peoples, originally from Southern Africa, into southern and western Tanzania. They brought in their wake considerable destruction, but they also provided an impetus toward social and political change on a considerable scale.

Northwestern Tanzania

The small kingdoms west of Lake Victoria continued to exist independently of each other for the most part. They often had to face pressure from more powerful neighbors to the north, first Bunyoro and then Buganda; while this at times placed some of them in a tributary position to the northern states, they never completely lost their freedom of action.

The two-class structure, similar to that of Nkore, continued to exist, with the Hima pastoralists and Iru cultivators forming the population of the kingdoms. This was an area well suited for cultivation as well as cattle raising, and most of the Haya states had become exporters of agricultural produce to neighboring areas by the nineteenth century. Interesting in this regard is coffee, which was cultivated with marked success by the Iru. It came to have an important place in the social system of the people as well as being exported to the kingdoms of Uganda. By the nineteenth century the region inhabited by the Haya had become involved in long distance trade. In fact, one of the kingdoms, Karagwe, became an important stopping point on the main trade route to Buganda from the East African coast.

Northeastern Tanzania

Like other parts of northeastern Tanzania, the Usambara highlands were the scene of numerous movements of peoples and waves of settlement. It was not until the eighteenth century that political change in this area led to the formation of a centralized kingdom. According to tradition, the Shambaa kingdom's origin resulted from the coming of a group known as the Kilindi under the leadership of Mbegha. Where they came from is unclear, but they appear to have provided a central political force at a time when it was needed.

Mbegha established himself as king; his capital was at Vugha. He fostered a process of centralization by taking a wife from every major clan. Kilindi chiefs were appointed to administer the various districts of the kingdom, but they were represented at court by non-Kilindi, an arrangement that provided a check on members of the ruling clan. Bughe, Mbegha's son, continued the work of centralization, and by military action he and his successors expanded the area of the Shambaa kingdom, especially toward the coast.

The greatest Shambaa ruler, Kimweri ye Nyumbai, further expanded and strengthened the kingdom in the nineteenth century. By placing a son over many chieftaincies, he brought about greater centralization and control by the king. He gained a reputation as a strong and benevolent ruler; many refugees sought his protection, and he increased his strength by enlisting them in his army.

Beginning in the 1860s, the strength and unity that Kimweri and his predecessors had forged in Usambara was undermined by new influences. The impact of increasing trade with the coast was felt during Kimweri's reign with an increase in wealth and the introduction of firearms. Vugha was not near the major trade route up the Pangani River valley from the coast, but Kimweri's son Semboja, as chief at Mazinde, was in a good position to dominate that trade. He was able to use his wealth to obtain allies, and he then overthrew Kimweri's successor at Vugha. A new kind of authority was manifesting itself here, as in other parts of Tanzania, one based on wealth and power derived from trade. Old types of authority based on kinship usually could not stand up to it.

The Pare Mountains were also a region to which peoples of diverse origins came between the sixteenth and nineteenth centuries. By the sixteenth century in Ugweno, north Pare, a loose political system controlled by clans skilled as blacksmiths had taken shape. After a civil war the blacksmith clan was eventually overthrown by a clan called the Wasuya. This seizure of power was led by Angovi, but it was his son, Mranga, who initiated the process of centralization by which the Ugweno state came into being. Mranga centralized the initiation system, created a hierarchy of councils, and made members of the ruling family the district chiefs. The political changes leading to this kingdom came from within rather than from outside, as was the case with the Shambaa kingdom.

For Ugweno the increase in trade and the advent of Swahili and Arab traders from the coast would ultimately have a divisive effect. The new economic activity aroused tremendous rivalry among the traditional rulers of the Pare hills for control of the trade and the chance to reap its benefits. Ghendewa, the ruler of Ugweno in the middle of the nineteenth century, attempted to assert the power of his kingdom in the face of such rivalry, but even outside help was not enough to enable him to hold it together. He was killed in war, and the kingdom split. In south Pare, where there had never been any large state, the new economic influence led to the formation of larger units. A ruler who could obtain wealth through trade in ivory and slaves, and thus have the means to employ large numbers of fighting men, could establish considerable control over territory. New states created by such means were almost always short-lived.

The Chagga living on the slopes of Mt. Kilimanjaro also experienced political change in the nineteenth century. The growing population of this fertile, well-watered region did not, however, produce a single large political unit. The Chagga continued to be organized in a number of chieftaincies. These often competed with each other and with neighboring peoples for land, livestock, and trade. By the second half of the nineteenth century the two most important Chagga chieftaincies were Kibosho, ruled from the 1870s by Chief Sina, and Moshi, ruled from the 1860s by Chief Rindi.

Southern and Western Tanzania: the Coming of the Ngoni

Northeastern Tanzania was not the only region to experience political turbulence and rapid economic and social change in the nineteenth century. Existing political units broke up and new ones formed over a broad belt of southern and western Tanzania. This social disruption and political change was largely the result of the destructive influence of the Ngoni from southern Africa.

The Ngoni who arrived in Tanzania in the 1840s originated in the Natal region of present-day South Africa. As a result of the rise of the Zulu kingdom under Shaka, a series of wars and population movements, known as the Mfecane, occurred during which many Bantu speakers of the Ngoni group left Natal to escape the might of Shaka's armies. Under the leadership of Zwangendaba, one such Ngoni group made their way north from Mozambique through Zimbabwe to Zambia, crossing the Zambezi river in 1835. Zwangendaba's followers spoke Ngoni, followed Ngoni customs, and employed Ngoni military techniques, but had their origins in diverse ethnic groups. They were absorbed into the community in the course of the trek north. Zwangendaba's Ngoni passed north through Zambia and Malawi, finally reaching Ufipa in southwestern Tanzania. There, in 1845, Zwangendaba died.

After the death of Zwangendaba, his followers split into numerous groups, some of which moved back into Central Africa. Those who remained in East Africa left Ufipa. One group, known as the Gwangwara, they moved east and south to the Songea area. Here they met another Ngoni group, the Maseko. Soon rivalry between the two broke out, and after a period of war the Gwangwara triumphed, driving the Maseko in various directions. After this, the Gwangwara divided, one group forming the Mshope kingdom north of Songea, and the other a kingdom further south. Between these two groups and the Maseko, they disrupted a vast area of southern Tanzania, as well as Mozambique and Malawi, with their warfare and raiding for stock.

A warrior people, the Ngoni effectively utilized the military techniques developed in southern Africa by the Zulu. Men of similar age were placed in territorial regiments; armed with the short, stabbing spears, they utilized the tactics of mass attack to envelop the enemy. These military techniques gave the Ngoni an advantage over the peoples of southern Tanzania who lived in small-scale societies.

The second Ngoni group to move from Ufipa in the 1850s was the Tuta. They too were a most disruptive force in the areas they touched. They moved north and then west to the shores of Lake Tanganyika, where they attacked Ujiji. Passing on north, they finally settled in Runzewe district, where they raided and plundered the Nyamwezi.

Map 19. Ngoni in Tanzania.

Thus, one of the most important effects of the Ngoni movements into Tanzania was disruption. Many communities and chieftaincies were destroyed. People were killed, forced to flee, or forcibly absorbed into Ngoni ranks. Cultivation was disrupted in several areas and trade routes were cut, leading to food shortages and famine. In the wake of the Ngoni, there often came chaos. Law and order broke down, and survivors had to fend for themselves; many joined bands of ruthless mercenaries, the ruga ruga, who roamed the countryside plundering and killing. When not raiding in their own right, the ruga ruga often hired themselves out as mercenaries to various chiefs and rulers.

While the coming of the Ngoni had negative effects, it also provided, along with the increase of coastal trade, one of the most powerful influences for change in nineteenth-century Tanzania. Many Tanzanian peoples, such as the Sangu and Bena, adopted the Ngoni military organization and tactics, and then used their armies to build larger states. Thus, a result of the Ngoni coming was a move away from small-scale political organization, such as the system of Ntemi chiefs, which had failed to effectively stand up against the invaders, in favor of bigger political units under kings.

An example of such political change occurred among the Hehe of central Tanzania in the latter half of the nineteenth century. From an area ruled by Ntemi chiefs, there emerged a strong kingdom under Munyigumba. Following the example of the Ngoni and the Sangu, he built a powerful Ngoni-style army and became a strong ruler, incorporating other chiefs in his domain. By the time of his death in 1879, practically the whole of the Hehe people were under a single ruler for the first time. His son, Mkwawa, proved an even abler ruler and expanded the kingdom to the north as he sought access to the main caravan route between the coast and the lakes. Mkwawa put up strong resistance to the German conquest in the 1890s.

Long Distance Trade in Tanzania

As has been seen for northeastern Tanzania, the nineteenth century witnessed a considerable upsurge of trade between the coast and the interior. One important factor in this was the move of Seyyid Said to Zanzibar, his encouragement of commerce with the mainland, and his establishment of a plantation economy with a demand for slaves on Zanzibar itself. Increasing numbers of trading caravans made their way into the interior, ranging as far as Lakes Tanganyika, Victoria, and Malawi. Led by Swahilis and Arabs, these caravans were often financed by Indian merchants. Increasingly, European merchants were attracted to the coast and Zanzibar as the volume of trade expanded rapidly over the first three quarters of the century.

The main trade arteries in Tanzania were the southern and central routes. The former ran from the southern ports of Kilwa and Lindi to the south and southwest through Yao country toward Lake Malawi. The latter led from the coast opposite Zanzibar to the west. In Nyamwezi country (Tabora), the route divided, with branches going north to Karagwe and Buganda, west to Ujiji on Lake Tanganyika, and southwest around the southern tip of Lake Tanganyika toward Zaire and Zambia.

Long-distance trade was not confined to Arabs and Swahilis. Several African groups also were involved, most notably the Yao and the Nyamwezi. The Yao had begun trading with people far away from their homes from at least the sixteenth century. Having been raided for slaves, the Yao themselves became involved in the trade; and as the demand for slaves increased in the nineteenth century, they exported increasing numbers along the southern route, a route they came largely to control. The Nyamwezi also occupied a position very favorable for trade. They sat astride the busy central trade route to Lakes Tanganyika and Victoria, and by the beginning of the nineteenth century Nyamwezi were arriving at the coast with ivory. As more Swahilis and Arabs began to trade in the interior, rivalry developed with the Nyamwezi.

The major items of trade were ivory and slaves. The ivory was largely for export outside East Africa, but slaves came to be in great demand for the plantations of Zanzibar and Pemba as well as for other Indian Ocean markets. By the 1840s something like 40,000 slaves per year were sold at Zanzibar, and this figure increased in the next two or three decades. Both the ivory and slave trades had the effect of increasing the number of firearms in the interior. They provided an effective way of killing elephants and capturing slaves.

As has long been recognized, the slave trade had particularly destructive effects. Many, if not most, slaves were captured as a result of wars and raids. Like the Ngoni invasion, therefore, the increase in slave trading as the nineteenth century wore on caused the breakup of community life, depopulation, and food shortages. This warfare and turbulence touched most parts of the interior as well as adjacent countries.

West-Central Tanzania: Trade and Political Centralization

As in the case of the Ngoni depredations, the effect of the slave trade was not entirely negative. Control of trade and the wealth it brought could provide the means for expanding the scale of political organization through the formation of larger and more secure states. Indeed, the military changes fostered by the Ngoni often combined with increased trading activities to strengthen the hands of ambitious rulers who wished to carve out larger political domains than had existed in west-central

Tanzania previously. It is important to note that in nineteenth century Tanzania there was a definite shift from political power based on kinship and religious authority to that based on military and economic power. External trade, and the wealth it brought, increased the opportunities for leaders to obtain fighting men and weapons with which to buttress and expand their authority. Moreover, the turbulence caused by the slave trade and Ngoni raids made people willing to follow a leader who could provide security and wealth.

One such leader was Nyungu ya Mawe. Although small and one-eyed, he was a brave warrior and leader. Taking control of one of the Kimbu cheiftaincies in the mid-1870s, he developed a strong army. For this he drew on ruga ruga. Welding them into an imposing fighting force whose very appearance was often enough to frighten an enemy, he built a large empire. He raided caravans and sold slaves, and with the wealth he obtained he increased his military strength. Under Nyungu ya Mawe all the Kimbu were united for the first time.

An even larger empire was carved out in an adjacent region by the Nyamwezi leader Mirambo. He used both the military lessons learned from the Ngoni (he spent some years among them as a youth) and the opportunities for wealth provided by increasing trade to buttress his position. By the 1880s he had established his hold on his father's chieftaincy, Ugowe, and he expanded it rapidly. Using Ngoni tactics and ruga ruga, he gained control over the main trade route from Tabora to Ujiji as well as to Karagwe. By controlling the trade routes, he could demand tolls from caravans—a practice that led to conflict with Arab traders in the 1870s. Mirambo also sent his armies to the north to raid cattle for his troops. By the 1880s Mirambo was the most powerful figure in western Tanzania. Although his empire did not long survive his death in 1884, Mirambo had combined military power with control of trade to greatly expand the territory under his control from a small Ntemi chieftaincy to a major empire. On a small scale this was typical of political developments in other parts of Tanzania during the nineteenth century.

The period between the mid-seventeenth and the mid-nineteenth centuries was thus marked by numerous significant political, economic, and social changes. By the end of the period most social formations had assumed the shape they would have in the following century and East Africa's peoples had moved into the regions they now inhabit.

These years, especially the nineteenth century, also witnessed an increasing impact of long-distance trade on East Africa. The impact of western capitalism was felt in several parts of the region as patterns of production and exchange were altered towards participation in wider markets. An important corollary of these economic processes can be seen in political changes leading to state building and the growth of larger and more complex political formations, most notably in Tanzania. Such influences often heightened the political power of established states and rulers, as in Buganda. Nevertheless, not all portions of East Africa experienced this kind of economic and political change. Kenya's peoples, for example, experienced little in the way of movement toward political centralization. The forces working for economic and political change thus produced in East Africa an uneven impact.

Some of the most important such forces were external in origin, as the nineteenth century was a time of increasing contacts with the world outside East Africa. These contacts will be examined in more detail in the next chapter.

Suggestions for Further Reading

Dunbar, A. R. *A History of Bunyoro-Kitara* (Nairobi, 1965).

Ehret, C. *Southern Nilotic History* (Evanston, 1971).

Feierman, Steven. *The Shambaa Kingdom* (Madison, 1974).

Karugire, S. R. *A History of the Kingdom of Nkore in Western Uganda to 1896* (Oxford, 1971).

Kimambo, I. *A Political History of the Pare* (Nairobi, 1969).

Kiwanuka, M. S. *A History of Buganda From the Foundation of the Kingdom to 1900* (New York, 1972).

Ogot, B. A., ed. *Kenya Before 1900* (Nairobi, 1976).

Ogot, B. A., ed. *Zamani* (Nairobi, 1974).

Roberts, A. *Tanzania Before 1900* (Nairobi, 1968).

Chapter 6

East Africa and
the Wider World
in the Nineteenth Century

THE FIRST EIGHT DECADES OF THE nineteenth century brought new and important actors onto the stage of East Africa, the most significant of them coming from outside Africa. In the first decades after 1800 Omani Arab influence was reestablished on the coast, and Arab and Swahili traders forged commercial ties with the interior of the region. By the middle of the century Europe was becoming more deeply involved in East Africa. Commercial relations were growing by the 1880s, and European interest in the region had become aroused through humanitarian motives which sought to utilize European technology and power to stamp out the slave trade and promote the planting of Christianity in East Africa. The interest generated, particularly in Britain, by these ventures, coupled with the propagandization of the many adventurers who found East Africa a popular and challenging place in which to make a name for themselves, served to attract considerable interest to East Africa in Europe.

Oman and the East African Coast

A major theme in the history of the East African coast in the first decades of the nineteenth century was the resurgence of Oman's power and influence. Although Omani forces had been instrumental in driving the Portuguese from the coast and the rulers of Oman claimed sovereignty over it, Oman had exercised but little control or influence over

111

the coast for most of the eighteenth century. For all intents and purposes, the coastal cities remained independent. Under Mazrui rule, Mombasa had come to exert considerable influence on the northern coast. This would change, however, after the accession of Seyyid Said as ruler of Oman.

Securing the throne by engineering the murder of his cousin in 1807, Said was at first not in a strong position. The interior of his domains were at the mercy of the Muslim Wahabi sect who controlled much of the Arabian peninsula, and at sea the Jawasmi pirates presented a severe threat to his naval position. Only in the early 1820s did his position improve through the defeat, with considerable outside help, of these two hostile powers. In the case of the Jawasmi pirates, the outside help was provided by British authorities in India, and this was of particular significance for the future of the East African coast.

Britain emerged from the Napoleonic wars as the dominant force in India and the Indian Ocean. It was fortunate for Seyyid Said that even during the wars with France he had backed the British. Cooperation in fighting against common enemies led naturally to British assistance to Said, including ships, naval technology, and British personnel to serve in Said's navy. An "alliance" was thus forged between the ruler of Oman and the dominant power in the Indian Ocean. Seyyid Said was to benefit tremendously from this arrangement; it was certainly a significant factor in his establishing control over the East African coast.

While cooperation between Britain and Oman provided advantages for Said, it was seen by British authorities as benefiting their interests as well. Not only was Said's help useful in promoting British trade in the Persian Gulf, but his claims to the East African coast could also be used by Britain. After 1815 British naval power was arrayed along the African coasts as one means of suppressing the export of slaves. British policy makers saw that influence with the rulers of the shores of the African continent also was necessary to effectively stop the slave trade. If Said's claims to the coast could be supported effectively, British anti-slavery interests could be furthered. Although the British were not ready to take control of the coast themselves, a series of treaties were made with Said in the first half of the century which sought to place limits on the export of slaves. Said thus became the British vehicle for anti-slave trade action.

Seyyid Said was favored in his quest for Omani hegemony over the coast not only by British assistance. Conditions on the coast were, at the beginning of the second decade of the century, favorable to the Omani ruler. Several coastal cities were resentful of Mombasa's dominance, and others were in no position to oppose Said's claims. Thus his sovereignty was initially recognized by Kilwa, Mafia, and Zanzibar. Moreover, Mombasa overreached herself in an attempt, in alliance with Pate, to include Lamu in her sphere of influence. At the battle of Shela in 1812, Lamu administered a decisive defeat to the invading Mombasa and Pate forces. This battle undercut Mombasa's position and opened the way for a revival of direct Omani influence on the coast.

Although events were moving in favor of Seyyid Said's claims to control the coast, he was forced to move slowly because of threats to his position in Oman. In addition, Mombasa's resistance under her Mazrui rulers proved a very considerable obstacle to the Omani ruler. After 1812 Said was able to establish his dominance over Pate, Pemba, and Lamu, all of which feared Mombasa, by combining skillful diplomacy with military force. It seemed only a matter of time before Oman took over Mombasa.

Seyyid Said's desire to take Mombasa and break Mazrui resistance, however, suffered a setback through the unofficial intervention of a British sea captain. In 1823 the city rulers had written to the British governor of Bombay asking for protection and, in effect, offering Mombasa to the British. The offer was not accepted, but in February 1824, with Omani ships attacking Mombasa, Captain W. F. Owen arranged, on condition that the Mazrui abolish the slave trade, for a British protectorate. Owen was in charge of a naval expedition charting the east coast of Africa. Seemingly unhappy with the effects of the slave trade, which he felt Said was doing little to suppress, Owen acted on his own to raise the British flag in East Africa. The British Protectorate at Mombasa was, however, short lived; British officials in London refused to accept Owen's action, and the protectorate was ended in 1826.

British intervention merely delayed the final conquest of Mombasa by Said's forces. Not willing to anger the British, he bided his time; in 1827 he launched a major expedition against Mombasa. Mixing diplomacy with force, the Omani ruler made an agreement with Mombasa's Mazrui ruler which he no doubt hoped would give him eventual control. In this he was disappointed, as his forces were driven from the island in 1828. Nor was Said successful in attempts to take Mombasa in 1829 and 1833. Finally, in 1837 he was able to exploit divisions among the Mazrui to make himself master of Mombasa. With the fall of Mombasa to Seyyid Said, Omani dominance of the East African coast had been clearly established.

Seyyid Said and Zanzibar

During the course of his lengthy campaign to gain control of Mombasa, Seyyid Said decided to make his permanent residence at Zanzibar. Although the exact date for Said's move from Oman to Zanzibar is disputed, by 1840 he had established himself on Zanzibar and had made the East African coast the center of his domains. There appear to have been several reasons for this shift. Zanzibar and the coast presented a less turbulent atmosphere than that of Oman. On more than one occasion, Seyyid Said was forced to break off his attempts to capture Mombasa as a result of the need to return to Oman to deal with challenges to his position there. The climate and water of Zanzibar also were more attractive to the Omani ruler. Economic considerations, however, must have played a very prominent part in Said's move. Zanzibar presented a potential source of great wealth through the development of a plantation economy, and the possibilities for developing trade along the coast and with the interior must have been very attractive.

Seyyid Said's move to Zanzibar had extremely important consequences for island and its neighbor Pemba, as well as for East Africa as a whole. Economically this can be seen, first of all, on the two islands. Even before taking up permanent residence on Zanzibar, Said recognized that the soil and climate of Zanzibar and Pemba made the two islands well-suited for the cultivation of cloves. Clove plantations were therefore established by Said and other Omani Arabs, with scant attention paid to the rights of the islands' inhabitants (e.g., the Hadimu and Shirazi on Zanzibar), who were forced to clear the land or were pushed into poorer areas. Arab landowners, relative newcomers to Zanzibar and Pemba, came to dominate the economy. As the plantations developed, slaves obtained from the mainland were increasingly used. Prosperity came rapidly to Seyyid Said as a result of the plantations that soon made the islands the world's leading producer of cloves, but the plantation system also brought evils, the slave system and the second-class status of the islands' inhabitants, in its wake.

The second important economic change that occurred as a result of Seyyid Said's shift to Zanzibar was an upsurge in trade between the coast and the interior. Said was not alone responsible for this, of course, but he played an important role in creating conditions conducive to such trade, as well as taking part in it himself. He united the coast in a single customs unit, and this helped to spur trade as did his encouragement of the plantation economy on Zanzibar and Pemba. Said recognized the need for capital and organization if coastal and inland trade was to be effectively developed. He therefore actively encouraged Indian financiers, the so called banyans, to move to Zanzibar and the coast. They provided the finance for the trading caravans sent into the interior. Said, moreover, encouraged trade along the coast and with merchants from further afield by levying a flat rate of 5 percent on all items in the ports of his domain. By the time of his death in 1856, Zanzibar's trade had increased tremendously, as is indicated by the figures for customs revenue, which increased fivefold from the end of the 1820s to the end of the 1850s.

114

Economic Impact of Nineteenth Century Trade

The trade between the coast and the interior and between Zanzibar and merchants from other parts of the world had important economic ramifications for East Africa. By the end of the eighteenth century such peoples as the Yao and the Nyamwezi had begun to bring ivory to the coast, and as it became clear that the trade in elephant tusks was potentially lucrative, many Arab traders, including Seyyid Said himself, were drawn to tap this trade in the interior after the 1830s. With Indian merchants and bankers providing capital in the form of loans to traders, Swahili and Arab merchants organized and led caravans into the interior. These caravans consisted of numerous porters who carried such trade goods as cloth, copper wire, beads, and guns which would be exchanged for ivory. The tusks, in turn, were carried to the coast by human porterage. It was not long, however, before caravans brought back captives as slaves for use on Zanzibar and Pemba and for export outside East Africa.

Most parts of the East African interior were affected by the commercial penetration fostered by the coastal and interior merchants, but the impact of such commerce was not the same in all regions. A considerable portion of Kenya, for example, received fewer direct trading caravans until the second half of the nineteenth century.

An important result of the developing commercial contacts between the coast and the interior in the nineteenth century was a considerable increase in economic production and commerce in both regions but most notably the interior. Until the arrival of coastal traders, Africans in the interior had not greatly valued ivory, and it had not been a significant item in local trade. Elephants had been hunted, but more to protect crops from damage than for ivory. As ivory became recognized as a source of wealth, so changes in patterns of elephant hunting took place; a great increase in the size of hunting parties and numbers killed resulted. Communal systems of hunting declined in significance as groups of professional ivory hunters, organized and led by individuals, emerged whose sole purpose was to produce ivory for sale.

With the intensification of ivory hunting went an expansion in the scale of African commercial organization. This was especially the case among the Nyamwezi of Tanzania. The coming of coastal traders to the interior in large numbers did not result in a decline of Nyamwezi trading; rather it seems to have stimulated long-distance trading among the Nyamwezi. They took an increasing part in all aspects of trade—as porters, elephant hunters, slave raiders, and caravan organizers and leaders. A significant portion of the Nyamwezi male population was involved in trade by the second half of the nineteenth century.

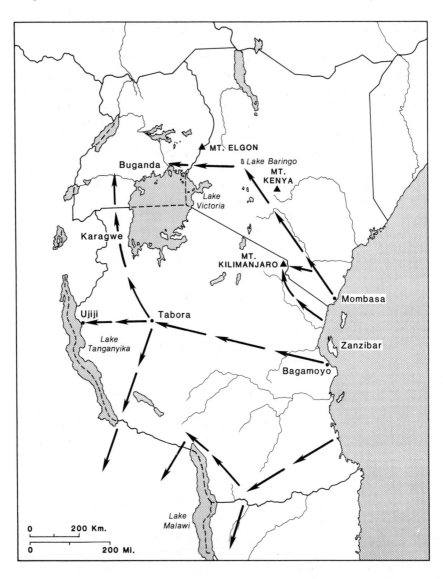

Map 20. Nineteenth Century Trade Routes.

The trade in ivory and slaves led to increases in production and trade of other products in the interior. Trade had been carried on between various states and regions before the arrival of traders from the coast. However, this trade in commodities such as salt, foodstuffs, and iron was normally carried on only within a short distance of their site of production. With the growth of coastal trade, demand for such goods grew greatly. Iron implements from the interior, for example, were in great demand on the coast. Caravans needed considerable food supplies, as did the population of trading centers and transit camps along the main trade routes. This demand helped to spur production of surplus foodstuffs for sale in many parts of East Africa. Moreover, the coastal traders helped to introduce new food crops to the interior, such as citrus fruits, pawpaw, and rice.

A transformation of economic production and commerce resulted from the growth in trade between the coast and the interior in the nineteenth century. New means of capital formation were begun, and a new range of consumer demands for imports was created. This change toward a market-oriented economy, and the integration with larger patterns of trade affected many peoples of the interior.

Growth of External Commerce

The expansion of trade between coast and interior was paralleled by a growth of trade between East Africa and the rest of the world. By the 1840s Zanzibar had become the headquarters of this trade. Goods from the coast and interior were exported to Europe, Asia, and North America, and imports from these areas passed into East Africa. Imports included cloth, wire, and gunpowder, while the most important exports were ivory, slaves, rubber, copra, and foodstuffs such as maize, millet, and sim sim.

Much of this commerce took place within the Indian Ocean region, as it had for many centuries past, but the nineteenth century witnessed an upsurge of commercial contacts with areas outside the region, most notably with Europe. This was primarily a result of Said's encouragement of European and American businessmen in his domains. He entered into commercial treaties with the United States in 1833, with Britain in 1839, and with France in 1844. These treaties regularized commercial relations and allowed foreign powers to open consulates at Zanzibar to look after the interests of their nationals.

Secondly, increasing commercial contacts with Europe and the United States were the result of the economic transformation the Industrial Revolution was bringing about in those parts of the world. As industrialization proceeded in the nineteenth century, Europe looked further afield for new sources of raw materials and markets for their manufactured goods. East Africa was thus one of many parts of the world to experience increasing commercial contacts with Europe. The leading role in this process, so far as East Africa was concerned, was played by Great Britain. Not only was Britain the greatest European industrial power in the first three quarters of the nineteenth century, but she had great seapower to foster and protect trade long distances from Europe itself. After the opening of a British consulate on Zanzibar in 1840, Britain played an increasingly important role in the European trade with East Africa, though not involved in the export of slaves. By the 1870s the British India Steam Navigation Company, under William Mackinnon, had established a regular service to Zanzibar.

Until the 1870s British and other European trading efforts were confined to the coast and Zanzibar. Few European traders made attempts to penetrate the interior, which was viewed, with good reason, as extremely unhealthy for Europeans and fraught with transport difficulties. Malaria and other tropical diseases made European travel and residence in the region difficult at best.

Nevertheless, in the latter part of the 1870s plans for European economic exploitation of the mainland were put forward by British merchants. With the aid of pressure from the British consul on Zanzibar, Sir John Kirk, William Mackinnon was granted a huge concession, to be developed by a European company on the mainland, by Sultan Barghash, Said's son. The scheme was never finalized, as pressure from the British government led Sultan Barghash to turn down the proposal the following year, but the incident is significant in demonstrating the growing economic interest of Britain in East Africa.

Two points need to be stressed, however, in assessing the importance of growing British economic influence in the nineteenth century. First, such economic influences cannot be looked upon in a vacuum, for British interests in East Africa also included missionary and anti-slavery activity. Both merchants and humanitarians recognized that European trade was linked closely to efforts to promote Christianity and stop slavery in East Africa. Thus, for example, Mackinnon's 1877 scheme for a concession (like his later Imperial British East Africa Company) had strong support from church groups and anti-slavery crusaders in Britain. Secondly, the total commercial involvement of Britain in East Africa formed only a very small percentage of total British trade. East Africa was not one of Britain's major trading partners.

Nevertheless, the development of European, particularly British, commercial contacts with East Africa was particularly significant for the future. It was one very important way in which Europeans had established interests in East Africa by the beginning of the 1880s. It is essential to recognize that in the developing commercial relations with Europe, East Africa came to occupy a subordinate role. East Africa was being turned into a supplier of raw materials, human and otherwise, for the benefit of others. Cheap manufactured goods began to undermine the demand for local, hand-made products, and East Africa was increasingly drawn into a subservient position to industrialized and capitalist Europe, often on very unfavorable terms of trade. This situation has changed little in the past century.

Anti-Slave Trade Impetus to European Involvement in East Africa

In addition to economic contacts, the effort to abolish the slave trade was an important way in which Europe, in this case Britain, was increasingly drawn into East African affairs in the nineteenth century. Following the abolition of slave trade in the British Empire in 1807, the British government sought to use diplomacy and naval power to stop slaves from entering British possessions and to convince other European and American countries to desist from the practice. The motives behind this British action were both humanitarian and economic. The religious resurgence highlighted by the evangelical movement at the end of the eighteenth century led to opposition to slavery as inhumane and unchristian. Pressure from religious groups in Britain was added to the weight of arguments of economists such as Adam Smith, who held that slavery was a wasteful and uneconomic form of production. It was thus partly for humanitarian and partly for economic reasons that Britain made the slave trade and later slavery illegal for her subjects and in her domains.

The major thrust of the British anti-slavery campaign was aimed toward West Africa and the Atlantic trade, but she also was active in the Indian Ocean. British authorities were concerned about the transport of slaves from the East African coast to the sugar-producing island of Mauritius, a British possession after 1815, and to India, the center of British interest in the region. To this end, in 1822 the British concluded the Moresby Treaty, named after its British negotiator. Under the treaty's terms, Arab slave traders could no longer ship slaves to India or Mauritius; the slave trade was to be confined to Said's domains and Arabia. The treaty gave British naval vessels the right to stop and search any ships that might be carrying slaves. Said was forced to agree to the British terms, as he needed their help and good offices in his attempts to take control of the coast.

Despite the treaty and the efforts of a small patrol of British ships, the volume of slaves exported, both within and outside Said's domains, steadily increased over the next two decades. British officials decided to seek a tightening of restrictions on the slave trade, as after 1833 slavery itself was outlawed in the British Empire. Using the influence of the British consul on Zanzibar, Colonel Hamerton, another treaty was agreed upon in 1845, which placed further restrictions on the export of slaves from East Africa. Thereafter, no shipments could be made north of Brava on the Somali coast. This closed off the Arabian trade. Within Said's domain along the coast and Zanzibar the trade could continue.

The conclusion of the Hamerton Treaty illustrated the power of Britain in the Indian Ocean. Although Seyyid Said and many of his officials disliked the limits placed on a lucrative commerce, they were forced to accept, and through the impetus of the anti-slavery campaign British influence in Zanzibar affairs came to be considerable. One could almost say that Seyyid Said brought the British to the East African coast.

After 1845 British influence over Zanzibar affairs increased. Following the death of Seyyid Said in 1856, the disputed succession involving his numerous sons was eventually settled through British intervention. By arbitration of the British Governor-General of India, Said's domains in East Africa were placed under a different ruler than those in Arabia. Moreover, British influence was heightened by the long and influential service of Sir John Kirk as British Consul on Zanzibar. He established a close relationship with Sultan Barghash, and by the end of the 1870s he had become what some scholars have described as "unofficial Prime Minister of Zanzibar." It was his influence and British power that brought a final agreement with Barghash which outlawed all slave trading in the Sultan's lands. Barghash was under great pressure from his subjects, and he was aware of the economic importance of the slave trade to his domain. However, by gunboat diplomacy involving threats of a blockade of Zanzibar and the shelling of his palace, the British forced Barghash to give in and decree the end of the slave trade in 1873. That the British were strong enough to force the Sultan to initiate a policy very unpopular with many in his realm illustrates the degree of influence Britain was able to wield at Zanzibar as a result of the anti-slavery campaign.

Missionary Impetus to European Involvement in East Africa

The same kind of religious feeling which fueled the anti-slavery campaign in Britain and elsewhere lent a major impetus to missionary work by European Christians. Around the turn of the nineteenth century, several missionary-societies were established in Britain, most notably the London Missionary Society (LMS) and the Church Missionary Society (CMS), which raised money to send missionaries to preach the gospel and bring about conversion in Africa. While these efforts had met with some success in West and South Africa by the middle of the century, very little was achieved in the way of conversion and the establishment of mission stations in East Africa.

Few missionaries were sent to East Africa in these years. Those who served mission societies there, such as the Germans Krapf and Rebmann, did much to spread knowledge about the interior in Europe but little in the way of establishing churches. Krapf, in the service of the CMS, came to Zanzibar in 1844, and he later established a mission station at Rabai near Mombasa. He hoped to build a chain of stations stretching from this coastal town into the interior, where he travelled in 1848 and 1849, visiting the Shambaa kingdom and Ukamba. Although Krapf's descriptions of these journeys and another in 1851 broadened European knowledge about the interior and his work on a Swahili dictionary was very useful to later Europeans, he achieved relatively little in the way of planting Christianity in East Africa.

Greater missionary interest and activity in the region came about beginning in the 1870s as a result of the experiences of David Livingstone and other European adventurers in the interior. Livingstone, who spent only the last few years of his life in East Africa, inspired a whole generation in Britain with his seemingly selfless wanderings in the heart of Africa. While Livingstone himself accomplished very little in the way of spreading Christianity, he stirred many with his lectures and books in which he painted a graphic picture of the social disruption attendant on the slave trade in the interior. He urged the opening up of Africa through commerce and Christianity, which he felt would do much to improve the lives of the people of East and Central Africa. The effect of Livingstone's example and his ideas can be clearly seen by his famous speech at Cambridge University in 1857. His call to the young men there to take up the work of Christianizing Africa led directly to the formation of the Universities Mission to Central Africa, which was later to make its headquarters on Zanzibar. At the time of his death in 1873, Livingstone was a national hero in Britain, and many more were inspired to undertake mission work in East Africa as a result of the dramatic manner in which his body was brought to the coast by his African companions on a journey of hundreds of miles through hot and difficult terrain.

In the 1870s, 1880s, and 1890s there was thus considerable mission involvement in East Africa, as a number of societies, British, French, German, and American, attempted to undertake the work of planting Christianity. Some established stations at the coast, where they gave considerable attention to the suppression of slavery and the rehabilitation of freed slaves. The Holy Ghost Fathers established one such station at Bagamoyo in Tanzania, and the CMS established another at Freetown near Mombasa in modern Kenya. Attempts were made to establish mission stations in the interior as well, though generally with less success. Perhaps the most significant missionary work in the interior was the planting of Christianity in Buganda through the efforts of the CMS and the White Fathers in the 1880s.

Christian Missions and Buganda

The invitation to Christian missions came from the ruler of East Africa's most powerful kingdom, Kabaka Mutesa I of Buganda. However, the impetus for his invitation was not primarily religious. By the middle 1870s, Mutesa had good reason to fear that the ambitions of Egypt to expand into the lakes region posed a threat to the integrity of his kingdom. He had earlier encouraged contact and trade with the coast, and with the Swahili and Arab traders came the influence of Islam in the 1860s and 1870s. Mutesa himself had, for a time, flirted with Islam, but though he never became a practicing Muslim, many of his subjects were attracted to the new religion. As well as seeking to enlist aid against the Egyptian threat, Mutesa may have desired to provide a counterweight to Islam in his call to Christian missionaries.

Mutesa made his willingness to accept missionaries known to the adventurer Henry Morton Stanley, who stopped in Buganda in the course of his circumnavigation of Lake Victoria in 1875. Having been convinced that Mutesa was interested in Christianity, Stanley sent a letter, eventually published in the London Daily Telegraph, to Britain calling for missionaries to take up the work of conversion. Considerable funds were donated to the CMS for this purpose, and in early 1876 a party of eight missionaries set out for Buganda, the furthest point in the interior that mission work had been attempted.

This mission met with many difficulties. Almost the entire initial party died during the rigorous safari to the lake region. However, other CMS missionaries arrived in 1878-79. Another difficulty was the attitude of the ruler. If he had ever been, Mutesa was no longer interested in becoming a Christian, as the threat of Egyptian expansion into Uganda was receding by the end of the 1870s. Soon after the arrival of the CMS, moreover, a party of French missionaries belonging to the White Fathers order arrived in Buganda. Almost from the first, there was mistrust and hostility between the English Protestant missionaries and the French Catholics which was heightened by the fact that the first missionaries could communicate with each other only after learning the local language. This divided missionary effort would have seriously divisive and unsettling effects on the history of Buganda over the next two decades.

Although they had little success in converting Kabaka Mutesa, the Protestant and Catholic missionaries did win a growing body of converts in the 1880s. In the highly competitive and mobile society of nineteenth century Buganda, foreign innovations were readily accepted as a means of improving one's position. Conversion was, in short, a path to progress.

The strength of the converts' faith was to be tested during the reign of Kabaka Mwanga, who succeeded his father in 1884. The introduction of the new religion had caused change and turmoil which undermined some of the foundations of the kingdom, most notably the power of the kabaka, which declined steadily after 1885—due in part, no doubt, to the weak and unstable character of the ruler himself. Although he had studied with both missionary groups, Mwanga soon initiated a policy of persecuting the Christian converts. In 1885 and 1886 many young Ganda Christians chose death rather than give up their faith, and as in other epochs this persecution strengthened rather than weakened Christianity in the kingdom.

Faced with Mwanga's hostility, the Protestant and Catholic converts joined with the larger group of Muslim Ganda to overthrow Kabaka Mwanga. They captured Mwanga's palace in 1888 and forced him to flee to the south of Lake Victoria. This inaugurated a turbulent year in Buganda history. A kabaka had been overthrown by his subjects, and a revolutionary process had begun by which political power would be transferred from the ruler to his chiefs, who were Christians. Mwanga's brother Kiwewa was made ruler, and the victorious parties divided up the offices of state and chieftaincies. Before long this alliance broke down, and conflict between Christians and Muslims developed in which the latter emerged victorious, driving the Christians and the missionaries out of the kingdom. Dissatisfied with Kiwewa, they put the Muslim Kalema, another of Mwanga's brothers, on the throne. Rather against their wishes, the Christians were forced to ally with Mwanga, and thanks to better supplies of arms and ammunition they defeated Kalema and the Muslims in 1889, restoring Mwanga as kabaka.

The year of the three kings, as 1888-89 is known in Buganda history, had clearly crystallized religious differences. The power of the kabaka was undermined, and a Christian revolution was underway. Increasing numbers of Ganda would become Christians. To this revolution was added a shift in political power from the kabaka to the Christian chiefs. Although victorious, the Christian parties would themselves soon split, and this would have an impact on the scramble for East Africa by European powers. Thus, while Christianity gained a lasting foothold in Buganda by the 1890s, it had also played a part in promoting turmoil and upheaval in the kingdom.

The foothold gained by Christianity in Buganda was not, however, paralleled in other parts of East Africa. For most of the region, Christianity did not provide the prelude to European control that it did in Buganda. It can not be overemphasized that successful missionary work came after the establishment of colonial rule in most parts of the region rather than before it. Still, missionary endeavors should not be lightly dismissed as precursors to colonial conquest. In Britain and other parts of Europe, the need to spread the European faith formed a very important justification for imperial expansion.

European Adventurers as Precursors of European Involvement in East Africa

As the nineteenth century wore on, increasing numbers of European adventurers or travellers made their way into the East African interior. The motives for the journeys undertaken by these travellers were diverse and not simply "discovery" as proclaimed by many past history books. For some, scientific motivation stood out; they wished to verify the main features of the geographic configuration of East Africa for the benefit of people in Europe and America and their own reputations. Others came to Africa in search of adventure and to make money, in addition to making a name for themselves. Some, such as David Livingstone, were motivated by high ideals of Christian service.

Without doubt, the geographic problem that engendered the most interest in East Africa was the source of the Nile River. Several European adventurers, beginning with Speke and Burton in the 1850s, made their way, financed and supported by the British Royal Geographic Society, into the interior to try to establish just where the White Nile began. Speke travelled to the source of the river via Buganda in 1861, but influential figures in the Royal Geographic Society, among them Burton and Livingstone, refused to accept Speke's identification of Lake Victoria as its source. It remained for H. M. Stanley, in the course of his journey across Africa in 1874-77, to show that Speke had been right.

Most travellers and adventurers published books on their return to Europe, and through these the literate public came to know more about East Africa. That the picture they received was in many ways biased and unbalanced is quite evident today. Many of the adventurers took little effort to try to understand the social and political systems of the people they moved among, and these were judged from a Victorian perspective which viewed Africa as a land of "savagery" and "barbarism." Indeed, the paternalistic and brutal attitudes that were to be so typical of European colonial rulers were first demonstrated by many of these individuals. The belief that might makes right and that Africans understood only force and physical violence were characteristic of men like Stanley as well as later generations of colonial administrators.

However biased their reporting, these nineteenth-century travellers did expand Europe's knowledge of Africa. In their descriptions of the economic conditions and potential of East Africa, they were acting, consciously or not, as agents of European governments and business interests. Even the missionary Livingstone's journeys were partially financed by commercial concerns and the British government. In addition to providing information, these travellers in their writing provided a picture of an underdeveloped and "primitive" Africa in dire need of aid from western civilization. In short, they, along with missionaries and anti-slavery advocates, handed European governments and politicians a powerful justification for the colonial intervention. Thus, by making more information available to influential people in Europe and by popularizing the image of African backwardness, these adventurers helped to pave the way for eventual European control.

The conquest of the coast by Seyyid Said and his decision to make his capital on Zanzibar helped to promote an increase in trade with Europe. European commercial involvement with East Africa would, however, have expanded markedly in the nineteenth century in any event. Developing European and American capitalism was seeking cheap raw materials and markets for its goods, and East Africa was one of several areas to experience expanding trade relations. These began to bring about economic change in the region during the nineteenth century, but they did not spur economic development on the European model. East Africa became a part of capitalist Europe's "periphery," a position in which the region would be firmly entrenched by colonial control in the twentieth century.

The leading role in European economic involvement with East Africa was played by Britain. To commercial links were added other ties between Britain and Zanzibar, most notably the result of the campaign against the export of slaves from East Africa. Missionary activity was another way in which Europe became involved in East Africa, and after the middle of the century increasing numbers of European adventurers made their way into the East African interior. Of the developing European contracts, undoubtedly the greatest number involved Britain. The most powerful European nation for most of the nineteenth century, Britain did not seek colonies in East Africa prior to the 1880s. New influences in the last two decades of the century, however, would drastically alter the stance of Britain with regard to the region.

Chapter 6

Suggestions for Further Reading

Alpers, Edward. *Ivory and Slaves: Changing Pattern of International Trade in East Central Africa to the Later Nineteenth Century* (London, 1975).

Ogot, B. A., ed. *Zamani* (Nairobi, 1974).

Oliver, Roland, and Mathew, Gervase, eds. *History of East Africa*, Vol. I (Oxford, 1963).

Wright, M. *Buganda in the Heroic Age* (Nairobi, 1971).

Chapter 7

The Scramble
for East Africa

BETWEEN 1880 AND 1895 BRITAIN AND GERMANY divided up East Africa
between them. Although their authority had yet to be made effective in
the territories they claimed, this "scramble for East Africa" involved a
distinct change in policy for the European powers. Thus, these years
were crucial in determining the fate of East Africa from a European
perspective.

Britain and Zanzibar: "Informal Empire"

By the end of the 1870s Britain had achieved considerable dominance in
Zanzibar affairs. Economic ties as well as connections established during
Britain's anti-slavery campaign gave her great influence. Although
nominally independent, Zanzibar was in many respects within the British
sphere of influence. Moreover, Britain was not loathe to press the claims
of Zanzibar over the East coast and the interior in the face of threats
from other European powers, notably France, to make inroads into the
region. By the late 1870s, moreover, Zanzibar's armed forces were under
the command of a British officer. Added to her paramountcy over
Zanzibar were Britain's missionaries and adventurers, certainly outnum-
bering those of any other European country.

For many reasons, therefore, Britain could get what she wanted in East
Africa (e.g., trade, mission stations, and anti-slavery decrees) without
having to formally annex it. Indeed, the feeling that colonial expansion
was unprofitable and unnecessary was quite widespread among political

leaders in mid-century Britain. Britain had sea power and a dominant position economically so there seemed no need to worry about potential colonies in East Africa. As already noted, the British government had opposed plans of British commercial interests to obtain a sphere of influence in East Africa through a concession from the Sultan of Zanzibar in the 1870s. Prior to the 1870s potential rivals such as France were kept too busy by events in Europe, such as the revolutions of 1848 and the Franco-Prussian War, to seriously challenge the British position. Germany had yet to be united in a single state.

The circumstances in which British influence had reigned supreme in Zanzibar and East Africa did not endure, however. By the end of the 1870s, strong, stable regimes had emerged in France and Germany with the capability of challenging the position of Britain. Before the end of the century, indeed, Germany would surpass Britain as the continent's leading industrial power. These countries would increasingly look to Africa for "a place in the sun." So too would the ruler of Belgium, King Leopold. Faced with new challenges from these quarters, Britain would be forced to alter her policy of dominating East Africa through Zanzibar.

Egypt and the Scramble for East Africa

The earliest attempts at imperial expansion at the expense of Zanzibar (and indirectly Britain) came not from a European power but from Egypt. Egypt's ruler, Khedive Ismail, planned, among other schemes for modernizing and expanding his domain, to extend his control south down the Nile valley into the southern Sudan and Uganda and along the coast of the Red Sea and the Indian Ocean. These were most ambitious undertakings for such states as Bunyoro, Buganda, and Zanzibar, among others, stood in the way.

To further these ambitions the khedive appointed an Englishman who had previously travelled down the Nile to the lakes region, Sir Samuel Baker, to be governor-general of Equatoria Province in 1869. It was intended that Baker would work to stamp out the slave trade which was bringing considerable instability to the Nile valley and also to extend the province's boundaries southward. Baker attempted to move into Bunyoro in 1872, but he found Mukama Kabarega determined to resist. Unable to bring Bunyoro into Egypt's sphere of influence, Baker soon left the Khedive's service.

He was succeeded by the more able and ambitious General Charles Gordon, who had made a reputation for bravery and determination in China. Gordon took up the governor-generalship of Equatoria Province, resolved to wipe out the slave trade, and expand the boundaries of Egypt southward. Indeed, he came to the conclusion that for the trade to be successfully attacked, Egyptian control must be extended right up to Lake Victoria. Gordon further envisioned a chain of Egyptian stations stretching from the lake to the east coast. While he thus attempted to push down the Nile valley, the khedive in 1875 ordered Egyptian occupation of the port of Kismayu on the Somali coast.

Standing in the way of the ambitions of Gordon and Ismail were Buganda and Zanzibar. From Gondokoro in the southern Sudan, Gordon sent two emissaries to Buganda hoping to gain a foothold in Mutesa I's kingdom, but the kabaka was suspicious of the Egyptian penetration. He knew what had happened in Bunyoro earlier, and coast traders at the Buganda court warned him of Gordon's motives. Mutesa met the challenge by skillful diplomacy, including his invitation to Christian missionaries through Stanley and a huge display of strength which forced Gordon to abandon his attempts to establish forts on Buganda's frontier. The sultan of Zanzibar, furthermore, strongly complained that Kismayu was a port under his jurisdiction, a claim supported by the British consul on Zanzibar, Sir John Kirk. British pressure thus helped force an Egyptian withdrawal. By the time Gordon left Equatoria Province in 1876, Egypt's plan for expansion in East Africa had been thwarted, and within less than a decade Egyptian administration would be driven from the Sudan by the revolt of the Mahdi.

Egypt would still play an important, though less direct, role in the scramble for East Africa. Khedive Ismail's expansion policy and improvement schemes, together with lavish personal spending and financial mismanagement, pushed Egypt deeper and deeper into debt to European banks and money lenders. By the middle of the 1870s not even the interest on Egyptian debts was being met, and Britain, France, and other European countries intervened to take control of Egyptian finances. With the purse strings in charge of foreigners, it was not surprising that many Egyptians began to support nationalist leaders who wanted to get rid of foreign domination.

In 1882 a nationalist revolt broke out under the leadership of Arabi Pasha. Britain and France, with the greatest financial stake in Egypt, did not wish to leave. Britain, moreover, had an additional reason for wishing to maintain a strong and influential position in Egypt. In 1875 the British government had bought the shares in the Suez Canal Company belonging to the khedive. With their important trade route to India at risk, the British decided upon military intervention. Prime Minister W. E. Gladstone dispatched an army, after France had declined at the last moment to join in an invasion, to crush Arabi's forces. Once they had done so, the British took over Egypt. Gladstone felt that the occupation would be only temporary, until Egyptian finances were put back in order, but as will be seen, this did not turn out to be the case.

Chapter 7

Germany Enters East Africa

While willing to take control of Egypt for financial and strategic reasons, Gladstone resisted any such British action in East or West Africa in the early 1880s. His government attempted to continue the policy of protecting British interests by using the claims of the sultan of Zanzibar, but Gladstone himself was averse even to this. In 1884 a young British naturalist, H. H. Johnston, had made treaties with African leaders in the Mt. Kilimanjaro region and wrote to urge colonization of the area by the British. Kirk suggested that Kilimanjaro be taken over by Zanzibar, but despite some support from the British cabinet, Gladstone refused to have any part of such a scheme "touching the mountain country behind Zanzibar with an unrememberable name."

Shortly after this, however, the British were placed squarely on the defensive by German intervention. Germany's decision to establish a colonial empire in the 1880s represented a change in thinking by Chancellor Otto von Bismarck. In the previous decade, he had on several occasions expressed his opposition to colonies for the newly united Germany. What made Bismarck change his mind is not entirely clear. He may well have become convinced that German merchants were correct in their arguments that Germany needed colonies for economic reasons. The decision to create German colonies doubtless served his diplomatic aims as well, for he was able, temporarily, to get on better terms with France at Britain's expense. Finally, it appears that Bismarck may have wished to show British leaders that they could not ignore Germany as a great power; Britain had done little to respond to his queries about southwest Africa (Namibia) in 1883, and the following year Bismarck made it Germany's first protectorate in Africa.

Germany's claim to a portion of East Africa would be the last she made to African territory. In this case the German government took advantage of the efforts of one of her most avid imperialists, Carl Peters. Long an advocate of German colonial expansion, Peters was one of the leading lights in the Society for German Colonization. In addition to propaganda, the society undertook a mission under Peters to promote German control of East Africa. Although he received little encouragement from the German government, Peters was not to be deterred in his maniacal desire to spread the German Empire to East Africa. He and his companions arrived in Zanzibar in November 1884 disguised as mechanics. They crossed to the mainland, obtained treaties with "chiefs" in the interior, and returned to Berlin in February 1885. Within a month Bismarck's government had made these treaties the basis of a German protectorate, the administration of which was to be entrusted to the society.

130

This German action brought to an end the British policy of dominating East Africa through her influence over Zanzibar. The Germans ignored or defied the sultan's rights and claims to the coast and interior of what would become German East Africa. The sultan was in no position to resist the Germans, and the British government was unwilling to take a stand on his behalf. Gladstone's government was faced with serious problems in West Africa, Egypt and the Sudan, and Afghanistan, and it could not afford to offend Germany. The Germans sent gunboats to Zanzibar to force concessions from the sultan, but Gladstone could do no more than wish Germany "God speed" on her way to becoming a colonial power.

With the end of "informal empire" through Zanzibar, Britain was forced to turn to diplomacy with a view to salvaging something of her influence in East Africa. Negotiations were undertaken with Germany in 1885-86. Bismarck was now more conciliatory, and an international commission was established to determine the exact boundaries of the domains of the sultan of Zanzibar. The commission's decisions, in which representatives of the sultan took no part, were very favorable to Germany. They were enshrined in the Anglo-German partition agreement of 1886.

This agreement marked the conclusion of the first stage of the scramble for East Africa. The sultan's domains were defined as consisting of the islands of Zanzibar, Pemba, Mafia, and Lamu, and the coastal mainland from the Ruvuma River in the south to the Tana River in the north to a depth of ten miles. North of this limit, the towns of Kismayu, Brava, and Merca were recognized as falling under the sultan's hegemony. The other important portion of the agreement divided the mainland into German and British spheres of influence. A line was drawn from the Umba River at the coast up to Lake Victoria, skirting Mt. Kilimanjaro so as to leave it in the southern, or German, sphere. With the exception of Witu, south of Lamu, the territory north of the line became a British sphere of influence.

Chartered Companies and the Scramble for Uganda

Having divided up a considerable portion of East Africa and kept other European powers out, neither Britain nor Germany was willing to take over direct control. Both left the immediate task of taking over the territories and starting European influence and administration to chartered companies. The companies involved themselves not only with moneymaking ventures but with the establishment of administration and control. The Society for German Colonization, given responsibility for the German sphere, developed into the German East Africa Company.

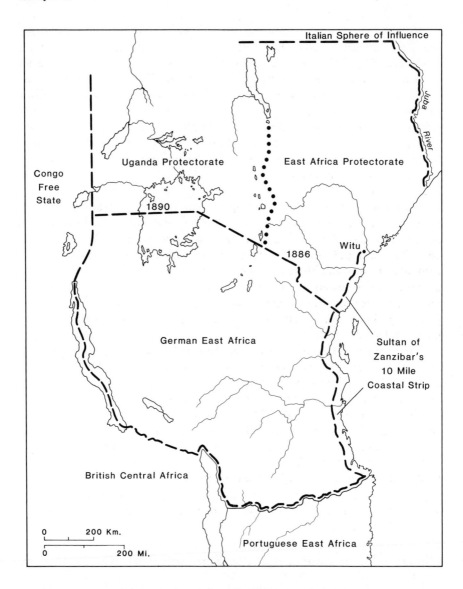

Map 21. Partition of East Africa to 1895.

With the British government now favorable, William Mckinnon was able to establish a chartered company, the British East Africa Association, which was a forerunner of the Imperial British East Africa (IBEA) Company. The association reflected a combination of commercial and philanthropic motives. Several of the directors were successful business-men whose concern was developing East Africa's resources for the benefit of Britain and their own pockets. Others, however, were churchmen and humanitarians concerned with stamping out slavery and promoting Christian work. Having obtained a concession from the sultan of Zanzibar granting full political and judicial authority and the right to levy customs duties in his domain, the association was granted a royal charter in late 1888 and became the IBEA Company

The IBEA Company established its administrative headquarters at Mombasa, but its attention soon was drawn far from the coast to Uganda. The 1886 agreement had provided for the division of East Africa only up to the eastern shore of Lake Victoria. Uganda was included in neither sphere. The British company feared it could be hemmed in through the linking up of the German protectorate of Witu with that further south via Uganda. Buganda was experiencing turmoil at this time, and British missionaries were resident in the kingdom. There was therefore consid-erable interest in Britain as to what would happen to Buganda. The IBEA Company decided to take steps to establish its control there.

British concern was heightened by the interest the German East Africa Company—and especially Carl Peters—showed in bringing Uganda into the German sphere. Peters, filled with imperial lust, was prepared to go to any length to carve out a large East African empire for Germany. In 1890 he set out for Buganda. In what is now western Kenya, he visited the camp of Frederick Jackson, leader of an IBEA mission, who was away from the camp at the time. A letter had arrived for Jackson from Kabaka Mwanga requesting assistance against Muslim attempts to drive him off the throne again. Peters read the letter and hastened to Buganda to conclude a treaty with the kabaka. When Jackson arrived in Buganda, he was too late to secure Mwanga's adherence to the British company.

Despite the success of Peters, the question of Uganda's place in the scramble for East Africa was decided over his head by diplomats in Europe. Lord Salisbury, the British prime minister and foreign secretary, had by 1890 come to the conclusion that Britain would have to remain in Egypt for a considerable time to come. From this decision, Lord Salisbury concluded that to secure her position there Britain must control the Nile, on which the prosperity and survival of Egypt depended. He feared another European power gaining a foothold in the Nile valley and damming the river. He therefore approached Germany and offered the Germans Heligoland Island in the North Sea in return for British control of Uganda. Much to the anger of Peters, an agreement to this effect was signed by the two powers on July 1,1890. The boundary separating the two spheres was extended to the west through Lake Victoria, leaving Buganda and the headwaters of the Nile in the British sphere. Germany also agreed to give up her protectorate over Witu and to accept a British protectorate over Zanzibar. In return, Germany gained control of Heligoland, which had strategic importance for her navy, and she was allowed to purchase from the sultan the ten-mile coastal strip earlier placed under Zanzibar's control. Moreover, Lord Salisbury made further agreements with Italy and Ethiopia to delimit the northern boundary of the British sphere.

From Chartered Companies to Protectorates

The 1890 agreement had finalized the division of East Africa between Britain and Germany, but, with the exception of the British protectorate over Zanzibar, neither government stepped in to take direct control of its sphere of influence. The chartered companies were left to carry on the task of administration until both rather quickly demonstrated that they were incapable of doing so.

Although undoubtedly doomed to a short life by poor management and undercapitalization, the IBEA Company hastened its own demise by setting its sights far into the interior on Buganda. Initially, this was to thwart German intentions, but even after 1890 the company was drawn, at great expense, into Buganda affairs. As in the late 1880s, these proved to be unsettled. As the Muslim threat receded, rivalry between Catholics and Protestants—heightened by the scramble with Protestant missionaries favoring Britain and the Catholics favoring Germany—led to friction and finally armed conflict. Many looked to the company to protect the British missionaries.

This was accomplished by Captain F. D. Lugard, who arrived in Buganda in December 1890 at the head of an IBEA Company expedition. Lugard signed a treaty with Mwanga which had the effect of placing the kingdom under the company, but he found the split between Catholics and Protestants (the Fransa and Ingleza as they were called at the time) widening and tension rising. The Muslims, though outside Buganda proper, still posed a serious threat. Lugard helped the Christians defeat them in May 1891, but the tension between Catholics and Protestants was not reduced as a result.

In the midst of this, Lugard went off to the west. In the course of the journey, he restored Kasagama to the throne of Toro, and he was able to persuade some 600 Sudanese troops to join him, considerably bolstering the forces at his disposal. These Sudanese or Nubian soldiers had been

134

left behind by the former Egyptian administration of the Sudan. Lugard then returned to Buganda, constructing a chain of forts enroute to protect Toro's independence.

Returning to Buganda in December 1891, Lugard found the Christian parties on the verge of open conflict. He also found instructions from the company to withdraw from Buganda because it had no money to carry on any sort of administration there. Lugard decided not to obey this order, and the CMS in Britain, stirred by their missionaries in Buganda, raised sufficient funds to enable the company to carry on until the end of 1892. In the end, conflict between Protestants and Catholics was inevitable; when it broke out, Lugard threw the weight of the company on the side of the Protestant Ganda to bring an end to the fighting. In a new agreement drawn up with Mwanga, Lugard provided for the principle of geographic partition of the kingdom by religion. The Protestants got a much greater share of government offices and counties than did the Catholics or Muslims.

Having "settled" Buganda for the time being, Lugard returned to Britain and joined others in mounting a public opinion campaign for the government to step in and take over Uganda. It was obvious that the IBEA Company could not continue. The British government sent Sir Gerald Portal, consul-general on Zanzibar, to Buganda to report on the situation there. Portal was highly critical of the company's administration at those points in the interior where it had set up stations. In 1893 Portal made a new agreement with Buganda which more equitably divided the offices of state between Catholics and Protestants, this time in the name of the British government. As a result of Portal's report and the pressure of public opinion in Britain, the government decided to declare a protectorate over Uganda in July 1894. One important development contemporary with the British takeover should be noted. This was the hostility toward Bunyoro which would mark the end of company influence. Deeply involved in Buganda, the British were drawn into conflict with Bunyoro.

The area between the Uganda border, which was drawn through the Rift Valley to the east of Lake Naivasha, and the coast remained under the IBEA Company, at least in theory. The company established a few stations in the area, the most important being Machakos in Kamba country and Fort Smith further west among the Kikuyu. Their major purpose was to supply caravans going to Uganda.

Machakos, started in 1889, was the first to be established. The company was not fortunate in the Europeans it initially placed in charge of this station. They used the firearms and small military forces at their disposal to steal food, and local Kamba attacked the small outpost in 1891. With the arrival of John Ainsworth as station superintendent in

February 1892, relations with the Kamba greatly improved. Ainsworth obtained assistance from the local people in building a larger and more impressive station, and he was able to obtain sufficient food supplies for passing caravans. He began to forge alliances with nearby Kamba leaders, but it would be wrong to say that he had established anything like European control over the region around Machakos by the time the British government took over the territory, naming it the East Africa Protectorate, on 1 July 1895.

Company relations were even more stormy with the Kikuyu than with the Kamba. Lugard, one of the few company officials to regard the Kikuyu in at all favorable light, constructed the first station at Dagoretti in 1890. He left a European official behind at the small fort he had constructed on the edge of Kikuyu cultivation, but hostility soon developed with the inhabitants of the area around the fort. Led by Waiyaki wa Hinga, they forced the evacuation of the fort in April 1891, destroying it after its abandonment. The IBEA Company still felt it was necessary to have a supply post on the edge of a productive region where caravans could obtain foodstuffs before crossing the more sparsely populated Rift Valley, so Captain Eric Smith was sent to build a new station later in 1891. Smith ordered Waiyaki out of his fields and sited the new fort, named Fort Smith after him, right in the midst of Kikuyu cultivation.

The establishment of Fort Smith did not lead to any improvement in relations with the Kikuyu, and the high-handed attitude of the company official put in charge soon led to further problems with the local people. As the company had little money to pay for food supplies, officials used the small military forces at Fort Smith to steal grain and livestock from the surrounding people. Waiyaki was tricked into coming to the fort and was seriously wounded when he tried to resist arrest. He died while being transported to the coast. This produced a particularly high level of Kikuyu bitterness toward Fort Smith. Sir Gerald Portal found it practically in a state of siege when he passed through on his way to Uganda in January 1893. He asserted that the company's raiding and looting in Kikuyu had "turned the whole country against the white man."

The situation at Fort Smith was thereafter stabilized somewhat by Francis Hall, who was able to get the upper hand with the assistance of Maasai to whom he had given refuge near the fort. Nevertheless, hostility and fighting continued to characterize relations between the company and the Kikuyu, and the violence directed toward the people around Fort Smith formed a most unhappy beginning for British relations with what would become Kenya's most populous and important ethnic group under colonial rule.

In the German sphere, company rule was even more short-lived than in the British. The Germans made an agreement with the sultan of Zanzibar in April 1888 giving the German East Africa Company administration over all the sultan's domains at the coast in addition to those claimed in the interior. The company moved in and almost immediately alienated the coastal population. Company officials behaved in a heavy-handed way, paying scant attention to local customs or feelings. The coastal peoples also rightly feared a loss of economic influence and trade as a result of the company takeover. Under the leadership of Abushiri bin Salim, numerous coast peoples took up arms in the second half of 1888 in an attempt to drive all Europeans from the coast. Company officials and German and British missionaries were forced out of the northern coastal towns except Dar es Salaam.

Alarmed by the Abushiri rebellion, which it was felt would undermine German prestige, the government in Berlin despatched a military force under Hermann von Wissman to restore European control. Wissman took the offensive against the rebels in May 1889. He regained control of the coastal towns; Abushiri was caught and hanged by the end of the year. As a result of this rebellion, however, the German government took over direct control of German East Africa from the company in 1890, and on 1 January 1891 formally took over the administration of the territory.

Thus, the fifteen years after 1880 concluded with Germany and Britain assuming control of East Africa. In some ways, this formal takeover was the culmination of the greater European involvement in the region that marked the nineteenth century. Other factors unique to the 1880s and 1890s conspired to produce the partition of East Africa. As the 1880s opened, Britain was in a strong position to dominate the region economically and politically, thanks to her influence over the sultan of Zanzibar, nominal ruler of the coast. The entry of Germany and the claims she made to the interior in 1885 forced Britain to end "informal empire" and stake out a formal claim to a portion of East Africa. Although at first on the defensive, by 1890 Britain was able to obtain Uganda and Kenya as spheres of influence, while Germany had her claims to mainland Tanzania (and also what is today Rwanda and Burundi) recognized.

Once the division of East Africa had begun, both Germany and Britain sought to control the region with as little expense as possible. Both therefore gave over the administration and economic exploitation of their spheres of influence to private companies. Although the British and German companies had some assistance from their respective governments, neither company was successful in its brief attempt to rule the vast area it was charged with administering. The German company was forced out of the field by the Abushiri rebellion and the consequent government takeover of January 1891. By July 1895 the British sphere had come under direct imperial rule as two separate territories, the Uganda and East Africa Protectorates. The British and German governments would, from the 1890s, control the destiny of East Africa for more than the next six decades.

Suggestions for Further Reading

Galbraith, J. S. *Mackinnon and East Africa* (Cambridge, 1972).

Ogot, B. A., ed. *Zamani* (Nairobi, 1974).

Oliver, Roland and Mathew, Gervase, eds. *History of East Africa*, Vol. I. (Oxford, 1963).

Chapter 8

The Establishment of European Rule: 1890s to 1914

BETWEEN THE OFFICIAL DECLARATIONS of protectorates in the 1890s and the start of the First World War, Germany and Britain established control of the East African territories they had laid claim to. With the exception of Zanzibar, this involved first and foremost the conquest of the region. Both Germany and Britain were able to bring the bulk of the territory under their writ by military force. The fact that colonial rule was established by armed conquest helped to determine the shape of that rule in East Africa. *acmel*.

Conquest and Resistance

The conquest of East Africa was a gradual process. The invading colonial forces fought engagements against individual ethnic or clan units, and only after a period of several years were all the major peoples of the region brought to acknowledge European dominance. One reason for the gradual nature of the conquest was the unwillingness of the European powers to expend huge amounts of money for military campaigns. Large-scale military expeditions, moreover, would have seriously undermined one of the main justifications for colonial rule in Europe: that the Europeans were bringing a better life to Africa by stamping out "tribal" wars and the slave trade. This, combined with fear of tropical disease, meant that neither Germany nor Britain utilized large numbers of European troops in the conquest. The European powers utilized African—and in the case of Britain, Asian—troops for the campaigns. They also allied themselves with African groups within the territories to subjugate other groups, following the dictum of divide and conquer.

The reaction of most East African peoples to the violent incursions of the Europeans was to resist. They took up arms and attempted to remain outside the domination of the invaders. They wished to safeguard their way of life and values and to maintain control over them. There were many variations on this theme from passive resistance to open fighting. Many groups put up a brave defense, and the colonial forces had to launch a number of campaigns, as with the Nandi of Kenya, for example, to overcome this primary resistance. Primary resistance, however, served only to slow down the European conquest, not to halt it. There were two important reasons for this. First, the forces employed by Britain and Germany had superior weapons. Although not all African peoples resisted the invaders with spears and arrows, even those with rifles did not have weapons as efficient as those of the European forces, with their repeating rifles, machine guns, and cannons. Secondly, as a result of the divide-and-conquer tactics of the invaders, the peoples of the region never put Up a united stand against them. The Europeans usually engaged other Africans, such as the Maasai of Kenya and the Ganda of Uganda, to help them in their campaigns of conquest.

The reaction of East Africa's peoples to the incursions of the colonial powers was thus characterized not only by primary resistance but also by collaboration. Some African individuals and societies saw it as in their best interests to cooperate with the colonial invaders. In the early years of foreign rule, some groups, such as the Ganda, benefited greatly from this collaboration. In a number of cases, moreover, peoples who had initially resisted the coming of European control later aligned themselves with the newcomers.

The Ecological Catastrophe

The last decade of the nineteenth century and the first decade of the twentieth were times of natural disaster in East Africa, especially in German East Africa and Kenya. Animal and human diseases, drought, and famine occurred on larger scales than in earlier periods, to some extent as a result of the European occupation and the warfare it produced. Population decline was followed by an expansion of the natural ecosystem of bush, game, and parasites at the expense of livestock and man.

The period of natural disasters began with a serious rinderpest epidemic which swept across Kenya and German East Africa beginning in the early 1890s. Huge numbers of cattle and wild game perished. Peoples such as the Maasai were especially hard hit. Smallpox followed in its wake as did locusts, which destroyed large amounts of sown crops. The 1890s were also a time of drought in several portions of the region, with resultant famine and death.

These natural disasters combined with changing settlement patterns, often produced by the colonial conquest (e.g., the movement away from large villages to scattered homesteads in what became German East Africa, and the removal of men to work on alien plantations), to bring about an ecological catastrophe. This affected all of East Africa, but probably German East Africa more than the two other territories created by colonial rule. From the turn of the present century, there appears to have been a retreat of men and livestock in the face of expanding bush, wild predators, and tsetse flies. Land under cultivation was steadily reduced, and the incidence of disease increased.

One of the most serious aspects of this catastrophe was the spread of sleeping sickness, carried by the tsetse fly, into much of East Africa. This was most notable in the region around Lakes Victoria and Tanganyika and in southern German East Africa. The rapid spread of the tsetse fly and the large-scale export of labor from population centers affected by sleeping sickness expanded the disease over a broad area. While it is not possible to precisely estimate the magnitude of these ecological setbacks, available evidence suggests that between the 1890s and 1914 the populations of Kenya and Tanzania declined disastrously.

Beginning Administration

The initial years of foreign control witnessed the establishment of the colonial state. At first, the governments established by Britain and Germany were small in scale and often makeshift. Only a handful of Europeans were engaged in the task of administering and governing the conquered territories. Generally speaking, these were divided up into administrative units known usually as provinces and districts. Sometimes, these divisions were based on geographical and ethnic boundaries, but just as often they were not. It was usual for these administrative divisions to be placed under the control of a few European officials (most often titled provincial and district commissioners) whose administrative responsibilities tended to be very broad. These were the "men on the spot" who often had to make decisions without policy guidelines or any but a passing knowledge of the societies with which they were dealing. They not only had to exercise administrative and judicial functions, but also to serve as agricultural, veterinary, and medical officers. The central bureaucracy, headed by the governor, tended to be small in the East African colonies. However, the colonial governors held immense powers in the first years of colonial rule, ranging from law maker to commander-in-chief of the armed forces stationed there.

Since the European governments involved in the establishment of colonial rule were unwilling to spend large sums of money to employ an extensive administrative staff, the colonial structure had, from the first, to rely very much on African manpower. This was, of course, what had happened in the course of the military campaigns, and it was continued in the administrative sphere. Africans were recruited by the colonial regimes to serve as communicators between their people and the colonial state. Often given the title "chief," these individuals were expected to make the wishes of the European administration known to the people within the areas they had been assigned. They were normally expected to maintain law and order and, some years after the conquest, to help in tax collection. Chiefs, and lesser officials known as "sub-chiefs" who were given responsibility for smaller areas than those assigned to a chief, would play an important role in the developing colonial structure.

In a number of cases these communicators were chosen from families which had been prominent in administration before the coming of colonial rule. This was true in Buganda and other Uganda kingdoms, where a system of Indirect Rule came to apply. The Europeans noted an already existing administrative structure and utilized it for their ends. Among those East African peoples who did not have kings or chiefs ruling them before the coming of the Europeans, it was not nearly so easy to utilize communicators. Within units recognized by the colonialists as tribes, for example, there were often several clan leaders, none of whom was recognized as leader by all. In other cases African rulers (for example, Kabarega) had led primary resistance to the Europeans, and they were excluded from the new administrative structure. Nevertheless, by 1914 a pattern was emerging all over East Africa of the colonial powers using African chiefs as a means of communication with and control of the peoples they were seeking to rule.

Another significant dimension of the system of colonial administration involved the creation of distinctive ethnic identities or "tribes". Although kingdoms such as those of the Ganda and Hehe presented seemingly easily identifiable ethnic units to the colonial rulers, in much of East Africa ethnic identity was much more fluid and could not in any sense be characterized as a tribe. The establishment of colonial rule forced many East Africans to adopt novel ethnic identities. At the location and district level, lines were drawn on the map which the colonial rulers expected to represent an ethnic purity which in fact had seldom existed previously.

As a result of this policy, ethnicity and "tribal" identity became essential attributes of the colonial experience. Developed and solidified in the initial years of colonial rule, ethnicity would form the basic framework for colonial administration and African political activity for decades to come as the colonial states practiced a system of divide and rule through the maintenance of a system of local administration based on ethnically distinct units. Ethnicity was particularly embedded in administration and politics in Kenya and Uganda, and to a lesser degree in German East Africa.

The establishment of the colonial state, however, did not mean an end to African resistance. Primary resistance was overcome through European military power, and most African peoples recognized that it would be almost impossible to successfully resist foreign domination by armed force. Nevertheless, many did not accept colonial rule, and as conditions under foreign domination became more and more oppressive, some, as in the Maji Maji rebellion, took up arms in an attempt to throw off the colonial yoke. Those who did not rebel often chose other forms of resistance, such as separatist churches, to display their continuing displeasure with the colonial situation.

Economic and Social Considerations

In addition to conquering and establishing an administration in their East African territories, Britain and Germany sought to make them pay. Conquest and administration involved the expenditure of funds by the European governments; both Britain and Germany hoped that by the encouragement of economic activity which would increase exports and thus bring revenue to the colonies, they might reduce, or eliminate, the necessity to call on European taxpayers to finance colonial control. Such previously significant exports as slaves and ivory were seen as not viable by the colonial regimes, and attempts were made to stimulate agricultural production for export. By 1914 the three mainland colonies had developed rather different approaches to agriculture. The Uganda administration was developing cotton grown by Africans as a major revenue maker; the East Africa Protectorate (Kenya) was developing an economy which favored European settlers who produced for export. German East Africa combined both these approaches. The economic transformation of East Africa had thus begun by 1914. Most parts of the interior had been more deeply touched by world capitalism than before the 1890s. As a result, new crops had been introduced, more European goods were being sold, and men were being drawn to wage labor in increasing numbers.

Wage labor evolved in early colonial East Africa as Africans were employed by colonial governments and missions in "new" occupations which required exposure to the educational system set up under colonialism. There also emerged, particularly in Kenya and German East

143

Africa, an African workforce undertaking agricultural production on land which the colonial state had made available to European settlers. Some of these Africans were squatters or resident laborers; others were short-term migrant workers.

In the British territories and to a somewhat lesser extent in the German, the economic rule of the day was largely to stimulate production by individual initiative in the usual capitalist sense while tying the territory's economy as closely as possible to that of the mother country and keeping it in a dependent position. Although the colonial state would be more active than its counterpart in Europe in the economy (for example, through the provision of transportation infrastructure), on the whole little was spent to aid what might be termed economic development. In the British territories, the colonial state involved itself little in providing educational, agricultural, and veterinary services which could have aided such development. While in German East Africa more was done by the colonial government to spur agricultural production, this did not amount to the large-scale effort to promote economic change which was to mark the final years of colonial rule. The kinds of economic activity embraced by the colonial authorities in this first period of their rule were not profitable, and both Germany and Britain continued to make grants-in-aid to their East African territories to cover the difference between revenue and expenditure.

Another effect of colonial rule in East Africa was the introduction of Christianity on a large scale. Except on the coast and in Buganda, missionaries had achieved little success prior to the 1890s. With the advent of colonial rule, however, conditions were much more favorable for the propagation of the gospel. Many Africans turned to Christianity as a path to spiritual salvation and/or political and social survival under the new conditions of colonial rule. For their part, the missionaries brought not only Western religion but also Western culture and values to East Africa. Prior to 1914 they provided, at least in Kenya and Uganda, practically all the Western education transmitted to Africans. Although their main mission was conversion, the missionaries, as propagators of Western culture and values, were also very important agents of social change.

Uganda

The development of the Uganda Protectorate under British rule prior to 1914 provides a good example of the gradual expansion of colonial control. Starting from Buganda, British influence spread slowly outward in all directions. In this expansion, the British remained closely linked to Buganda.

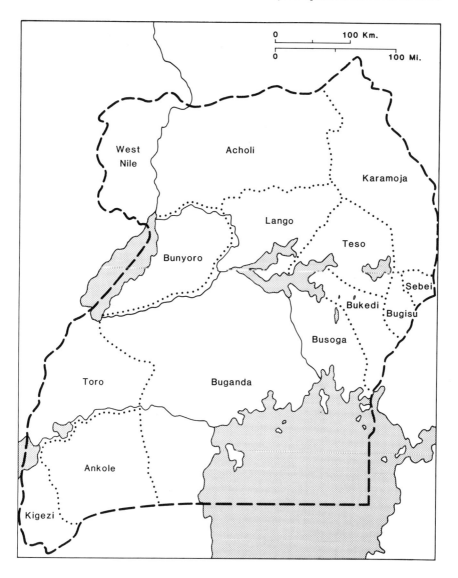

Map 22. Colonial Uganda.

Chapter 8

Britain and Buganda

In officially taking control of Buganda in mid-1894, the British government inherited an unsettled situation. The kingdom was in the throes of
what has been called the Christian revolution whereby political power
passed from the kabaka to the major chiefs. Buganda chiefs had accepted
the British, and this served to enhance their power; the most influential
chiefs in Buganda were Protestants. Feeling his loss of influence and
power even more keenly under British rule and blaming the Europeans
for this, Kabaka Mwanga eventually rebelled. In July 1897 he left his
capital at Kampala and made his way south to Buddu, where he attracted
a number of supporters. Seeing Mwanga as a danger, British authorities
sent an armed force of Sudanese troops and Ganda against him. The
kabaka was defeated and forced to take refuge in German East Africa. A
month later the administration deposed Mwanga and placed his infant
son, Daudi Chwa, on the throne. Three Christian regents, the most
important of whom was Apollo Kagwa, the katikiro, or chief minister,
were appointed to rule during the young kabaka's minority. This marked
the final downfall of the king's power from its pinnacle just a few decades
earlier. As later events would show, it was the Christian chiefs who held
political power; and with the kabaka a mere boy, there was little
challenge to their position for many years to come.

The British had already seen the advantages of taking over the
existing Buganda administrative system and using it for their own
purposes. The hierarchy of chiefs was an effective mechanism for control.
The new colonial administration had little money to spend and only few
European officers available. The missionaries already in Buganda wished
to see their followers holding influential positions continue to do so.
These factors thus combined to convince the first British administrators
to keep the Buganda system intact by backing the major chiefs against
the kabaka. The chiefs in turn were to gain from this association.

Only Mwanga was the loser. He left German East Africa in early 1898
and made his way north to join Kabarega, mukama of Bunyoro, in the
latter's guerilla campaign against the British. These two former enemies
held out against the colonial forces until they were captured in 1899.
Mwanga was eventually exiled to the Seychelles islands in the Indian
Ocean.

A greater threat to the British position in the new protectorate was
the mutiny of the Sudanese troops who had been serving the colonial
authorities since Lugard had brought them from the west. They had
played a major part in the defeat of Mwanga and his supporters in 1897,
but soon after this engagement they were marched east to Eldama Ravine
(in what is today Kenya) to join an expedition to the north. At Eldama

Ravine the Sudanese troops refused to go any further because many of their grievances, such as arrears in pay, had not been dealt with. They mutinied and returned to Busoga where they were joined by other Sudanese stationed there. As it turned out, the British position was rescued through the initial help of the Ganda chiefs. Kagwa led a large force of Ganda to Busoga, and helped to pin down the mutineers until imperial forces from India could arrive to finally quell this danger to colonial rule.

Buganda Sub-imperialism

Another way in which Buganda and her emerging Christian elite were important to the British was in the extension of colonial authority. Here the actions of ambitious Ganda leaders were more important than British activity. The western kingdoms of Toro and Nkore were brought under colonial authority through treaties between their rulers and Britain, but colonial rule came to Bunyoro and much of south-eastern Uganda through the agency of Buganda expansionism.

Mukama Kabarega had proven a major opponent of British expansion even before the formal declaration of a protectorate. In 1893 he had attacked Buganda and Toro, whose independence of Bunyoro had been provided by Lugard. As a result, British officials became convinced that Kabarega was their greatest danger, and a major campaign was launched against him at the start of 1894. The attack on Kabarega was a joint effort between the British and the Ganda who provided the bulk of the troops. They took Kabarega's capital in February 1894 and cut his kingdom into two with a line of forts. Kabarega took the offensive in attempts to drive the invaders out of his kingdom, but he was unsuccessful and he was eventually forced across the Nile into Acholi and Langi country. From there, joined by the deposed Kabaka Mwanga, he carried on a guerilla campaign against British and Ganda forces. He was captured in 1899.

These hostilities against the British and their allies had disastrous consequences for Bunyoro. The fighting brought much destruction and devastation. Agriculture and trade suffered, and famine occurred as a result. In the long run even more unfortunate was the political settlement imposed on Bunyoro by the victorious allies. As a reward, Buganda was given additional land at Bunyoro's expense. A good deal of this was inhabited by Nyoro, and it even included territory containing the tombs of mukamas. Thus was created the problem of the "lost counties" which bedevilled the British down to the end of colonial rule. Moreover, the conquest imposed on Bunyoro an administration in which Ganda were very prominent.

Perhaps the most outstanding example of Buganda sub-imperialism, however, can be seen in the exploits of Semi Kakunguru. A military leader who had participated in the campaigns against Mwanga and Bunyoro, he launched a dramatic campaign of expansion after 1895. Kakunguru was ambitious, but he found his way to the top of the Christian elite in Buganda blocked by Apollo Kagwa and others. He therefore set out to make a name for himself in areas outside the kingdom. He turned his attention north and east. He first moved north of Lake Kyoga. With his armed followers, he established control of Langi and Teso country. Tacitly encouraged by the British, he built and garrisoned forts in these regions and established Buganda-type administrations. Counties (saza) and sub-counties (gombolola) were established, with Ganda acting as chiefs and sub-chiefs. Thus Kakunguru not only conquered these areas, but he introduced a new type of administration operated by Ganda agents. He himself set up his headquarters at Budaka in Bukedi, and so well entrenched was he by the turn of the century that Sir Harry Johnston would refer to him as the "Kabaka of Bukedi."

In 1902, however, Kakunguru's headquarters were taken over by the British, who now assumed the administration of the region. Kakunguru moved north to establish himself at Mbale, which became an important center for controlling the Gishu. Here, too, he introduced a Buganda-type administration with Ganda as chiefs. When the British took over the district in 1903, they used these Ganda not as chiefs but as agents or advisors to Gishu. Kakunguru now transferred to Busoga. European rule had been accepted there, but the system of administration had not pleased British officials. Kakunguru became president of the Busoga Lukiko in 1906, and he set about introducing a Buganda-type administration.

As time passed, however, Kakunguru grew dissatisfied with his role. There were no new worlds to conquer, and collaboration with the British came to be less and less pleasing to him. By the time of his transfer back to Bukedi in 1913, Kakunguru was bitter against not only the British administration but also Christian missionaries, and he became involved in the separatist and anti-European church, the Bamalaki, which he helped spread. Nevertheless, his contribution to the inauguration of colonial rule and Buganda influence in many parts of Uganda was immense.

The Buganda Agreement of 1900

During the first years of British rule in Buganda and neighboring regions, little had been set down, either in London or East Africa, in the way of overall policy. Moreover, the administration of the protectorate was proving rather costly. In 1898-99, for example, a British grant-in-aid of more than £300,000 was necessary to meet the cost of administration. In 1899 the Foreign Office, which controlled the affairs of the Uganda and East Africa Protectorates until 1905, appointed Sir Harry Johnston as special commissioner to—among other things—cut the costs of administration, put the finances of the protectorate in shape, and investigate the raising of revenue by the imposition of a tax on Africans. One of the first Africanist scholars, Sir Harry had travelled widely in Africa and had played a key role in the establishment of British rule in Malawi.

As a result of his investigations, Johnston concluded that the kingdoms under British control should be left to govern themselves as allies of the British with a minimum of interference. He put this premise into effect in the settlement he reached with Buganda. The Buganda Agreement of 1900 was drawn up after discussion and lengthy negotiations with the regents and Christian chiefs, and it is probably not too much to say that it completed the transfer of power to that group.

Buganda became a province within the protectorate, but the administration of the kingdom remained virtually intact. The kabaka became, in effect, the chief communicator between the British and his people; he would have to remain loyal to the colonial authorities if he wished to retain his throne. The Lukiko was now formally constituted as a legislative body and final court of appeal. The Ganda leaders agreed to the introduction of a tax on houses (called the hut tax), but no further taxation could be imposed without the consent of the kabaka and the Lukiko.

A most significant part of the Buganda Agreement was the land settlement, which altered the system of land tenure in a revolutionary way. Land was granted on a freehold basis to the kabaka and his chiefs. Previously, land had been held at the pleasure of the kabaka and normally a service was rendered to him in exchange for use of the land. Now chiefs could claim a clear title to land and pass it on to their heirs. Approximately half the land of Buganda was divided up in this way; the rest was recognized as crown land. The county and lesser chiefs, numbering some 4,000 were the great beneficiaries of this part of the agreement, the peasant farmers the losers.

It would be difficult to overestimate the importance of the Buganda Agreement in the colonial history of Buganda. It gave Buganda a special place in the protectorate enjoyed by no other kingdom or province, and this helped to promote a feeling of superiority and separateness among the Ganda in their relations with the rest of the country. Within Buganda, it completed the Christian revolution, giving considerable control in government and land to the Christian chiefs. The land settlement not only increased the chief's control of the peasants who became tenants on their land, but it opened the way to great economic advantages for them, especially with the introduction of cash crops. In the decades to come, this land settlement would engender considerable hostility and opposition from the bataka, or clan heads whose rights to land were overridden by the agreement.

Having made a settlement with Buganda, Johnston turned to the western kingdoms. Since Toro had been friendly and loyal to Britain, Johnston signed a similar agreement with its ruler, Kasagama, in 1900. Territory was added to the kingdom, and all land was made crown land. Freehold grants were made to the king and more important chiefs. Johnston initially felt that a similar agreement could not be made with Nkore, and only in August 1901 was such a settlement formalized. The mugabe was recognized as ruler and the surrounding principalities were joined under his rule as part of Nkore. Johnston did not visit Bunyoro, since it was deemed a conquered territory, and no agreement would be made until 1933. The kingdom continued to be ruled by British officials aided by Ganda agents.

Further Resistance to British Rule

Neither the conquest of the major kingdoms and the southeast of Uganda by the British nor the signing of these agreements brought an end to opposition to colonial rule. Dissatisfaction was not demonstrated by open fighting; it took other forms, but it left no doubt that those involved did not accept the colonial situation with anything like open arms. One of the first manifestations of resistance took place in 1905 in Nkore, where the highest British official was stabbed to death by an assailant whose identity was never established. The colonial authorities viewed this as symptomatic of hostility and dissatisfaction on the part of chiefs. The British suspended the 1901 agreement for some seven years, and they imposed heavy fines in cattle. It is impossible to say just how far-reaching the opposition to the British really was, but the episode showed that not all in Nkore were happy with the new order.

Such feelings were demonstrated even more forcefully in Bunyoro. Ganda chiefs and agents had been brought in by the British after the conquest, and their presence was increasingly resented by the local people. In expressing their dislike of colonial rule, they focused their wrath on its most hated symbols, the Ganda agents, many of whom, like James Miti, had amassed great influence by the middle of the first decade of this century. The Nyoro began to feel that the whole of their kingdom might be taken over by Buganda. To this fear was added a dislike of Ganda cultural imperialism, which manifested itself in the use of Luganda rather than Lunyoro as the official language of state and church.

In 1907 this disenchantment flared into the so-called Nyangire rebellion (after the slogan Nyangire Abaganda—"I have refused the

Ganda") led by Nyoro chiefs. The Nyoro refused to cooperate with or obey Ganda chiefs. Most of the Ganda chiefs fled to Hoima, the Bunyoro capital. The British supported the Ganda chiefs and ordered their reinstatement, but the Nyoro chiefs were willing to accept arrest rather than aid in this order. British military force secured the restoration of the Ganda, but no more were appointed. Eventually, all were retired or removed and replaced by Nyoro. In the long run, this rebellion was successful in altering the character of, though not in eradicating, colonial rule, and in this it was to be typical of many kinds of what might be termed secondary resistance in East Africa. Nor would Bunyoro be the last to oppose "alien" chiefs.

A somewhat different reaction to colonial rule may be seen in the growth of separatist churches. These reflected an acceptance of Christianity but a rejection of European missionary control in all matters including doctrine. The Bamalaki were the most notable example of a separatist church from this period. Breaking with the mission churches, the followers of the Bamalaki rejected, among other things, the long waiting period for Christian baptism and bans on polygamy, which the mission churches insisted were prerequisites for membership in the Christian community. They also rejected Western medicine. Most notably, they rejected inoculations even in the face of government insistence. The doctrines of the Bamalaki reflected a rejection of attempts to force Western values and mores on Uganda Christians.

Further Expansion of Colonial Rule

Prior to 1909 the Uganda administration exercised relatively little control over the northern regions of the protectorate. British claims had been recognized by other European nations through diplomatic agreements, but although posts had been placed in Acholi and Madi country, no effective administration had been established. Administrators, such as Governor Sir Hesketh Bell, felt the north was an economic liability.

After 1909 colonial rule would be expanded beyond the kingdoms and the areas conquered by Kakunguru. The finances of the protectorate now seemed to warrant military expeditions to the north, and from posts on the edge of Langi country, new government stations were set up in Acholi and adjacent regions. Lango District was created in 1911, and by 1913 civil administration had been established in Acholi. As in previous instances, Ganda agents came with this expansion of colonial rule, and the Buganda model of administration was introduced even into these regions as well as in the south. The Ganda also helped introduce cotton cultivation around Lake Kyoga with marked success.

Expansion of British control also took place in the southwest. This was accomplished, in considerable measure, to check any claims the

Belgian authorities of what is today Zaire might have had on the area. Kigezi District was established as a result, and Ganda agents and their administrative structure were the vehicles chosen to effect British rule as in other areas.

Here, too, the reaction against Ganda domination was not long in coming. This anti-colonial reaction demonstrated the dislike of peoples in Lango, Teso, Acholi, Kigezi, and elsewhere to a colonial system which put Ganda over them as rulers. The protest had not only a political dimension but also a cultural one, as strong opposition to Luganda as the language of administration and education surfaced. In 1910 and 1911 numerous conflicts between Ganda agents and local populations took place in Kigezi, Lango, Teso, and Bukedi districts, resulting in a number of deaths and injuries. The system continued to be under fire during World War I, but the colonial authorities undertook the gradual removal of Ganda agents and their replacement in positions of responsibility by local individuals. By the end of the war, this transition was virtually complete in most parts of the protectorate.

The Colonial Economy

Prior to 1903 little had been accomplished in the way of economic expansion under British rule. The economy of Uganda remained essentially a subsistence one. As has been noted, government revenue proved inadequate to meet expenditures. There was thus considerable impetus for protectorate officials to develop the economy by finding a means of production for export. It happened that at the same time textile manufacturing interests in Britain were showing considerable interest in cotton growing in the British Empire. Worried about a possible shortage of cotton on the world market, they formed the British Cotton Growing Association in 1902 to pressure the British government to encourage the inauguration of cotton cultivation in favorable parts of the empire. This pressure helped to spur administration support for cotton growing in Uganda.

Cotton seed was first distributed on a substantial scale in 1904. Government and private companies provided seeds which were placed in the hands of chiefs, mostly in Buganda. Cotton grew well in the soil and climate of Uganda, and the protectorate was fortunate in that prices for raw cotton were steadily rising at the time of the crop's introduction, thus providing an attraction and incentive to growers. The initial attempts to introduce cotton were largely on a do-it-yourself basis. Little instruction in planting and care was given, several different types of seed were distributed, and hand gins, which were not easy to use, were sold or given to chiefs to provide for preparation. The result was that, although cotton production grew rapidly in these first years, the quality of cotton grown and processed drew criticism in Britain. The British Cotton Growing Association, in particular, complained to government authorities about quality control in 1907.

This prompted strong and decisive action from the governor, Sir Hesketh Bell, in 1908. Never one to shrink from drastic action if he thought it necessary, as when he ordered the forced removal of much of the population of the Buganda and Busoga lake shore in an effort to check the ravages of sleeping sickness, Bell issued new cotton-growing rules. As only one type of seed would thereafter be grown, all cotton plants were destroyed. All hand gins were collected; ginning would now be done at central ginning stations to which growers would bring the crop. Such was the authority of the Ganda chiefs and agents that these drastic measures were carried through with little overt opposition. If the success of cotton growing owed much to the chiefs' authority, they, as land owners in Buganda, gained great economic advantages from cotton cultivation.

As a result of Bell's reforms, cotton of satisfactory quality was produced at increasing levels. Cultivation spread from Buganda to the east and to the Lake Kyoga region, where the Soga and Teso took up the crop. With more growers, exports expanded. Valued at £60,000 in 1909-10, cotton exports rose in value to over £350,000 by 1914-15. With increasing exports came greater prosperity for the protectorate, and a reduction and eventual termination of the grant-in-aid from Britain.

The success of cotton would have some negative effects as well. The Uganda colonial economy developed largely for the purpose of supplying the needs of the British textile industry, and this produced a very unfortunate kind of dependency. No encouragement was given to local textile manufacturing; imperial authorities saw Uganda's role as that of a producer of primary products. Throughout the colonial period the Uganda economy would be largely dependent on world prices for cotton, over which the peasant producer had little or no control.

The intrusion of Asian (as used here the term Asian refers to individuals of Indian or Pakistani descent) middlemen in the cotton trade can perhaps be seen in the same light. The colonial authorities encouraged the settlement of Asian traders in Uganda from the earliest days of British control. Asians opened shops and provided a link in the economy that officials felt Africans were unable to fill. With the start of cotton growing, Asians came increasingly to serve as middlemen who bought the crop from the African growers and then sold it to ginners. During and after World War I the ginneries, initially opened by European firms, came to be largely owned by Asian businessmen. The economic and social effects of the position of the Asian middleman would be reaped in later years.

Although African peasant-grown cotton was Uganda's most successful cash crop before 1914, cotton growing did not necessarily exclude other forms of economic activity. Some protectorate officials hoped that plantation agriculture could succeed in producing exportable quantities of rubber, coffee, and other tropical produce. Although Europeans had started plantations in Uganda before the First World War, their numbers were not very great. Unlike in neighboring Kenya, where many European settlers acquired land, restrictions were placed on the alienation of land to non-Africans. Missionaries in Uganda were not highly supportive of European agriculture, nor were Governor Bell and other influential officials. Moreover, the demand for crops other than cotton produced on European plantations was not very strong or buoyant. Rubber prices, for example, had collapsed to almost uneconomical levels by 1914.

Despite the lack of a numerous European planter class, no firm decision had been taken by protectorate authorities for or against plantation agriculture. African grown cotton was far and away the most important export by 1914, but Uganda was yet to be seen clearly as the domain of the peasant producer. Only after World War, in the face of considerable pressure for the extension of European settlement, would the imperial authorities finally decide in favor of a predominance of African agriculture.

Missions and Western Education

Christian missionaries had, of course, begun work in Buganda before the establishment of colonial rule and had played a significant part in bringing the territory under British control. As the 1890s drew to a close, increasing numbers of Ganda became members of Protestant or Catholic churches. By the end of the first decade of the twentieth century, Buganda Christians greatly outnumbered Muslims and followers of the traditional faith whereas a decade or two earlier the Christians had been a minority. The turbulence of the times and a desire to get ahead in the new era now dawning help to explain this very rapid Christianization.

Christianity went hand in hand with Buganda sub-imperialism. As Ganda agents carried colonial rule to other parts of the protectorate, Ganda preachers and cathecists carried Christianity. As in Buganda, many were drawn to the Christian church as a way of ensuring success in the new, European-dominated world.

In this regard, Western education was especially important. Missionaries established schools to train their followers in the scriptures and to transmit the rudiments of Western education. Such mission schools became very popular in Buganda. They were important symbols of the age of improvement and were seen as a means by which Africans could improve themselves and learn to cope with the changes colonial rule was

154

bringing. After 1900 boarding schools were opened by the missions to provide spiritual and practical education. These became the foundation stones which would produce in Uganda by far the largest number of Western-educated Africans in the East African territories by the end of the colonial period.

Kenya

As in Uganda, the extension of European control in Kenya (known before 1920 as the East Africa Protectorate) represented a gradual process of conquest. Here the building of the Uganda Railway played an influential part in shaping the early history of the protectorate. Construction of the rail link to Lake Victoria took precedence over organized military campaigns of conquest, and the need to make the railway pay for itself shaped the future economic structure of Kenya.

The Uganda Railway

With the decision to take up a protectorate over Uganda, the British government decided that a rail line should be constructed to link it to the east coast. Although there was opposition in the British parliament to the immense expenditure this would entail, construction began at Mombasa in May 1896. One reason for the high cost of construction was the difficult terrain to be crossed. There was the dry Nyika; the steep escarpment of the Rift Valley had to be negotiated; many rivers had to be bridged. A satisfactory terminus on Lake Victoria had to be decided upon. Added to these problems were the need to import coolie labor from India, the threat posed by lions in the Tsavo region, and the hostility of the people along the way, most notably the Nandi.

Despite these difficulties, construction reached a point some three hundred miles from Mombasa in June 1899. Here on the level plain on the eastern side of the Rift Valley, railway engineers decided to establish the headquarters and workshops for the line. This site, Nairobi, was later to become the capital of the protectorate. With considerable difficulty the Rift Valley escarpment was surmounted and the railway reached Uganda, then just west of Nairobi, in 1900. By December 1901 the rail line had been completed to Kisumu (then called Port Florence) on Lake Victoria.

The completion of the line had an important impact on the development of Kenya. Prior to its completion, British authorities had made little attempt to expand their control over the peoples of the interior. The East Africa Protectorate was ruled from Zanzibar by Sir Arthur Hardinge, British consul-general there, who doubled as commissioner of the protectorate. Any extension of British control was

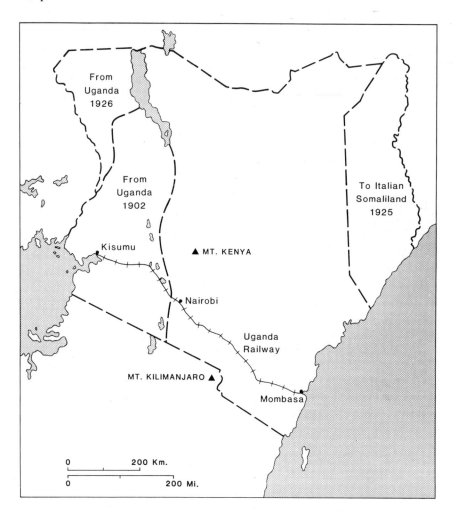

From
Uganda
1926

From
Uganda
1902

To Italian
Somaliland
1925

Kisumu

▲ MT. KENYA

Nairobi

Uganda
Railway

MT. KILIMANJARO ▲

Mombasa

0   200 Km.

0   200 Mi.

Map 23. Colonial Kenya.

the work of local administrators. After 1900, however, completion of the railway link with the coast made it much easier for the colonial authorities to move troops into the interior to undertake a more systematic conquest. Because of the railway; moreover, the size and character of the protectorate was altered in 1902. So as to keep the railway under a single administration, the Eastern Province of Uganda was transferred to Kenya; thus, the east shores of Lake Victoria and most of the Rift Valley highlands were taken over by the administration of the East Africa Protectorate.

The Conquest of Kenya

The conquest of Kenya's population, as noted above, did not take place on any significant scale until after 1900. Before that date the extension of colonial control was accomplished by the actions of administrators who had previously occupied stations of the IBEA company. The amount of influence over surrounding peoples achieved by John Ainsworth at Machakos among the Kamba and by Francis Hall at Fort Smith among the Kikuyu was based on the forces they could raise locally and the success of their policies of divide and conquer.

In this regard, it is important to note that the 1890s were a time of tribulation for the major peoples of the East Africa Protectorate—the Kamba, the Kikuyu, and especially the Maasai, pastoralists who had a reputation as fierce fighters. In the nineteenth century, civil strife, animal mortality, and human disease severely reduced the number and strength of the Maasai, and the decline continued into the 1890s. Inter-Maasai fighting caused hardship and social disruption. Rinderpest reduced the numbers of Maasai cattle, and smallpox took its toll of the human population.

By 1895 the Maasai could not have effectively resisted British penetration of the interior. They chose to join forces with the Europeans and aid in the conquest, seizing the opportunity to raid other peoples (e.g., the Kamba and Kikuyu) to replenish their herds. The help of the Maasai was welcomed by British officials such as Ainsworth and Hall as the forces at their own disposal were weak. Moreover, they believed erroneously—that the Maasai could prove a great danger to the British position if they took up arms against the Europeans. This inflated British estimate of Maasai power led the British to pursue a policy of collaboration. Thus, the 1890s saw an alliance forged between the Maasai under the olaiboni Olenana and the British.

Even with Maasai help, the conquest went slowly. Ainsworth at Machakos gradually extended his rule over the surrounding Kamba by the selective use of rifles and a successful policy of divide and conquer through alliances with the Kamba near Machakos. The rinderpest epidemic and a great famine in 1898-99 finally broke the back of Kamba resistance to British rule. Similar factors operated for the extension of authority over the Kikuyu around Fort Smith; in addition, a smallpox epidemic in the late 1890s helped to weaken resistance.

The first severe challenge to British claims to control came from the prominent Mazrui family at the coast. Some Mazrui at Mombasa came to resent British control as inimical to their own position and aspirations. Trouble began in 1895 over a succession dispute involving a Mazrui claimant. The British backed a rival, and Mbarak bin Rashid, the disappointed heir, raised the Mazrui against the new colonial order. The Mazrui burned several towns and for a time controlled a portion of the coast, but fortunately for the British not all the Arabs at the coast joined the rebellion. In early 1896 imperial troops arrived from India to put down the threat to British control.

After 1900 expansion to the north to bring the Kikuyu people under British rule was speeded up. A series of so-called punitive expeditions were launched by the protectorate's military forces. By 1906 most of the Kikuyu and Embu had been conquered, and the Meru were subsequently brought under British control.

In the western portions of Kenya, until 1902 part of Uganda, British influence was initially extended from the station established at Mumias by the IBEA company. Here with the active collaboration of the Wanga ruler, Mumia, control was established over the Luhya, utilizing a policy of divide and conquer with the various Luhya clans and sub-tribes. A similar approach was utilized to bring about the conquest of the Luo living along the shores of the lake and Nyanza Gulf.

The most serious resistance in western Kenya came from the Nandi. Unlike the Maasai, they were not weakened by the events of the 1890s. Their power had been growing in the latter half of the nineteenth century. In addition, the main caravan route to Uganda ran through their territory, and the railroad, when constructed, skirted the edge of the lands they occupied. Nandi resistance thus served to disrupt communications to and from Uganda. Initial hostilities with the British were the result of what can properly be termed barbaric behavior on the part of British traders. When one of them was killed by the Nandi in 1895, an expedition was launched by the Uganda authorities to punish those responsible. Another was despatched against the Nandi in 1897. Three more British military expeditions were sent against the Nandi before their resistance to British rule was finally ended in 1905.

The last of the major western Kenya peoples, the Gusii, were conquered in 1908, but the northern portions of the protectorate inhabited by pastoral peoples such as the Turkana, Oromo, Samburu, and Somali were hardly troubled at all by British authority. Only in what was known as Jubaland Province (much of which was transferred to Italy after World War I) did the colonial authorities attempt to exercise some control. The Somali living there put up strong resistance, however, and despite several large military incursions into the region the British never really established effective control.

Following the conquest, the colonial authorities established an administrative structure based upon a division of the protectorate into provinces and districts. As in Uganda, shortages of European staff and money necessitated the use of Africans as communicators between administration and people. Unlike in Uganda, however, there were no well-established kingdoms, other than Wanga, in Kenya. Most peoples in Kenya were not even ruled by chiefs. Nevertheless, the colonial authorities appointed chiefs and sub-chiefs to serve as part of the administration. Though taking the form of Indirect Rule on the Buganda or Nigerian model, this administrative system was in reality a kind of direct rule, as many of the men who were made chiefs had little if any traditional standing, and they were allowed little initiative in controlling the affairs of their localities. Supervised by European officers, their major functions came to be the maintenance of order, collection of taxes, and the production of able-bodied men to work for European settlers.

European Settlement and Land

Upon completion of the Uganda Railway, colonial officials needed to find a way to make it pay. The British taxpayers had provided a great deal of money to build the line, but until 1902 it was operating at a heavy loss because neither Kenya nor Uganda were producing much in the way of exports. In order to spur production for export, the government of the East Africa Protectorate decided in 1902 to encourage the settlement of European farmers in the highlands around Nairobi and further west in the Rift Valley just transferred from Uganda.

The decision to pursue development through European settlement was largely the work of Sir Charles Eliot, who had succeeded Hardinge in 1900. He took a dim view of the productive potential of the African population and he believed that they could not for a long time be brought to produce economic products for export. He therefore began to advertise the possibilities of the protectorate for white settlement, particularly in South Africa, and the availability of large tracts of land on easy terms.

Land was given to Europeans for farms under the terms of the Crown Lands Ordinance of 1902. This provided for the alienation of "public land" in the protectorate to Europeans on ninety-nine-year leases. In practice, "public land" was taken to mean all land not inhabited by Africans at the time. When settlers began to arrive in 1903 and 1904, clamoring for land to begin farming, land grants were made without proper survey. The Kikuyu were the first to feel the brunt of European settlement. Considerable portions of their land were alienated to Europeans while they were forced into reserves where it became next to impossible for many to obtain land of their own. This drove many Kikuyu to become "squatters" or resident laborers on settler farms, and it served to heighten distinctions in Kikuyu society between those who had land and those who did not. The effect of this plus rapid population growth was evident as early as 1914; the lands reserved for the Kikuyu after European settlement were not adequate to support the people. The situation worsened in succeeding decades.

The Maasai in the Rift Valley also suffered as a result of European settlement. Here too, Eliot made huge grants along the railway line to whites, caring little that the pastoralists grazed their herds there. Opposition to such grants and irregularities surrounding them drew criticism from the Foreign Office and forced Eliot's resignation in 1904. It was left to his successor, Sir Donald Stewart, to deal with the settlers' claims to Maasai land. Following the advice of his senior officials, Stewart made a solemn treaty with Maasai elders under which some of the herders would move north of the rail line to the Laikipia plateau, thus creating two Maasai reserves. This left the land along the railway for alienation to Europeans. This treaty was to be in effect as long as the Maasai "as a race shall exist."

As it turned out, the agreement lasted only seven years. Settlers cast covetous eyes at Laikipia, and pressure built up from the administrative officials to reunite the Maasai in a single reserve. Governor Sir Percy Girouard forced another treaty on the Maasai in 1911 by which they "agreed" to move south to join their brethren already there. Despite an abortive attempt to accomplish this in 1911 when the Maasai refused to complete the move, the Maasai were moved from Laikipia in 1912. The following year Maasai elders hired a European attorney and filed a case in the High Court asking for the return of the Laikipia plateau under the terms of the 1904 treaty. The case was rejected by the court on the grounds that since the treaty was between Britain and a foreign power (the Maasai), the court was not competent to hear it. The Maasai thus lost both their grazing grounds near the railway and Laikipia to European settlement.

The incoming settlers, most of whom were from South Africa (British and Boers) and England, demanded not only plenty of land but exclusivity of ownership. The demand was directed not so much against Africans at this time as against the other immigrant community, the Asians. Eliot had reserved all land between Kiu in the east and Fort Ternan in the west exclusively for white occupation. When the Colonial

Office took over responsibility for the territory in 1905, pressure was brought to bear to give this division legal sanction. Eventually, in 1907, the secretary of state for the colonies, Lord Elgin, gave what came to be known as the Elgin Pledge—that the area should indeed be reserved for Europeans. This broad belt of land thus became known as the White Highlands.

The Colonial Economy

Until 1914 European agriculture could hardly be said to have prospered. Many of the immigrant farmers had brought little capital with them and were unable to adequately develop the farms they obtained. Others found the environment decidedly hostile to their attempts to introduce European crops and cattle into the heart of Africa. Only such tropical crops as sisal and coffee were successfully established as money makers by the outbreak of the war, but even with these, production had not reached significant levels. In short, European settlement had not proved itself economically by 1914.

Many of the Europeans tended to view their economic problems in a very simplistic light, equating them with a lack of African labor. Unwilling to undertake manual labor in Africa themselves, they became convinced that African men, whom they viewed as habitually lazy, should work for them. Almost continuous pressure was put on the colonial administration to force Africans take jobs on European plantations. Periods of severe labor shortage, such as those which occurred in 1908 and 1912, led to noisy demonstrations and collisions with the administration. The settlers called on the government to raise taxes demanded from Africans in order to force them to work, and in fact a Poll Tax was levied in addition to a Hut Tax. Settlers called for direct government recruitment of labor and the active discouragement of agricultural production in African reserves. This selfish demand for cheap labor was to some extent camouflaged by rhetoric extolling the redeeming qualities of work and manual labor. In general, heavy coercive pressure was placed on African men to force them to leave their homes to work on European estates.

Some administrative officers, most notably John Ainsworth, did not support this move toward forced labor or the idea that African agriculture for export should be discouraged. As provincial commissioner of Nyanza Province, the most populous of the protectorate, from 1907 until the start of the war, Ainsworth strongly encouraged Africans to grow new crops, such as cotton, sim sim, and maize, which could be sold for cash. The settlers came to regard him as a great enemy since his policy implied that Africans could just as well work on their own lands and produce badly needed exports for the protectorate. Indeed, by 1914,

Nyanza Province was the leading exporter—notably of maize and sim sim—of the East Africa Protectorate and its greatest source of revenue through tax collection. The province was also a leading producer of laborers who worked away from home, usually on short-term contracts.

In practice, African agriculture was in many ways more profitable than European agriculture in this first period of colonial rule. This was not an accident, as African commodity production was encouraged by the colonial state. It came to provide an important source of government revenue and was a means of providing "legitimacy" to colonial rule. In the two decades after 1914, on the other hand, European agriculture won a striking pride of place; African growing of cash crops was discouraged and government policy was increasingly bent toward the export of labor from African areas. The reasons for this were both economic and political. The settlers gained influence which enabled them to obtain their wishes from the colonial administration.

As in Uganda, the means by which African production was channelled to the world market was Asian merchant capital. Asian migrants to Kenya from the 1890s to 1914 were even more numerous than Europeans. Contrary to popular myth, the Asian population was not largely the descendants of the coolie laborers who built the Uganda Railway; most of these laborers had returned to India. Rather the immigrants came mainly from the west of India and Pakistan, many of them from families who had long had commercial connections with the East African coast. They moved into the interior after the completion of the railway, settling largely in the towns. They came to dominate wholesale and retail trade, and helped to carry European imports and the cash economy all over the protectorate. The Asian migrants also tended to concentrate in skilled and semi-skilled trades and crafts and to occupy lower-level clerical jobs with the state. The Asians were thus an important element in the colonial economy.

Despite their rapid integration into the economy of Kenya and the vital role they came to play there, Asians tended, as in Uganda and German East Africa, to mix little socially with other groups. They preserved their own cultures and languages. This made it easier for Europeans to successfully press their demands for residential segregation and the color bar against the Asians.

Missions and Western Education

Even more than in Uganda, Christianity made inroads in Kenya after the establishment of colonial rule. Given the conquest and the considerable political and economic changes that came in its wake, the appeal of Christianity is not surprising. Nevertheless, not all the major population groups in Kenya were deeply affected by mission work and attendant

Western education. The mission effort began in Kenya fully a generation after it had taken root in Uganda, and this fact helps to account for the uneven impact of the missions. Some peoples, such as the Kikuyu, Luo, and Luhya were deeply touched by mission influences prior to 1914; others, such as the Gusii and most of the Kalenjin, who were brought under British control later and had yet to experience the full brunt of the colonial economy, were hardly affected at all.

As in Uganda, the Christian missions were the primary agents of the age of improvement. They brought Western education to those African populations which were receptive to Christianity. The colonial government provided aid only for schools catering to European and Asian children. Unlike in Uganda, there was considerable diversity in the mission effort in Kenya, particularly on the Protestant side. Whereas in Uganda the CMS dominated, in Kenya a number of Protestant mission societies from Britain, Europe, and America were at work.

Social and Political Dominance of the European Settlers

While their economic position was not overwhelming by the start of World War I, the European settlers had attained considerable political and social ascendency. Almost from the first, they had pressed for a share in the administration of the protectorate, setting for themselves the goal of minority self-government on the South African pattern. As a result of this pressure, a legislative council was established in 1907 with two settlers among the membership. Although never a majority in the council, the settlers, under men like Lord Delamere and Ewart Grogan, came to exercise influence, thanks to their incessant pressure and the sympathy or weakness of Kenya's earliest governors. They soon were calling for an unofficial majority and elections for European members to the council. Although Asians were more numerous, Asian political influence was hardly comparable to that of the Europeans before 1914.

As many of the settlers had been born or lived in South Africa, it was natural that South African attitudes, including the ugliest disregard of Africans, should dominate the social and judicial spheres. As mentioned earlier, segregation was insisted on in the White Highlands and towns. The desire to "show the African his place" also marked European attitudes, with harsh corporal punishment relatively common. As the outspoken racist Ewart Grogan demonstrated in flogging Africans in 1907, Europeans could take it upon themselves to physically punish Africans and the administration would do little to stop them. The settlers also were successful in obtaining a differential system of justice on the South African model. Europeans alone had the right to trial by jury, and in no case did a jury find a European guilty of murdering an

African despite several blatant killings of Africans by whites in these years.

By 1914, therefore, Kenya was developing as a plural society of various racial and ethnic groups. Given the settlers' increasingly dominant political and social position, there was certainly a strong possibility that the protectorate would follow in the footsteps of South Africa. In the following years, European influence expanded even further. Kenya, however, did not go the way of Zimbabwe and South Africa, as opposition from administrative officials and especially from Africans and Asians forced the colonial government to intercede and put a brake on European aspirations for a "white man's country."

German East Africa

The German government took over responsibility for its sphere in East Africa after 1890. As in the British territories to the north, the process of European conquest was gradual, and the Germans were forced to make use of local people in the administrative structure they created. German colonial administration was brutal and heavy handed, differing from that of Britain only in degree, not in kind. A major difference with British policy in East Africa can be seen in the German approach to economic development and education, which the government actively promoted so that the colony would not just pay for itself but would produce a profit. Also, the Germans, unlike the British, had to face a major rebellion in their territory.

The Conquest of German East Africa

The German authorities began to establish their control in the early 1890s, but the process was gradual and not complete until the end of the decade. They occupied the coast first and then moved inland along the major trade routes, using a combination of military force and alliances with African peoples. Neighbors were often turned against each other to aid the German conquest. The chiefs drawn to the Germans attempted to use their power against former and present enemies for their own benefit. Yet the advantages gained were usually short-lived; for while some gained ascendancy over rivals with German help, they themselves eventually lost their freedom of action to German control.

Several of the kingdoms which had been founded in the nineteenth century resisted the German conquest. Mirambo's successor in Nyamwezi country, Isike, took up arms in an attempt to stop German incursion into this region. He closed caravan routes and initially defeated the forces sent against him. However, a large German force stormed his headquarters in January 1893, and Isike blew himself up rather than face capture.

The most serious and sustained resistance to the German conquest came from the Hehe people of the south-central region under their leader, Mkwawa. The Hehe kingdom was one of the strongest in the interior by the 1890s, and Mkwawa had established control over the central trade route to the coast from Tabora. As the Germans desired free access to the interior along this route, a source of conflict quickly developed. Mkwawa heavily defeated the first German force sent against him in 1891, and for the next three years he was free of German threats. He strengthened his defenses and fortified his capital, building a high wall and deep ditch around it. A large German expedition attacked Mkwawa's capital in 1894 and took it only after fierce fighting. The king escaped and carried on a guerilla campaign for the next four years. Then, facing capture, he shot himself rather than fall into the hands of his enemies.

By 1898 most parts of the territory had been brought under German control, a hut tax had been introduced, and an administrative structure had come into being. At the head of the administration was a governor who oversaw the colony and was responsible to the German government in Berlin. The imperial parliament, or Reichstag, closely controlled the finances of the colony. German East Africa was divided up into twenty-two districts by 1914. As European staff were few in number and communications with the capital, Dar es Salaam, were poor, German officers in charge of the districts often were left very much on their own in the exercise of administrative responsibilities. The administration, with the assistance of a small force of troops, was responsible for maintaining order, collecting taxes, and settling disputes. Being often left on their own and possessing great power, many district officers became too zealous; they overreacted and used harsh methods of corporal punishment at the least sign of discontent.

The Germans did seek to use reigning chiefs and rulers where possible in their administrative system. In well-ordered kingdoms, Rwanda and Burundi, for example, little was done to change the existing pattern of administration. Elsewhere, some Africans were unable to meet German expectations as administrators, and Swahilis and Arabs were used as akidas (agents) who served as communicators between the German administration and the people. The akidas often were able to build up considerable power and influence, but they had no traditional authority or ties to the local people. They tended to use their power forcefully and without consultation, and were much hated for their despotic and cruel behavior.

Chapter 8

The Colonial Economy

Much earlier and in a more substantial way than in the British territories in East Africa, the Germans pushed to make their colony pay. Investment of government funds was not shunned, and development was fostered by a varied approach. Plantations, backed by both public and private capital, were encouraged for the production of tropical crops. European settlement was encouraged and assisted, and Africans were forced to grow cash crops which could be exported. German East Africa thus adopted characteristics of both the peasant production of Uganda and the settler-dominated economy which came to characterize Kenya.

To promote economic development, medical and agricultural research was fostered through the posting of outstanding scientists to the territory. Perhaps the most conspicuous example of this was the establishment of the Amani Institute for agricultural research in 1902. The results of such research were passed on to European and African farmers. The administration also took the lead in the provision of communications, initially through the construction of a railway line from Tanga to the interior, and after 1904 by laying the central line, which by 1914 stretched from Dar es Salaam to Lake Tanganyika.

The first European plantations and farms grew coffee, but this crop was not as successful as sisal, a plant yielding a strong fiber used to make rope and twine. Imported from the new world early in the 1890s, sisal proved well suited to the soil and climate conditions of German East Africa. Spurred by rising prices, it had become the most important cash crop of the territory by the end of the first decade of the twentieth century. Sisal was grown primarily on plantations owned by European companies rather than by individual settlers. For a time rubber attracted the interest of European planters due to the high prices resulting from a great world demand. However, thanks partly to competition from the plantations of Southeast Asia, rubber production had become unprofitable by 1914.

As in Kenya, European settlement brought in its wake the problems of land and labor. Initially, settlement was concentrated (starting in 1898) in the Usambara highlands, and later spread to the areas around Mounts Meru and Kilimanjaro. In these areas Africans, notably Maasai, were moved aside to make way for the European farmers. Labor was demanded by these planters, especially those involved in the sisal industry, who seemingly could never get enough. To hold down labor costs, the plantations used migrant labor. Constant pressure was placed on the administration to provide workers for settler estates and to loosen safeguards for workers provided in labor legislation. Africans living near the plantations were able to sell food to them to meet their tax responsibilities, and so migrant workers from much further away, such as the Nyamwezi and southern areas, were utilized.

African cash crop agriculture was encouraged in several parts of the colony. Coffee was introduced in the Kilimajaro area by missionaries and was rapidly adopted by the Chagga. In the Haya area west of Lake Victoria, coffee had been grown prior to colonial rule, and exports from this region began as early as 1898. As in the British territories, the marketing of coffee and other African crops would increasingly fall to Asian merchants.

The other major cash crop pushed by the German administration was cotton, which was introduced in Sukuma country south of Lake Victoria and proved very popular. German officials also launched a major scheme to promote cotton growing in the south of the colony after 1902. African heads of villages were ordered to establish cotton plots, and adult males were forced to work on them. This system produced more hardship than profit, and it was a major factor in igniting a huge rebellion against German rule in 1905.

The Maji Maji Rebellion

The Maji Maji rebellion began in southeastern German East Africa in precisely those areas where hostility to the forced cotton growing scheme was strongest. In late July 1905 the people of the Matumbi hills northwest of Kilwa attacked the headquarters of their akida, and they later turned on any European, Arab, or Asian in the area. The uprising spread rapidly from the Rufiji River valley to other areas south and west, bringing together such diverse peoples as the Ngindo and Ngoni. By September 1905 most of the peoples of southern German East Africa had taken up arms and were attempting to force all foreigners associated with colonial authority out of the region.

The Maji Maji rebellion represented a new form of resistance to colonial rule, a mass movement of protest, rather than rebellion by individual ethnic or tribal groups. The integration of diverse peoples into a united movement was made possible by religion. The prophet Kinjikitile Ngwale, living at Ngarambe, became recognized as a spokesman for Bokero, the chief deity of many peoples living in southeast German East Africa. Kinjikitile declared that by sprinkling a special water (rnaji) on people he could give them immunity to German bullets. Religious authorities carried this message and the water all over southern German East Africa in much the same way they had previously provided fertility medicines.

After initial setbacks the Germans counterattacked. They launched major expeditions against the rebels at the end of 1905 and succeeded in dividing the hostile area into two. In 1906 they turned to the reconquest

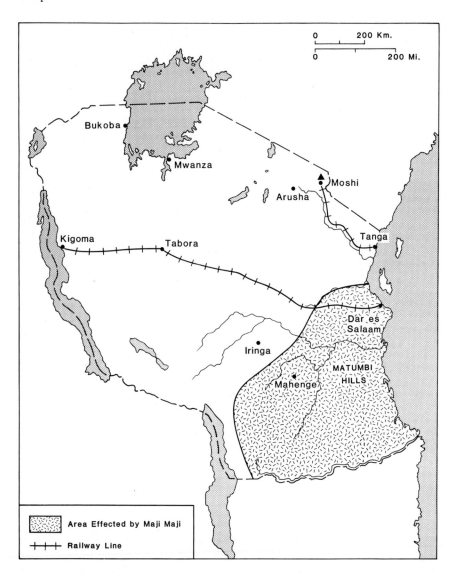

Map 24. German East Africa.

168

of both areas. When it became clear that the maji did not provide protection from bullets, the rebels were forced to rely on guerilla tactics to harass the Germans, who responded by destroying crops and laying waste a considerable portion of territory. Resistance finally collapsed in 1907 in the face of devastating famine in the south. More than 75,000 people lost their lives as a result of the rebellion and its suppression.

The rebellion had important consequences. The movement provided an experience of united mass action that would be drawn upon by later political leaders. Many Africans, not only in the south, now subtly changed their methods of dealing with the Germans. Instead of seeking to resist and restrict the European impact, many now began to seek an improved position within the colonial system by acquiring European skills and using them to better their position in their own societies. What has been termed an age of improvement thus followed the Maji Maji rebellion for some of the colony's people.

The rebellion also forced the German government to rethink and alter its colonial policies. Bernhard Dernburg, who became colonial minister in 1906, undertook several important reforms in the colonial administration, eradicating abuses such as excessive corporal punishment and forced labor. He appointed a new and reforming governor, Albrecht von Rechenberg, who made it the cornerstone of his policy that an event like the Maji Maji rebellion would never occur again.

Reform and Development Under Rechenberg

Rechenberg believed that one way to prevent further unrest in the colony was to press ahead with schemes of economic development. He felt that the African farmer would respond to economic incentives. If he was given a market for cash crops, the African would produce more; possible discontent would be tranquillized by prosperity. From early in his governorship, he decided in favor of encouraging African agriculture rather than that of European settlers. African peasant agriculture was, from the government's point of view, cheap and much less risky than settler agriculture. Compulsion was no longer applied to make Africans grow cash crops. Rechenberg favored economic incentives to encourage the production of indigenous crops by established methods. Further encouragement was given to Asian merchant capital to set up a marketing system for African produce. The governor saw the economic potential of the lakes region, and for this reason strongly—and in the end successfully—urged the extension of the central railway line to Tabora. The success Rechenberg achieved with his policies was considerable. The trade of the colony tripled between 1905 and 1911-12, and the imperial grant-in-aid was considerably reduced. African taxes collected shot up to some three million marks in the same period.

Rechenberg's policies met strong criticism from the European settlers in the colony. These increased in number as the years passed, and although they were confined largely to the highlands in the north, by 1914 they were more numerous than the whites in Kenya. As in Kenya, these settlers pressed for government aid in labor recruitment and for a greater share in running the colony. A governor's council had been established in 1904, and though only advisory, it was a major forum for settler complaints against the administration in labor recruiting and for calls for an end to African production of cash crops. Even though, as in Kenya, plantation agriculture had not proved itself by 1914, the influence of settlers on officials in Berlin and Dar es Salaam was considerable.

Rechenberg's successor, Heinrich Schnee, believed that the interests of the Africans and Europeans could be balanced, but it was the settlers who gained most of the advantages under his administration. Asian immigration was restricted in response to European demands, land alienation for settlement was made easier, labor contracts were lengthened, and district councils with unofficial European majorities were elected in 1913. These advances, together with greater influence in the governor's council, brought German East Africa very close to being a white man's country on the southern African model. Only the coming of the First World War halted the process.

Thus, by 1914 German East Africa was also developing as a plural society in which both African agriculture and European settlement were making contributions to the colony's exports. An economy oriented toward the export of primary products such as coffee, cotton, and sisal had taken shape. Little or no serious attempt was made to establish processing of food crops or manufacturing based on the colony's raw materials. As in the British territories, such manufacturing was carried out in Europe for import into East Africa, a situation which would generally continue after the war. Indeed, Andrew Coulson maintains that the economic structure established by 1914 was "in all but detail" that which would pass to independent Tanganyika in 1961.

African Improvement and Education

After the Maji Maji rebellion, many Africans in the colony began to adopt a new attitude to the colonial regime, showing more receptivity to Western influences, particularly education. Some Africans saw that it was necessary to adopt new techniques to redress their technological inequality vis à vis the Germans and to improve their positions in their own societies. Chiefs and their families were particularly drawn to Western education and to new technologies such as cash crop agriculture.

Western education was initially provided, as in the British territories, by Christian missionaries. The German government, however, went much further than the British in providing financial aid to the mission schools and in establishing schools themselves. Making wide use of Swahili as the medium of instruction, the German authorities established schools throughout the colony. After World War I these helped to produce a new generation of young and educated men who would claim to be more effective communicators between Europeans and Africans than the official chiefs.

Zanzibar

At the time of the 1890 agreement with Germany, Britain had declared a protectorate over the islands of Zanzibar and Pemba. This, of course, merely confirmed a situation that had been in existence for some time; Britain had been the power behind the throne for internal as well as external affairs. Nevertheless, as a result of the protectorate the sultan became even more a puppet ruler than before.

Zanzibar remained under the Foreign Office longer than Britain's mainland territories. At first Zanzibar was regarded as important enough that the British consul-general stationed there also governed Kenya as well. After 1900, however, the commissioner and consul-general moved his headquarters to Mombasa, and after 1904 the two jurisdictions were made separate. The consul-general thereafter was responsible only for the islands and served as the sultan's chief minister.

The initial years of British rule witnessed a fairly rapid end to Arab political dominance in Zanzibar. When Sir Gerald Portal arrived as consul-general in 1891, he took control of the sultan's finances and placed Europeans in control of all government departments. The sultan and the Arab aristocracy were shocked by this but could do little to regain their political clout. This was made clear in 1896 when one of Sultan Barghash's sons tried to seize the throne and throw off British rule. A British naval bombardment of the sultan's palace ended this attempt to assert independence of foreign control.

While the first years of British rule thus brought a huge decline in the power of the Arab ruling class, in the social and economic spheres Arab domination continued. The British saw Zanzibar and Pemba as separate communities, with the Arab land-owning class at the top of the social scale. In British eyes the Indian traders were next, with the African population, whether the Hadimu or those freed from slavery by British decrees, at the bottom of the social ladder. The Hadimu, the most numerous African group, had developed peasant agriculture on the less productive eastern side of Zanzibar, but many were forced to become clove pickers on Arab estates. The freed slaves were the next largest population group; most were unable to become independent producers and worked for Arab plantation owners, often as squatters. Still, freed slaves and Hadimu did not provide enough labor for the clove harvest, and between 3,000 to 4,000 migrant workers from the mainland had to be brought in. Little was done then or later to alter the export-oriented economies of Zanzibar and Pemba, dependent on a single crop, cloves, which provided up to 80 percent of export earnings.

Some significant administrative changes were made after 1905. The consul-general was made more like a colonial governor. Finances and courts came under stricter control. Departments of Education and Agriculture were established. Finally, in 1913 the protectorate was transferred to the Colonial Office. A new post, that of British resident, was created, combining the functions of consul-general and chief minister to the sultan. A Protectorate Council was set up, presided over by the sultan but dominated by British officials. Thus, by 1914 Zanzibar's administration had become more like those of the British territories on the mainland, even as the importance of Zanzibar declined greatly in relation to that of the Uganda and East Africa Protectorates.

The period from the 1890s to 1914 witnessed the establishment of direct European rule in East Africa. Britain and Germany conquered the region and imposed on it a new and authoritarian political structure which would remain in place for a long time to come. Some Africans played a part in the administrative systems created by colonial rule, but their role, with some exceptions, was that of subordinate communicators.

Africans would also occupy a subordinate position in the plural societies that colonial rule produced in East Africa. Europeans moved into the region in greater numbers as administrators, missionaries, and settlers. They achieved pride of place socially and to a considerable degree economically, though in neither the East Africa Protectorate nor German East Africa had European settlers gained real power. Asians also settled in East Africa during these years, and even though they played a role in colonial administration, their most important role was that of a merchant petty bourgeoisie.

By 1914 the colonial economies of the East African territories had assumed the shape they would long maintain. The colonial powers established a communications infrastructure to facilitate the export of agricultural produce and the import of cheap European manufactured goods.

The initial years of foreign rule also witnessed the importation of European social and cultural influences into the region on a much larger scale than before. Christian missions from Europe and North America successfully gained a foothold, bringing to East Africa new ideas and belief systems. The missions also were major purveyors of Western education.

Thus, in the social, political, and economic spheres, the patterns established by 1914 would have a long and deep impact. The authoritarian colonial political system, the emerging Christian elites, the dependent economic systems, and the continuing missionary influence would mark the next period of colonial rule in East Africa just as they did this initial one.

Suggestions for Further Reading

Coulson, Andrew. *Tanzania: A Political Economy* (Oxford, 1982).

Harlow, V., and Chilver, E. M., eds. *History of East Africa* Vol. II (Oxford, 1965).

Iliffe, John. *A Modern History of Tanganyika* (Cambridge, 1979).

Iliffe, John. *Tanganyika Under German Rule, 1905-1912* (Nairobi, 1969).

Ingham, Kenneth. *The Making of Modern Uganda* (London, 1958).

Mungeam, G. H. *British Rule in Kenya, 1895-1912* (London, 1966).

Ochieng, W. R., ed. *A Modern History of Kenya* (Nairobi, 1989).

Sorrenson, M. P. K. *Origins of European Settlement in Kenya* (Nairobi, 1966).

Chapter 9

East Africa from
the First World War
to the Second: 1914-39

DURING THE FIRST WORLD WAR and the years that followed, the political patterns and structures in East Africa continued along the lines they had assumed by 1914. The war formed a brief, albeit destructive, interruption in the development of this pattern. The interwar years would be characterized by consolidation rather than innovation. Although colonial rule now came to touch regions previously loosely administered, such as northern Kenya, and the British assumed control of German East Africa, renaming it Tanganyika, colonial administration changed little for most Africans. The authoritarian structure and statist tendencies that had marked the pre-war era continued largely intact. The British had introduced legislative councils in all three mainland territories by 1939, but Africans played virtually no role in these organs of "national" politics.

Indeed, the British gave little concern to democracy during these years. Stability and controlled change were the goals of administrative policy. While the goal of eventual self government for the colonies might be laid down in Britain, little was done to work towards such an end in East Africa. In the name of efficiency, order and welfare, Africans were acted upon, not consulted with, by the colonial rulers.

In addition to the almost total absence of democratic initiatives between the wars, the colonial states' administrative and political policies continued to support trends that fostered regional differentiation. From the earliest days of colonial rule, some African households

175

responded more rapidly to the economic pressures and incentives that followed the establishment of colonial rule than did others. This, in most cases, was because of their proximity to railway lines, trade routes, or to the new urban centers established as a result of colonial rule. These households were drawn into commodity production, wage labor, or a combination of both, while others were not. The former were, more often than not, among the first to experience the impact of christian missions in the shape of conversion and the establishment of schools. Moreover, between the wars those areas where capitalist and missionary penetration had the greatest impact were invariably the ones to experience the most extensive political activity.

In terms of political activity, a truly nationalist movement in the shape of a political party with a large, representative membership with the goal of ending colonial rule and establishing an independent government representing and drawing support from the people of the colony had not emerged by 1939. Political activity between the wars was more characterized by segmentation. This rested on the economic divisions brought by colonial rule that produced white capitalist farmers, Asian merchants, African workers, commodity producing peasants, and a straddling petty bourgeoisie. Such segmentation rested not only on class, however. Ethnic, regional, religious, and racial segmentation also characterized the period as diverse interests found expression in various forms of political activity. By the end of World War II as a result, East African societies were far less united than four decades earlier.

Those most involved in such political activity had usually experienced the economic, political, and social impacts of colonial rule more profoundly than other inhabitants of East Africa. More often than not, they constituted what can be broadly termed the beneficiaries of colonial rule. In this category may be placed, for instance, Kenya's European settlers, East Africa's Asians, and the emergent petty bourgeoisie or African middle class in the three mainland territories. All had made gains as a result of colonial rule, and they sought to protect those and to enhance their economic and social positions through political activity of various types.

The class and ethnic divisions that had manifested themselves as a result of colonial rule had substantial impact on forms of African political organization and activity. For example, most political activity was "local" in nature in that it focused on localities normally inhabited by a single ethnic group. For the most part, political activity between the wars did not bring together people of differing ethnic identity; rather local political activity involved peoples now recognizable as belonging to the same "tribe". Nevertheless, the arena of local politics was diverse. The domain of local political articulation varied from mission station to chief's baraza, to a district-wide political organization. This kind of protest encompassed the movements of organized groups as well as the spontaneous actions of individuals.

Although types of protest were diverse, some common threads emerged. Most local political protest sought not the overthrow of colonial rule but rather to work within the colonial system. Those involved accepted the reality of colonial rule and sought to deal effectively with it. They tried to make colonialism's impact less harsh and to improve their position within the alien system of rule rather than trying to drive the British out of East Africa.

Much protest between the wars was also characterized by being motivated by the drive for modernization. It reflected a desire of individuals and groups to improve their ability to cope with the colonial situation by obtaining greater access to western education, agricultural improvement, enhanced opportunities in commerce, greater employment opportunities, and more equitable treatment when employed. These types of drives for modernization could be reflected in the activities of political organizations, separatist churches, or ethnic based protest groups. While the drive for modernization reflected a desire to adapt more fully to western civilization, those involved never completely cut themselves off from their traditional culture and values.

Local political activity as expressed in the organization and agitation of political associations was an important form of African protest between the wars. Such associations were usually made up principally of the western educated petty bourgeoisie that had emerged in each territory. Such individuals were normally employed as teachers or clerks and were involved in trade and/or commercial agriculture. These were men who had been most affected by colonial rule at the local level. In the 1920s, the petty bourgeoisie membership of political associations often included chiefs and headmen, but before long rivalry developed between the state-backed chiefs and the non-chiefly petty bourgeoisie. This rivalry, a key factor in the local political dynamics of interwar East Africa, developed largely because the colonial states favored the chiefs and were unwilling to cater to the interests and needs of their rivals. A significant factor in such local rivalry between competing petty bourgeoisie was competition for access to local resources and control of them. Another significant factor in local political activity was the existence of patterns of clientage. Poorer men lined up behind the wealthy, often within the context of existing kinship ties. Thus class and ethnicity became important determinants of political activity in interwar East Africa.

The economic pattern of the first years of colonial rule also continued with little alteration down to 1939. In Kenya the settler economy was given pride of place, but African production continued to be important even though African farmers would not be allowed to grow high value cash crops such as coffee. In Uganda, African production for export held sway, in Tanganyika African and settler production was encouraged, and on Zanzibar and Pemba Arab plantation owners were most favored. Just as before, East Africa's role in the world economy was a dependent one in which Europe, particularly Britain, enjoyed the advantages of unequal exchange (raw agricultural commodities from East Africa in exchange for manufactured goods). These years would witness the first attempts to bring about a union of the mainland territories, all now under British rule. Supported by the Kenya settlers and the Colonial Office in London, what was termed Closer Union never became a reality. It foundered on the rocks of Buganda hostility as well as that of the government of Tanganyika.

Of all the territories, the most controversy, particularly in Britain, was associated with Kenya. This grew mostly out of the attempts of the settler community to achieve political and economic domination. The settlers' aim was clearly to create a southern African style system of white supremacy. The British government reacted by intervening in the colony's affairs to a much greater degree than those of Uganda, Tanganyika, or Zanzibar, attempting to follow policies which would strike a balance between the claims of the settlers and those of the Asians and Africans, who were also vocal in setting forth their demands. As a result, the settlers' demands for a self-governing Kenya under their rule went unheeded.

Tanganyika

The War and German East Africa

Although in no way decisive to the outcome of the conflict, military operations in German East Africa and adjacent territories lasted even longer than those in Europe. While other German colonies were quickly taken over by allied forces, German military power in her East African territory was never completely broken. Although most of the fighting took place in German East Africa, Kenya, Mozambique, and Zambia also were the scenes of battles.

Once war broke out in Europe in August 1914, it quite rapidly spread to East Africa. The German forces in their colony made the first important incursions into Kenya in an attempt to cut the Uganda Railway. The German commander, General P. von Lettow-Vorbeck, understood that, given the fact that the British would deny him significant supplies from Europe, he could not hope to drive the British from the East African territories. What he did hope to do was to tie down as many British troops as possible in East Africa so as to keep them from the major theater of the war in Europe. In this he was quite successful.

In the initial stages of the conflict, 1914 to 1916, the Germans held the iniative. Firmly in control of their territory, they launched a number of raids and patrols into Kenya, and for some time installed themselves in the southeastern corner of the colony. British forces in East Africa were ill prepared for the conflict; they were fewer in number than the German troops and much more poorly led. This continued to be true even with the arrival of troops from India. An attempt to make a landing at the German port of Tanga in November 1914 ended in a debacle for the British.

The British finally came to the conclusion that von Lettow-Vorbeck would be overcome only by the deployment of substantial forces. By the beginning of 1916 a large army had been assembled for the invasion of German East Africa from Kenya. Soldiers were drawn from other parts of the British Empire, most notably white South African soldiers, in addition to East Africa. Jan Smuts, the South African soldier and politician, took command, and the move into German territory commenced. Von Lettow-Vorbeck was forced out of the northern highlands of the German colony and driven south to the central railway line, but try as he might, Smuts was never able to encircle the German and defeat him in a decisive battle. By the end of the year, the Germans had been driven south of the central railway, and with the invasion of Belgian troops from Zaire, they lost the western portion of the colony as well.

As the conflict dragged on, heavy demands were made on the resources of East Africa, especially manpower. Most of the European settlers in German East Africa and Kenya were drawn to military service, and large numbers of Africans, particularly in German territory, were taken for war duty. Even more numerous, however, were those men drafted to serve as carriers or porters. As communications were poor, motor transport scarce, and the environment of German East Africa rather unhealthy for draft animals, African men were used as a major source of transport. This was particularly true in 1917-18, when the Germans were driven into the southeastern portion of their territory. Here communications were difficult, and the conflict became a "carriers war." Most of the porters for the British force were recruited into the Carrier Corps in Kenya. Men were forcibly taken for service, and the conditions in which they worked in the German colony were far from good. Many died or became sick and disabled.

During 1917 von Lettow-Vorbeck was forced further and further south. Although the allied forces enjoyed a large advantage in troop strength, they were never able to defeat von Lettow in a decisive engagement. In

November, running out of space and ammunition, his force crossed the Ruvuma River into Mozambique. He stayed there for some ten months; living largely off the land and captured ammunition, he briefly returned to German East Africa before moving into Zambia. He and his men were still in the field there when the war ended in Europe in November 1918.

The conflict caused considerable damage to German East Africa. Agricultural production for export collapsed as settlers and Africans were drawn from their farms to the war effort and the competing armies swept across the territory, taking what they could. The result was not only a fall in cash crops but also a shortage of food crops, which inevitably led to famine in some areas of the colony. Infectious diseases proved a menace in such an atmosphere, as the rather meagre health services set up by the Germans no longer functioned after their withdrawal to the south. There can thus be no doubt that an important effect of the war was to reduce the population of the German colony. To those killed as a result of the fighting must be added those who died as a result of famine and disease.

The major political impact of the war was the end of German authority. After 1916 German civil administration broke down in the face of enemy invasion. Moreover, communications were damaged and slowed, and many schools were closed. In the wake of their invading armies, the British and the Belgians sought to establish administration in their conquered areas. This proved a prelude to the takeover of German territory by these two victorious powers. At the Paris Peace Conference after the war, all of Germany's colonies were taken from her.

German East Africa was divided between Belgium and Britain. The former took possession of the kingdoms of Rwanda and Burundi, while the rest of the territory passed into British hands. Although it had been suggested that German East Africa be given to India or the United States, it was perhaps inevitable that Britain should take over. However, British rule was not established on the same basis as in Uganda and Kenya. The territory, now to be known as Tanganyika, was made a mandate of the newly formed League of Nations.

The Start of British Rule in Tanganyika

League of Nations supervision did not have great impact on the character of British rule in the former German colony. Tanganyika was a mandated territory. The Permanent Mandates Commission of the League had only general supervisory powers and could in no way interfere in the administration of the territory. The mandatory power, in this case Britain, had to submit an annual report to the commission. The latter normally discussed it and then, if necessary, passed on recommendations to the administering power. While policies and trends could be criticized in this way, Britain had no obligation to alter them.

In taking over German East Africa, the new British administration under Sir Horace Byatt, who had since 1917 been in charge of the areas conquered by Britain, followed a policy of caution and gradual recovery. Byatt realized that the war had caused great destruction and dislocation, not to mention loss of life, and he felt that nothing should interfere with a policy of gradual revival with the help of grants from Britain.

In the administrative sphere, there was relatively little break with the previous structure. The twenty-two districts established by the Germans were retained and so too were the services of the experienced chiefs and akidas. Byatt did get rid of the Germans, however; by 1922 there were virtually none in the territory.

In the area of economic recovery, progress was slowed by the economic slump of 1920-21, but Africans continued to be encouraged to grow cash crops and had considerable success, notably the Chagga of the Mt. Kilimanjaro region. They had by 1924, with the encouragement of some British administrators, formed themselves into a coffee growers union, the Kilimanjaro Native Planters Association. Although British settlers were allowed to move in to take up German property, Governor Byatt did not show great favor to European settlement. The settlers became critical of Byatt and his lack of sympathy for their demands for land. Only in early 1923 was a land ordinance promulgated, and it provided for limits on farms and no grants of freehold. Only leases would be available to settlers. This led to further attacks on Byatt, but he believed the economic future of Tanganyika lay in developing African agriculture.

Byatt's rather conservative policy was justified by the recovery achieved under his governorship. Helped by grants from Britain, by 1924 exports had risen to surpass the levels of 1914. Sisal and coffee were most significant in this respect. By 1926, after Byatt's departure, revenue was sufficient to cover expenditure. Communications had been restored and improved, and approval had been given to extend the railway line north from Tabora to Mwanza on Lake Victoria.

Sir Donald Cameron and Indirect Rule

Sir Donald Cameron took over the governorship of Tanganyika in April 1925. Unlike Byatt, who had shown little interest in district administration, Cameron believed in action and positive reform in that area. He quickly set about remodeling the administrative structure of the territory. In so doing, he was greatly influenced by the seventeen years he had spent in Nigeria, part of the time working under Lord Lugard (formerly Captain Lugard of the IBEA Company). It was in Nigeria that Indirect Rule had been consistently applied as an administrative dictum, and Cameron was convinced that it would be appropriate to introduce such a system in Tanganyika.

In its classic, or Nigerian, form, Indirect Rule essentially involved using traditional African authorities to provide the basis of local government in the colonies. African rulers or chiefs would be put into positions of responsibility similar to those they held before colonial rule, and they would be given a budget with which to provide local administration, courts, and public works from taxes collected locally. Another part of Indirect Rule was the "native court," in which cases would be decided according to African, as opposed to European, law. By building upon the traditional system, Cameron hoped to avoid a breakdown in "discipline" and the unfortunate results he felt would come with too rapid Westernization. Administration economic and social reforms would also be more effectively carried out if promoted through traditional chiefs.

One of the first things Cameron did after his arrival in Tanganyika was to inaugurate a Legislative Council to serve as a law-making body for the colony. He appointed a majority of official (government) members, but he also named seven unofficials—five Europeans and two Asians. Cameron felt that there were no Arabs or Africans who could qualify for membership. The knowledge of English of the "right" kind of Africans would not be sufficient, and he felt that he and his officials could adequately look after African interests. When he increased the unofficial membership in 1929, he still made no move to include African members.

One reason for this, of course, was Cameron's feeling that African interests should be confined to local affairs at that time. It was in this area also that he introduced sweeping changes. He swept away the old system of twenty-two districts and created in their place eleven provinces. To oversee African administration and development, he created the new post of secretary for native affairs. The first two holders of this post, Sir Charles Dundas and Philip Mitchell, would both serve as governors in East Africa in their own right.

At the local level, Indirect Rule was introduced. This involved, first of all, finding out who the traditional rulers were. Cameron believed that German brutality had destroyed chiefs' powers. European administrators were ordered to search for and find the "true" African authorities in their regions. In some cases this was relatively easy to do, but in others, at the coast and among stateless societies having no chiefs, it was not easy to implement this aspect of Cameron's policy. Nevertheless, he insisted that every "tribe" have its "chief." By the Native Authority Ordinance of 1926, African chiefs were given certain executive functions, such as maintaining order and collecting taxes. A proportion of the taxes was returned to the chiefs' government to be used, together with fines from court cases, to meet the costs of administration. The 1929 Native Courts Ordinance established African courts under the chiefs' jurisdiction which were part of the administration rather than the judicial system of the territory. Here cases would be heard and decided in accordance with African law and custom, and appeals could be heard by European administrative officials rather than the British type courts established in Tanganyika.

Cameron regarded this introduction of Indirect Rule as largely successful. Certainly local administration was put on a more stable and regularized basis than before. On the other hand, the new system brought with it many problems, both practical and long range. These had not become clearly visible by the time Cameron left as governor in 1931, but his successors would have to grapple with them.

Cameron's concern for the reform of African administration made him, not surprisingly, unpopular with European settlers in the territory. Despite their criticism, however, it was certainly true that Cameron was not anti-settler. He appointed settlers to his first Legislative Council, giving them a voice in the government of the territory. He also opened up new areas for settlement, notably in the Iringa area, and he even allowed German settlers to return to the colony.

African education was one area in which the British administration was not able to reestablish the conditions of German times. By 1924 there were only seventy-two schools in the rural areas, far fewer than in the German period. With an improving revenue situation, Cameron was encouraged to expand the government's contribution to schools through a system of grants-in-aid to the mission bodies. In five years expenditure for education rose by almost £65,000, but this still only made schooling available for extremely small numbers of pupils.

An important issue throughout Sir Donald's period of office was the question of Closer Union, or a federation of the three East African territories now that they were under British rule. Economic benefits were initially urged as a major reason for such a federation, and L. S. Amery, Conservative Party secretary of state for the colonies, was a strong advocate. Three commissions dispatched to East Africa from Britain during the 1920s had as a major part of their charge the question of Closer Union. The first of these (the Ormsby Gore Commission) found suggestions of a federation to be premature, but Amery appointed Sir Edward Grigg governor of Kenya with the expectation that the latter would facilitate federation. By 1925, moreover, European settlers in Kenya under the leadership of Lord Delamere had begun to espouse the cause of Closer Union. They felt that a federation, which would add the European population of Tanganyika to that of Kenya, would improve the settlers' chances of achieving ultimate self-government on the Rhodesian model.

From the first, Cameron opposed Closer Union because he felt it would endanger his program for recasting the African administration of Tanganyika. When in Britain in 1927, he made his opposition to federation known to Amery, and he lobbied members of Parliament against the scheme, going so far as to threaten to resign. Even though many settlers in the north of the territory gave their support, Cameron made known his opposition to the Hilton-Young Commission in the same year and to Sir Samuel Wilson in 1929. He sent three Africans who shared his opposition to testify in London before the Joint Select Committee of Parliament in 1931. By the end of Cameron's governorship, the idea was dropped. His was not the only strong opposition to Closer Union, as will be seen, but it was influential in bringing about the defeat of Amery's and Delamere's dreams.

The Depression and After

By the end of 1930 the effects of the Great Depression were being felt in Tanganyika. Like other producers of primary products dependent on the world market, Tanganyika was hard hit by falling prices and loss of markets. The main export crops of sisal and coffee both fell in value in 1930 and 1931 even though the volume exported rose. Sisal prices, for example, fell from £32 a ton in 1919 to £21 in 1930 and as low as £12 a ton in 1931. During this period government revenue fell by some £200,000. European settlers were particularly hard hit, and they reduced wages and laid off many of their African workers.

The initial response to these trends by Cameron's successor, Sir Stewart Symes, was retrenchment and belt tightening, coupled with a drive to increase agricultural production. Even in the face of low prices, the government took an active role in promoting such increases, particularly among African growers. More effort than in the past was given to improving techniques of cultivation and marketing. As in Kenya, the depression made the government more aware of the need to increase the output of African agriculture, but this had negative aspects, as expanded planting was pushed at the expense of proper land care.

Economic recovery began in mid-1933. Prices for the major crops rose, and by the end of 1935 the value of sisal exported exceeded £1 million. A revival of cotton growing occurred, and two new plantation crops, tea and sugar, were introduced with success in the 1930s. Gold mined in the territory also gained a place in Tanganyika's exports by the end of the 1930s. Nevertheless, little economic progress occurred and the export-oriented nature of the economy continued. Thus, the 1930s were a time when colonialism in Tanganyika lost momentum.

Improvement and African Politics

For most of the interwar years, political activity took place at the local level rather than at the national. This was what would be expected, given the push toward Indirect Rule, but local issues went beyond the mere maintenance of order by the chiefs set in power by the British. A good deal of competition developed over what may be broadly termed improvement and who should have access to it.

Between the wars, education and cash crop agriculture were the main sources of improvement. Africans who had access to one or both could better themselves in the material sense and often within the colonial system. Neither was easy to obtain, for education and access to cash crops often involved a considerable struggle. The government-appointed chiefs normally had easier access than did other people. As the initial communicators, they thus gained the benefits of cash crops and Western education and became, in effect, the first modernizers in African societies.

After World War I, however, their position would be challenged by others who obtained access to improvement. These found themselves in competition with the chiefs and resented the privileges the chiefs enjoyed. Conflict often developed. It was most bitter in the Chagga and Haya areas, where coffee growers formed growers' associations to better protect their interests. These associations became a vehicle for competition and conflict with the chiefs. This was not a contest between rich and poor between the best educated and most wealthy Africans in the rural areas. It has been accurately termed a conflict between "competing modernizers," and it was a key feature of the local political struggles in many parts of Tanganyika.

The Haya region provides a particularly good example of this competition. There chiefs had early access to Western education and coffee growing, and they were in effect a privileged group. In 1924 other educated Haya formed the Bukoba BuHaya Union, which called for equality of opportunity in access to education and the profits of coffee growing. They strongly opposed the land tenure system by which the chiefs enriched themselves. Under the leadership of men like Klemens Kiiza, a Catholic-educated coffee grower who attempted to move into the coffee-processing business, the union competed with the chiefs in the local arena. In 1936 the union led protests against the chiefs' enforcement of new coffee rules, and the protests developed into riots. The British administration stepped in the following year and jailed the leaders. Men like Kiiza gained much during these years, but limits established by the colonial system held them back from further improvement.

For most of the interwar years, African political activity and interests focused on this competition between rival modernizers at the local level. Among a few individuals, however, the vision of a unity wider than that at the tribal or district level prompted action to forge broader ties: Those who had such vision were normally civil servants working for the British dominated central government. One such individual was Martin Kayamba. Educated by British missionaries, he had worked in Kenya and Uganda before the war, and when the British took over Tanganyika, he was given a place in the new administration. In 1922 he founded the Tanganyika Territory African Civil Servants Association (TTACSA). This was not a political organization but an association of educated Africans which cut across tribal and regional lines. It organized libraries, bought newspapers, and sponsored a soccer team. Although Kayamba and his fellow members formed a mutual improvement society, they had aspirations of unity which were central or territorial in focus rather than local.

It was out of such feelings that the Tanganyika African Association was born in 1929. Several members of the TTACSA took part in its formation. The Tanganyika African Association made contact with several improvement organizations around the country and helped coordinate their aims while adopting an interest in Tanganyika as a whole. By 1939 nine branches had been established.

Cash crop agriculture and mission education had initially provided new opportunities for improvement in Tanganyika. Yet Africans were finding by the end of the 1930s that improvement beyond a certain point brought them into conflict with the colonial government. Only political activity beyond the local level could change this situation in the years after World War II.

Uganda

The East African campaign of 1914-18 had little direct impact on Uganda. No battles were fought there, and far fewer of the population were taken into the army or Carrier Corps than in Kenya and Tanganyika. As in Tanganyika, local rather than national political activity predominated during the interwar years. Buganda was particularly the focus of such activity. More often than not, British officials found themselves prisoners of the 1900 Agreement, as their alliance with the chiefs left little room for maneuver. An unhappy result of all this, and especially the movement to promote Closer Union, was to increase Buganda separatism.

Peasant or Plantation Agriculture for Uganda

An issue of some importance that occupied official circles during the war years and after was of whether European settlement should have been encouraged to promote plantation agriculture as the most important segment of the export economy. Africans were not involved in the discussions that led to proposals for the encouragement of plantations, a debate within the Uganda administration and the Colonial Office in London which dragged on for several years. In fact, this was not only a Uganda question; the issue of peasant versus plantation agriculture was important in other parts of the empire.

The leading protagonist of settlement and plantation agriculture was the protectorate's chief justice, Sir William Morris Carter. He felt that the government should take steps to facilitate development through plantations, and as chairman of the Land Committee, first set up in 1911, he pressed for the easing of restrictions on the alienation of land to Europeans. Instead of being encouraged to grow cash crops, Africans would work as wage laborers on European estates. Carter's views won the backing of Sir Frederick Jackson, governor from 1912 to 1918, and, for a time, Sir Robert Coryndon, who was governor from 1918 to 1922.

Other officials and missionaries took the view that African cash crop agriculture should be encouraged rather than European settlement. This faction strongly backed the view that in Uganda it was better to place the burden of economic development on the African peasant. Cotton had already achieved success. The land and labor policies necessary for the promotion of plantation agriculture would prove disruptive and block African advancement.

Despite these views, the proposals of Carter's committee for the promotion of settlement were approved by Governor Jackson and forwarded to London in 1915. The Colonial Office, however, was not willing to accept these suggestions. The secretary of state for the colonies turned them down early the following year, noting that they were not in the best interests of Uganda and its African population.

The secretary of state's veto did not put an end to attempts by Uganda officials to encourage settlement. Jackson merely referred the matter back to Carter's committee, and although it remained dormant for some time, new proposals for the encouragement of plantations were put forward after the war. It seemed that in 1919 and 1920 a more favorable atmosphere existed in Britain for an economy based on European enterprise. With the Colonial Office under Lord Milner's stewardship and with Sir Robert Coryndon, who had experience in Southern and Central Africa, as governor, the tide seemed to have swung in favor of the proposals turned down in 1916. In 1920 virtually the same proposals were drafted and sent to London, where they received a much more sympathetic hearing.

Yet, in the end, the dream of a Uganda based on plantation agriculture came to naught. Several factors played a part in this. Uganda agricultural officials strongly supported peasant production. Coryndon came to agree, and the Colonial Office dropped all support for plantation agriculture in 1923. Opposition to policies encouraging plantation agriculture was also expressed by the Buganda government and by missionaries there. Perhaps the most influential factor of all, however, was the economic collapse, after 1920, of the plantations already established in Uganda. Coffee and rubber prices dropped to such an extent that their cultivation by European planters became virtually unprofitable. After this there was little interest in obtaining land for plantations in Uganda. From 1923, therefore, the Uganda administration was committed to a policy which recognized the security of African land and the primacy of the African peasant as the basis for Uganda's economy.

African Discontent and Politics

Between the wars, most African discontent focused on local issues. There was little national political organization, and, as in Tanganyika, the local discontent often focused on competition between modernizers. This was certainly characteristic of much of the political protest generated in Buganda against the privileges enjoyed by the chiefs under the terms of the 1900 Agreement.

One such issue of contention involved land in Buganda which had been placed under the ownership of chiefs by the agreement. In 1918 the bataka or clan heads, began to agitate against the system which had deprived them of their rights to land. They formed the Bataka Association and took their grievances to the kabaka, Daudi Chwa. The bataka were the real spokesmen of the common people against the chiefs. In this instance Daudi Chwa suggested a compromise which was rejected by the chiefs, but the bataka also voiced protests over the chiefs' increasing the traditional levies of busulu (labor obligation) and envujo (tribute in produce). As the Lukiko, dominated by the chiefs, rejected their claims, they took them up with the British authorities at the protectorate level. The British investigated the matter and showed sympathy to the claims of the bataka. However, the whole matter was eventually passed to London for decision. Secretary of State Amery criticized the chiefs for abusing their powers, but he felt it was impossible to reopen the question of land allocations or a reduction in the chiefs' privileges at this date. The British had allied themselves with the chiefs, and they did not feel that they could openly go against their wishes.

Still, criticisms of busulu and envujo continued and were the source of serious strain between chiefs and the European administration. Chiefly land holders were, in the 1920s, levying envujo not only on food crops but on cotton as well. Finally, a compromise was worked out by the British. They forced a busulu and envujo law through the Lukiko in 1927 which placed limits on the demands that could be made by chiefs. Considerable pressure was needed to force the chiefs to accept this act.

Such British action led almost inevitably to conflict with the chiefs who, as the 1920s wore on, felt that their status was being diminished through increasing British interference in Buganda administration. This issue came to the breaking point in the bitter clash between the katikiro, Sir Apolo Kagwa, and the provincial commissioner of Buganda. The actual cause of the dispute was a minor one, but Kagwa objected to receiving orders straight from the British official. The British were determined to be the bosses even if it meant casting aside a former collaborator. Kagwa's antagonism grew so great that he resigned, a bitter man, in 1926.

In the type of political activity that has been described, the common people ranged against the chiefs, often appealing over their heads to the colonial officials. In other instances, however, chiefs and people stood together to demand changes in aspects of colonial policy that were widely disliked. A good example is provided by the agitation in the north against Ganda agents. The British normally bowed to such protests led by traditional authorities.

Perhaps the most important grievance of this type was one that the British were unable to solve. This was the agitation for the return of the Lost Counties to Bunyoro. Hostility to Bunyoro no longer formed a part of British policy, and in 1933 an agreement similar to those made with Nkore and Toro regularized relations between the kingdom and the colonial power. However, the Lost Counties were a part of the Buganda Agreement, and the British were unable to do anything to accommodate this protest.

As noted earlier, there was little national political activity in this period. The British, pursuing a policy of divide and rule, did not encourage national consciousness. When a Legislative Council was introduced in 1921, no African members were appointed. Not until 1945 were any named. Although it was in theory the national legislative body, the council had little to do with African policy or interests. Most ordinances concerned with African issues passed with little debate. This kind of practice discouraged national loyalty and consciousness.

Religion was perhaps the only non-traditional allegiance in African societies at this time, and political enmity based on Catholic-Protestant divisions was extremely important. In Buganda and elsewhere, these two groups continued to live in separate communities. Schools were either Catholic or Protestant, and marriage patterns reinforced the religious division. It should be noted that in most parts of Uganda, Protestants dominated in local government. In the four major kingdoms the ruling establishment was entirely Protestant. If Catholics were a political outgroup, the Muslims were even more completely denied access to power; they had no political influence and received little in the way of educational assistance from the central government. This division by religion would continue to be important in Uganda politics.

The issue of Closer Union, or the creation of a possible East African federation, provoked a good deal of protest, especially in Buganda. Unfortunately, it promoted not national but rather tribal consciousness. The Ganda, both chiefs and people, were strongly opposed to any federation. They felt, no doubt correctly, that such a union would be dominated by Kenya settlers. They were aware of the kind of economic and social system that this implied, and they wanted no part of it. Above all, they feared losing their land to white settlement if Closer Union was initiated.

In fighting against federation, however, the Ganda placed great emphasis on the separate status that the 1900 Agreement had given them. They fought Closer Union not as Ugandans but as Ganda. Holding to the terms of the agreement, they maintained their special and unique place, which could not be easily altered to fit in a federal scheme. Buganda's hostility was a key factor in the eventual defeat of the proposals. British officials made no attempt to challenge Buganda separatism, also manifested in the Ganda's refusal to use .Swahili in their schools. For the future, this was an extremely important development: probably no other political issue would be of greater importance after World War II than Buganda's separatism.

Education

Mission societies had provided almost all the Western education in Uganda prior to World War I. After the war the government began to provide increasing money for education through block grants to missions. In 1924 a director of education was appointed for the protectorate, and with state support a uniform system of education was begun. Schools remained under mission control, as the government did not want to establish its own schools, but they were subject to government syllabus control and inspection. Catholic and Protestant schools developed to serve each sect. Provincial and district education boards were established, under the supervision of administrative officials to oversee all schools.

The Department of Education started technical schools which provided training in trades and crafts. One of the most significant of these was opened at Makerere in Kampala to train carpenters and mechanics. Government attempts to establish technical schools encountered opposition, however, from both missions and Africans. At the heart of this opposition was the issue of academic versus technical education—one of the most fundamental education issues in colonial Africa. Those missionaries and Africans felt that an emphasis on technical education was a reflection of second-class status. They wanted Africans to have an academic education in the British public school tradition. They wanted Africans to have the same educational opportunities as Europeans.

The arrival of Sir Philip Mitchell as governor in 1935 resulted in an expansion of secondary and higher education with an academic bias. In the long run, Mitchell's educational reforms were more significant than those he instituted in the area of local government. Looking to the emergence of an educated African elite with much less hostility than his predecessors, the governor succeeded in obtaining the appointment of a commission under Earl De La Warr in 1936 to make recommendations for the future development of higher education in East Africa. From these came the proposal to eventually develop the Makerere technical school to university status. Mitchell also worked for an expansion of secondary education, and as a result of greatly increased government activity, secondary school enrollment shot up from less than 250 to more than 1,300 in the last four years of the 1930s.

Uganda's Asians

Although it encouraged Asians to come to Uganda, the colonial administration did not show great interest in the affairs of the Asians in the country. When the first Legislative Council was opened in 1921, for example, only one Asian was appointed as an unofficial member as against two Europeans, even though the Asian population was much larger. As a result, Asian leaders boycotted the council for five years. In other areas, the British attitude was even more prejudicial. Asians were seen as temporary residents of the protectorate whose presence marked a potential road block in the path of African advancement in business, trades, and the civil service. The British did little to integrate the Asian minority into Uganda, and it is not surprising that the African population also developed a prejudice against the Asians.

Another area which proved fertile in breeding resentment against Uganda's Asians was the organization of the cotton industry. After 1916 Indian businessmen and firms came increasingly to occupy the position of middlemen in the cotton industry. Indian capital flowed into Uganda for the purpose of obtaining more cotton for the growing textile industry in

India. By 1925 Indians owned some three-quarters of the existing ginneries. African growers' discontent about prices and the monopolistic nature of cotton buying came to focus largely on these Asians. Although this was not always reasonable, world prices being beyond the direct control of middlemen, Africans continued to resent the economic role of the Asians.

The Colonial Economy

After World War I cotton continued to be the most important export of Uganda. Despite problems with middlemen and ginneries, it proved very resilient to the changing economic climate of the interwar years, and indeed Uganda was probably less affected by the Great Depression than her two sister colonies. There was a great increase of acreage in cotton in Eastern Province, and improved transportation spurred expansion in other areas.

The postwar years also saw the successful introduction of other cash crops. In the 1920s large sugar cane plantations and processing plants were established by Asian entrepreneurs such as N. K. Metha and M. Madhvani. Sugar had an advantage over cotton and coffee in that it found a ready and expanding local demand, and did not have to depend on exports to distant markets. The industry made rapid progress.

Coffee also became a viable cash crop after World War I. Starting in the early 1920s, acreage planted in coffee by African farmers rapidly expanded. By the 1930s, coffee ranked second to cotton as a money-earning export. While most coffee grown in Uganda was robusta, indigenous to the area, a major exception was the arabica grown by the Gishu on the slopes of Mt. Elgon, where the crop thrived. By the start of World War II, Gishu coffee farmers were producing some 4,000 tons per year.

As a result of the growing prosperity of peasant cash crop production and also to further encourage it, communications were greatly improved. New roads were constructed and old ones upgraded. By the middle of the 1930s, almost all the major towns and economic centers were linked by good roads, and the railway had been extended directly to Kampala through western Kenya.

It is worth emphasizing that the revenues and exports of Uganda consistently surpassed those of her neighbor Kenya for all the interwar period. Despite European settler claims, the peasant-based Uganda economy was thus stronger and more buoyant than that of Kenya. On the other hand, the Uganda economy underwent no fundamental economic revolution. Dependency on export markets continued. Cash crops had merely been attached to the traditional subsistence economy, and

Uganda peasants enjoyed what has perceptively been described as a life of "easeful poverty."

Kenya

The East Africa Protectorate, renamed the Colony and Protectorate of Kenya in July 1920, suffered greater damage in the war years than Uganda, and during the interwar years was a far greater center of the colonial power's attention than Tanganyika, Zanzibar, or Uganda. The war years witnessed heavy calls on Kenya's African population to be porters for the military effort; the period also witnessed growing European settler political and economic domination. This domination reached such a high level in the early 1920s that the settlers' goal of an unofficial majority and eventual self-government seemed possible to achieve. However, strong political pressure from Africans and Asians in the colony checked the settlers' ambitions.

As in Uganda, African political interest focused on local competition, but in Kenya the disadvantages the Africans faced were so great and the threat of white domination was so real that Africans sometimes became involved in activities focusing on the central government and even pressed their claims in London. Such activity, however, did not fundamentally alter the economic structure of the colony, which during the interwar years was clearly slanted in the settlers' interests.

Kenya Africans and the War

After the initial German invasions of 1914, little fighting took place within the protectorate. This did not mean that the war had little effect on the people of Kenya. It had indeed a very profound effect in that thousands of African men were recruited between 1914 and 1918 to serve in the Carrier Corps as porters for the British armed forces.

Few porters were recruited in the beginning, as military operations were largely confined to Kenya itself. At first, recruitment was voluntary, but not enough men volunteered to join the Carrier Corps and forced recruitment was begun in 1915. Chiefs and their assistants pressed Africans into war service by outright armed force. As the allied troops advanced into German East Africa in 1916 and 1917, the need for carriers increased, and the administration in African areas more aggressively sought out able-bodied men.

Service in the war was often an extremely unhappy experience for the Africans, who were shipped to Mombasa in cattle cars and then put on ships for German East Africa. Many died or were disabled. By 1918 the continued calls for military labor had caused severe population loss and dislocation in many parts of Kenya. Not enough men were home to provide adequate cultivation; famine and social distress resulted. Many men never returned, dying in a war of little concern to them.

Toward European Domination

European settlers gained considerable economic and political advantages during the war and in the immediate post-war years. Some had only an indirect negative impact on the African population, while others affected the Africans directly. The cumulative effect was to move Kenya much further along the road to white supremacy than was the case in 1914.

One of the first gains made by settlers at the expense of African rights was the promulgation of the Crown Lands Ordinance of 1915. This met many settler demands which had long been pressed on the local authorities and on London. Under the ordinance, 999-year leases for land were provided, and all land, even that included in what were now called African reserves (in theory for African occupation only), was classified as crown land. The legislation also gave legal standing to the concept of the white highlands since the governor had a veto power over any land sales there.

The Native Registration Ordinance also was passed in 1915, though the war delayed its implementation until 1919. It provided for a system of registration by Africans that had long been demanded by Europeans. Every African male was to be issued identity papers, commonly known by the Swahili word kipande (piece—in this instance, of paper), which he was required to carry at all times in a metal container, usually hung round his neck. The kipande was one of the most disliked innovations made by the government in response to settler demands for aid in obtaining increasing supplies of African labor.

Settlers also gained greatly in political influence during the war. Even before 1914 they had called for increased representation in the Legislative Council, with the right of election for themselves alone. These demands were not granted by London, but the war gave settlers an opportunity to reassert their claims for more participation—and indeed control—in the running of the protectorate's affairs. Settler pressure forced the weak and ineffectual Governor Sir H. C. Belfield to establish a War Council in 1915. The council, although advisory, developed power and influence that helped strengthen the settlers' voice in the administration of the war and in the territory's government. As a result of such influence, the governor successfully pressed the Colonial Office to accept the principle of European elections to the Legislative Council. Deferred until the end of the war, electoral rights were first exercised in 1920 when whites only were allowed to elect eleven members to the Legislative Council. This was bitterly resented by the Asian population, who were denied electoral rights and equality of representation.

The settlers achieved an even more advantageous position under Governor Sir Edward Northey. A general during the East African campaign. Northey took up his appointment as Kenya's governor in January 1919 as a response to European demands for a military governor. He immediately showed a strong bias in favor of settler demands and against the claims of the Asians and Africans of the territory he renamed the Colony and Protectorate of Kenya in 1920. This change of name and status (the protectorate referred only to the ten-mile coastal strip technically the possession of the Sultan of Zanzibar) seemed to make settle self-government, as would be practiced in colonies such as Southern Rhodesia, a strong possibility. Northey also went far to meet settler wishes on the question of labor recruitment. He ordered the beginning of African registration, and in October 1919 he issued a labor circular which called for active assistance by administration officials in the recruitment of labor for private undertakings. Northey also rapidly implemented the Soldier Settler scheme, which brought many European veterans to Kenya by providing land on easy terms.

Under Northey, other measures were taken which benefited the settlers far more than any other group. This was certainly true of the currency changes Northey advocated in 1920 and 1921. When actually carried out, the change from rupee to florin to shilling reflected a definite bias on the part of the colonial state to aid the economic interests of the settlers rather than those of Africans, who faced the possibility of seeing the value of the subsidiary coinage they held cut by half until the intervention of the imperial government forced the scrapping of what had been an attempted "shilling swindle". Taxes paid by Africans were raised during and after the war, while Europeans, having successfully opposed the introduction of income tax, paid little in the way of direct taxation. With the support of the state, moreover, European employers were able to reduce wages paid to Africans after the war.

Clearly, during and after the war, in both the political and economic spheres, African and Asian interests suffered by comparison to those of the European settlers. Largely neglected during the war, African agriculture was now relegated to the back burner, as Northey placed great emphasis on the need for the African population to work on European farms rather than their own. By the early 1920s, therefore, the settlers seemed poised on the threshold of even greater gains which ultimately could put them in control as a governing minority, as in Southern Africa. That this did not occur was the result of protest and political resistance by Kenya Asians and British humanitarians, but of greatest significance was the colony's financial position and the emergence of African protest.

The Asian Question

Nothing focused more attention on Kenya after World War I than the political controversy that raged over Asian (usually referred to as Indian at that time) demands for equality of treatment with the European population, demands provoked by the advantages being gained by the settlers with the open support of Governor Northey. Although more numerous than the white population, Indians were given fewer seats in the Legislative Council and not allowed the right of election. Asian leaders demanded the right to vote and a common roll: all qualified voters, Asian and European, would vote for the same slates of candidates rather than separate slates, as settlers desired. Asians also called for an end of land reservation in the white highlands, an end to segregation in the towns, and free immigration to the colony for all.

For the first half of the 1920s successive British secretaries of state for the colonies grappled with the conflicting claims of the Asians and the European settlers. In the battle to move the British government in the direction they desired, both the Asians and the settlers mobilized influential support. The Europeans found sympathy among many in imperial circles in Britain and among missionaries in Kenya itself, while the Asians gained strong support from the government of India, which emphasized the implications that negative policies towards Asians in East Africa would have on continued British rule in India.

During both Lord Milner's and W. S. Churchill's periods as secretary of state, no solution could be found, as they could only propose measures favorable to the settlers. In response to the Asian demands, the settlers, through their main political organization, the Convention of Associations, put forward an "irreducible minimum" in 1921, calling for strict controls on Asian immigration, two nominated Asian members to the Legislative Council, residential segregation in the towns, and the sanctity of the white highlands. Both sides sent delegations to London in 1921 to press their claims. In January 1922 Churchill made a speech at an East African dinner in London in which he hinted at a preference for the European claims by stating that the British government would regulate Asian immigration, maintain the white highlands, and look forward to self-government as a reasonable ideal for the colony. Such statements, combined with Northey's favored treatment of the settlers, led the Asians to redouble their efforts.

Toward the end of 1921, however, the movement toward greater white supremacy began to slow down. This was seen initially in the area of labor policy. Churchill, bowing to pressure from church and humanitarian groups in Britain, decided, after consultation with Kenya administrative officers, to scrap Northey's labor circular of 1919 and its amended versions which had called for government aid in labor recruitment for the settlers. Northry's sympathy for the European settler positions in the Asian Question and, more particularly, the disastrous impact of his economic policy of placing state resources behind settler production to the total detriment of African agriculture brought about his recall as governor in June 1922. His successor, Sir Robert Coryndon, the former governor of Uganda, had no trouble supporting expanded African production as he became a strong advocate of the so-called Dual Policy, already reluctantly proposed by Northey, which provided state support for both European and African agriculture.

Shortly after the recall of Northey, settlers received another shock in the form of the Wood-Winterton (the under-secretaries of state for the colonies and India respectively) proposals to settle the Asian question. While not granting all the Asians' demands, the proposals were much more in line with their claims. The Wood-Winterton proposals represented London's recognition that if African agriculture was to be encouraged, Asian merchants were needed to provide an outlet for that produce. The Colonial Office was also concerned to avoid any repetition of African protest that had culminated in March of 1922 in the violent suppression of demonstrators in Nairobi advocating the release of Harry Thuku. Despite initial rejection by the European settlers, the Duke of Devonshire, who replaced Churchill as secretary of state in October 1922, pressed governor Coryndon to achieve their acceptance. The settlers and Coryndon reacted with fiery talk of armed resistance and the kidnapping of the governor.

Faced with what seemed to be a settler rebellion that they were ill equipped to suppress, London officials decided to invite the governor together with representatives of the Asian and Euorpean protagonists to London in early 1923 for discussions aimed at the achievement of a mutually agreed upon settlement. The Duke of Devonshire and his colleagues at the Colonial Office had already decided to come down completely neither on the side of the settlers or the Asians, but rather they pitched their settlement around the concept of African paramountcy. This made a virtue out of the idea that the British government was trustee for Kenya's African population. In July 1923, a white paper, commonly known as the Devonshire Declaration, was issued by the Colonial Office which emphasized that Kenya was primarily an African country where the interests of the indigenous people must be paramount. Neither the Europeans nor the Asians were completely happy with this doctrine, but both had argued that they would be the best trustees to guide the development of the African majority, so neither could come out openly in opposition.

In the settlement of the dispute between the settlers and the Asians, neither group could claim a victory. The white highlands would remain closed and there would be no common roll elections. Five seats in the Legislative Council would be filled by Asian-only elections. While this disappointed many Asians, urban segregation was not sanctioned, nor was Asian immigration controlled. The significance of the Devonshire Declaration was that it brought an end to the fiery political controversy between Asians and Europeans, though Asians boycotted the communal seats for some years. In view of what happened in Southern Rhodesia in the same year (settler self-government), it is clear that in Kenya the Europeans suffered a loss: the British government's declaration of African paramountcy closed the door on any possibility of the European settler community gaining political control of the colony. There were far fewer settlers in Kenya than in Southern Rhodesia, and Asian and African opposition had greater impact on imperial policy towards Kenya.

African Political Activism after the War

The increasing predominance of European settlers in the political and economic life of the colony, coupled with the negative impact on Africans of the many measures the settlers were able to win from the administration, led to African political activity. This protest generally did not involve the bulk of the African population but rather those who had been touched most by the colonial system—colonial chiefs and the mission educated. As in other East African territories, moreover, these two groups sometimes cooperated to pressure the colonial government, but they also competed for dominance in the local arena.

The political protest of Harry Thuku in Nairobi and the nearby Kikuyu areas provides a good example of this point. As a young man, Thuku was drawn to a Christian mission in Kiambu District, and he received his first contact with Western education. After some years he left the mission to seek work in Nairobi about 1911. There he held a variety of jobs, notably working as a compositor and machine minder for the settler newspaper The Leader of British East Africa. He was able to observe first-hand the organizational and agitational aspects of settler politics. After the war he obtained a position as a clerk and telephone operator for the government treasury. It was from this vantage point that he launched his political career to campaign against the administration, the settlers, and the Kikuyu Association in 1921. The Kikuyu Association had emerged after the war as a protest movement led by the government-appointed chiefs. Their major grievance was that land had been taken from the Kikuyu and the people were now faced with a land shortage. The chiefs campaigned for more land and security of tenure for those who had it, mainly themselves and other well-off Kikuyu.

Although the immediate cause of his entry into politics was the cut in African wages in 1921, the protest that Harry Thuku led was directed not only at specific abuses which the colonial government could remedy but also against the role of chiefs as spokesmen for Kikuyu unhappiness. In forming the Young Kikuyu Association and its successor, the East African Association, Thuku was also influenced by the political agitation surrounding the Asian question. He made common cause with Asian leaders, and he received advice and material help from them. Following a meeting held by the Kikuyu Association in June 1921, Thuku sent a cable to the Colonial Office to express the unhappiness of those at the meeting without having consulted the leaders of the association. This got him into hot water with them, and also with many missionaries. He had stated in his cable that the Asians were the Africans' "best friends" after the missionaries. Thuku also attempted to forge ties with members of other tribes living in Nairobi, including Ganda, and his choice of the title East African Association for his organization is testimony to this fact. He sought to attract Muslims, Christians, and followers of traditional religions.

By the end of 1921, Thuku had begun to build a protest organization. He published a broadsheet expressing grievances over land, labor, and the political voicelessness of the literate African. Influenced by his Ganda friends, Thuku called for a paramount chief for the Kikuyu. He was able to reach the new generation of Africans educated in mission schools, and by early 1922 he had developed support both in Nairobi and in the Kikuyu rural areas.

He also began to call upon Africans to take actions, such as dumping kipandes and doing no work for Europeans, that the government interpreted as civil disobedience, and these were used to order his arrest in March 1922. He was placed in a Nairobi jail and when a large crowd of African supporters and sympathizers gathered to demand Thuku's release, the police guarding the jail opened fire, killing or wounding a considerable number of Africans. Thuku's East African Association was banned, and he was detained in the northern portion of the colony for several years. It would be some time before another African leader would attempt to press the colonial regime for reform while uniting diverse ethnic groups. As noted earlier, however, this protest would have a very significant impact on the British government's decision to sack Northey and officially adopt a policy of African paramountcy.

Political protest also emerged in western Kenya among the Luo and Luhya after World War I. Here, too, missionary education had considerable impact. At first, both the chiefs appointed by the colonial rulers and the mission-educated elite were united in protest. The colonial administration saw the chiefs largely as tax collectors and labor recruiters. After the war, the chiefs experienced an increase in their duties and a decrease in their independence. This placed them more and more at odds with the people they were supposed to communicate with. Thus they were at one with many of the mission-educated young men, almost all trained by the Church Missionary Society, in opposing greater benefits for the settlers while promoting African progress. Influenced by the example of Buganda, these young men also looked to the creation of a paramount chief as a means of protecting African interests and controlling local affairs in the face of greater settler demands for land, labor, and taxation.

At the end of 1921, young mission-educated Luo men organized a meeting which led to the formation of the Young Kavirondo Association. This body drew up a memorandum for transmission to the colonial authorities, the first part of which urged the establishment of a paramount chief. As a result of these meetings and resolutions of protest, the administration made certain concessions, including the lowering of poll tax, easing of labor recruitment, and the establishment of meetings of Luo chiefs. At the same time, the administration put pressure on mission societies to control and curb the political activities of their adherents. The CMS, under the leadership of Archdeacon W. Owen, attempted to find means of influencing and controlling their members, who made up the bulk of the adherents of the Young Kavirondo Association.

Unique among Kenya missionaries, Owen was not afraid to take a pro-African stand. He worked closely with the Young Kavirondo Association, and in 1923 it was remodeled, with Luo and Luhya membership, as the Kavirondo Taxpayers Welfare Association. Owen himself served as president. Under Owen's influence, the body turned slowly but surely from politics to social improvement and welfare matters.

The Kavirondo Taxpayers and Welfare Association typified a major thrust of African local politics after 1922. Avoiding agitation and an interest in central or national issues, Owen steered the body to welfare, relegating political matters, Owen said, "to their proper place." Members of the association had to undertake such measures as tree planting, sanitary improvement, and using Western-style utensils. The association also sought to promote close cooperation with the administration. Its major demand was for more government services at the local level.

This local focus was increased by the decision of the colonial regime to introduce Local Native Councils in the colony after 1924. Africans in western Kenya had high hopes for these local representative bodies. The educated hoped to use them to promote local development, but they were disappointed, in large measure because the councils had little power or influence. The bodies were headed by the local district commissioner and were largely under his control.

After 1925 the Kavirondo Taxpayers Welfare Association began to wane. There were splits between chiefs and other members, and also a split between Luo and Luhya members which led to the establishment of a separate organization for each people. Moreover, land shortage was not felt to be a major problem by the Luo and Luhya up to the end of the 1920s. This, together with a lessening emphasis on labor recruitment, helped reduce interest in political activity. Owen ultimately failed to bridge the gap between African expectations for improvement and the administration's continued emphasis on white supremacy.

In central Kenya after Thuku's arrest, interest in politics shifted markedly to the local area. The land issue, however, still stirred discontent. In mid-1924 a number of educated Kikuyu young men formed the Kikuyu Central Association (KCA), and the following year, when the governor, Sir Edward Grigg, visited the Kikuyu districts, they made their concerns known to him. They complained of a loss of land and land rights, called for the release of Harry Thuku, criticized the chiefs' abuse of power, and lamented the lack of opportunity for Africans to grow cash crops such as coffee. The administration was not sympathetic to the KCA. Although members gained election to the Local Native Councils set up in the 1920s, British officials saw the KCA as an irresponsible body.

Nevertheless, the KCA continued to gain support among the mission-educated men in Kikuyu country and Nairobi. From the first, the KCA drew its adherents from what may be termed the Kikuyu middle class: individuals who owned shops, carts and lorries and who farmed for the market and milled grain for sale. Many of the membership were also employed as teachers or clerks. As KCA members strove to maximize their economic interests at the local level, they found themselves engaged in rivalry with a competing group of modernizers, namely the state-appointed Kikuyu chiefs. The latter had the advantage of state patronage, and in the 1920s they utilized the Kikuyu Association as the vehicle for pressing their political and economic interests in rivalry to the KCA.

One of the most important adherents of the KCA was the young, Church of Scotland educated Johnstone Kamau, later to be known as Jomo Kenyatta. He took up the position of general secretary of the KCA in 1928 and served as the first editor of its journal, started in the same year. Kenyatta was also chosen as the representative of the association to take their grievances and demands to London for placement before the secretary of state for the colonies. In London, Kenyatta pressed the KCA's land claims and called for African representatives in the Legislative Council. However, he received scant attention in official circles, and he returned to Kenya in 1930 having accomplished little.

From 1928 another issue occupied the KCA, and thrust it into what has sometimes been termed cultural nationalism. The KCA increasingly championed the cause of traditional Kikuyu values in the face of European missionary attacks. The issue that generated the most heat was female circumcision. Partly on health grounds, the various Protestant missions, under the leadership of the Church of Scotland, launched a strong attempt to do away with this important traditional practice marking the accession of a girl to wOmanhood. Disregarding government advice to go slowly, the missionaries pressed their converts to disassociate themselves from the practice or give up church membership. Many Kikuyu Christians, with the support of the KCA, chose to leave their mission churches. This controversy contributed to the growth of inde-pendent churches and schools in the 1930s.

Settler Politics, Closer Union, and the Colonial Office

Even after 1923 most European settlers continued to press for an unofficial (settler) majority and ultimately self-government. After 1925 this effort was linked to the issue of Closer Union for the three East African territories. Here the settlers took up an issue dear to the heart of the Conservative Party secretary of state for most of the period 1924-29, L. S. Amery. He appointed Sir Edward Grigg as governor in 1925 with the hope that the latter would bring about federation. Grigg also showed himself sympathetic to the settlers' demand for an unofficial majority. The settlers, led by Lord Delamere, reciprocated Grigg's sympathy for their aims as they saw that the addition of further Europeans in Tanganyika and Uganda to a united British East Africa could strengthen their claims for self government. Although he had previously opposed federation, Delamere sponsored meetings of settlers from East and Central Africa in 1926 and 1927 to drum up support.

Grigg's push for an expansion of European influence in Kenya's affairs was not easily accomplished. Asians continued to oppose it, and, strong opposition to Closer Union continued in Uganda and Tanganyika. Moreover, the Hilton-Young Commission appointed by Amery to make recommendations on future British policy in East Africa did not support his and Grigg's point of view to the degree they had hoped. A majority of the commission disagreed with Sir Edward Hilton-Young after their visit to East Africa, declaring that the 1923 Devonshire Declaration on the paramountcy of African interests should stand and that Europeans could hope only for "partnership not control." Only if African interests were adequately represented could an unofficial majority be considered.- The commission threw cold water on any implementation of Closer Union, and not even Amery's dispatch of his permanent under secretary,

Sir Samuel Wilson, to East Africa in 1929 could salvage any such scheme.

By the time Wilson reported, moreover, a Labour government had come to power in Great Britain. The succession of Lord Passfield (Sidney Webb) to the Colonial Office marked a departure from Amery's excessive favoritism for the settlers and Closer Union. Although not a colonial expert, Passfield forced Grigg to take a less obstructionist line to African economic development and to put through a Native Lands Trust Ordinance in 1930 which was much disliked by Kenya's European politicians. In July 1930 Passfield produced two white papers setting out the Labour government's position on Closer Union and African policy. Responsible government was recognized as a goal for the future Kenya, but Africans would have to be represented. The memorandum on African policy insisted, moreover, that trusteeship responsibilities rested with the British government alone.

These policy statements prompted strong settler opposition. This, combined with sympathy in Britain, led the minority Labour government to place the white papers before a Joint Select Committee of Parliament for consideration and decision on East African policy. The committee heard testimony in London from officials, missionaries, settlers, and three Africans from each of the territories, and their report in 1931 buried the question of Closer Union for more than a decade and put an end to any hopes for an unofficial majority and eventual European self government. This report closed what George Bennett has called the first theme of Kenya's political history, "the direct possibility of an independent settler governed state." The committee also called attention to certain African grievances such as the prohibition of coffee growing, the kipande, and land issue, and the committee urged the appointment of a committee to examine the land question in detail.

The Colonial Economy

Throughout the 1920s European agriculture held pride of place in Kenya. African production of crops, a significant factor in exports before the war, now shrank somewhat in importance. Following the postwar slump, European agriculture achieved a more stable footing after 1922. Nevertheless, the colony continued to be a country of large farms with many acres not planted in any crop. For most European farmers, the most important crop of the 1920s was maize. Output of maize and wheat grew rapidly, but the concentration on these crops to the point of monoculture was not altogether wise. Moreover, neither crop achieved a consistent level of profitability without a high level of government support. Export of maize, for example, was dependent on the lowering of railway rates to the breaking point and below; a high protective tariff was necessary, on the other hand, to protect the important wheat and flour industry started by settlers between the wars. The local and East African market for dairy products was also secured only with an uneconomic amount of government support.

In the industrial area, food processing (grain and dairy products) was the major area of manufacturing to develop in Kenya. The industrial concerns begun by settlers (individually or in groups) were normally small in scale and required high protective tariffs and other preferential treatment to achieve even modest success. Additional markets were obtained in Uganda and Tanganyika, however, as goods manufactured in Kenya were able to enter both neighboring territories free of duty. Several large British trading firms also moved in behind the tariff walls to set up operations in Kenya. This helped to give Kenya a head start in industry over the other two colonies.

Kenya's most important exports were plantation crops: coffee and sisal. These constituted approximately 50 percent of Kenya's exports by the end of the 1920s, and although prices were deeply affected by the Great Depression, coffee continued as Kenya's premier export during the 1930s. This decade also saw the introduction of tea as an important plantation crop.

The Dual Policy enunciated under Governor Croyndon provided, in theory, for government support for both European and African agriculture. In practice, European production was clearly favored in the 1920s, and more government revenue was spent on improving communications in settler areas and in providing specialized agricultural and veterinary services for white farmers. While not prohibited by law, cash crops such as coffee were not allowed in African reserves. An emphasis continued on the export of labor from African areas for work on settler farms. The result was that for most areas production for sale outside the African reserves expanded at nothing like the pace it had before 1914.

Beginning in the late 1920s, the economic situation in Kenya turned increasingly sour. Locusts invasions in 1928 and 1929 caused widespread crop damage. In the next two years drought hit several parts of the colony. At the same time, the world depression caused a drastic drop in the price of agricultural exports. The settlers were very hard hit, as most had borrowed heavily and not diversified their holdings to a significant extent. Total European land under cultivation fell by almost 150,000 acres in the early 1930s. Only a high level of government support saved the settler economy from complete collapse. Loans, refunds, rebates, and price supports were provided on a very generous basis. New cash crops, such as pyrethrum, were introduced to diversify holdings and move away from maize monoculture. One important consequence of the Kenya government's attempt to salvage settler agriculture was that it stimulated African production.

It was hoped that Africans could be induced to grow cash crops for export and thereby help the colony out of the depression. The colonial state hoped that African farmers with increased income would purchase greater amounts of European flour and dairy produce, thus broadening the market for settler agriculture. To accomplish this, an increased level of agricultural and veterinary services was provided in the African reserves, though these services were still not comparable to those in European areas. Despite strong settler opposition coffee was introduced in selected African areas (though not Kikuyuland) beginning in 1933.

The 1930s were thus a period of transition. African production did not rise to challenge European crops as the major exports of the colony, but an important change away from exclusive emphasis on settler agriculture occurred.

African Protest in the 1930s

Among the Kikuyu the KCA continued to attract support. It pressed demands for land reform, for permission to grow cash crops, and for greater political participation. While not a true mass movement, the KCA enjoyed support all over central Kenya as a result of-the controversy over female circumcision. Kenyatta spent the 1930s in London, where he combined lobbying for the KCA with further studies. He authored an important exposition and defense of Kikuyu culture, *Facing Mount Kenya*, in 1938.

A significant development in the 1930s was the emergence of independent schools and churches among the Kikuyu. This was a direct result of the conflict with Protestant missions over the female circumcision issue, as Christians driven from the mission churches established their own churches and schools. The Kikuyu Independent Schools Association was one body formed to provide a link among the various schools, which tended to be strongly anti-mission and, in time, anticolonial.

The major issue for the KCA and the Kikuyu in the 1930s remained land. They wanted more land, control of reserve land to lie with the Kikuyu, and compensation for lands lost to European settlement in earlier decades. Many Kikuyu were squatters living on settler farms, especially in the Rift Valley. The appointment of the Kenya Land Commission in 1932 raised hopes that some of the Kikuyu claims would be settled. The commission, under the chairmanship of Sir William Morris Carter, an early advocate of European settlement in Uganda, largely disappointed these hopes in their report issued in 1934. Although the commission heard many witnesses and collected a huge amount of testimony, its recommendations disregarded many Kikuyu claims and recommended less compensation than the Kikuyu had hoped. Moreover, the commission recommended that Europeans be given greater security in the white highlands, seemingly firmly entrenching the principle of segregated land holding.

A significant rural protest occurred in the 1930s among the Kamba. The administration decided that the problem of soil erosion and over-grazing in the Kamba reserve required drastic action, and in late 1937 the government introduced a policy of compulsory destocking under which Kamba farmers were forced to sell their livestock for slaughter. Kamba leaders drafted a petition of protest to be sent to the secretary of state for the colonies and to Jomo Kenyatta as well. The most important leader of this protest was Samuel Muindi, better known as Muindi Mbingu.

As the numbers of cattle sold grew, so did discontent. Muindi and other leaders formed the Ukamba Members Association. Money was collected and an oath taken not to cooperate with the administration. At the end of July 1938, several thousand protesters marched to Nairobi and refused to leave before they saw the governor. That official did not prove very sympathetic, but he did concede the end of forced sales in favor of voluntary transactions. Muindi, however, was arrested and detained at the coast. The kind of rural radicalism demonstrated by the Kamba protest would be repeated in the years after World War II.

The first strong indication of urban discontent also appeared in the late 1930s. Reacting to low wages and poor working and housing conditions, workers in Mombasa went on strike in late July 1939. Police were called in to disperse and arrest many of the strikers, but urban unrest would emerge again.

Zanzibar

Initially, the British did, little on Zanzibar to alter the basic political and social patterns that had been established prior to colonial rule and was shaped by Arab domination in administration and land ownership. The Asian population of Zanzibar and Pemba dominated trade and commerce, while Africans filled the role of workers on plantations and in the towns. Politically, the British authorities saw Zanzibar as primarily an Arab settlement, even though this was hardly the case in terms of numbers of people. The colonial power had neither the desire nor the power to change the prevailing social patterns, and the Legislative and Executive Councils established in 1926 only reinforced the status quo. The sultan was a member of the Executive Council, together with several other government officials. In the Legislative Council there were six unofficial members (in addition to ten official members)—three Arabs, two

Indians, and one European. No Africans were appointed to the body until 1945.

Segregation by racial groups was not confined to the political structure. In education, for example, there were schools for Arabs, Indians, and Africans which used different languages and emphasized different fields of instruction: for Arabs, agriculture; for Asians, commerce; and for Africans, industrial training.

During and after World War I, Zanzibar's two major exports, cloves and copra, did very well. Prices rose, and this meant increased profits for the Arab landowners. The British authorities paid particular attention to protecting the economic interests of this group, which included Arabs who formed a Clove Growers Association in 1927.

Beginning in 1929, Zanzibar suffered from the effects of the Great Depression. Clove prices fell steeply, and the Arab growers were hard hit. The Clove Growers Association pressed the British administration for protection, and the growers were granted preferential treatment through financial aid and a new export tariff. The Asian merchants who sold almost all the clove crop, and therefore paid the tax, were unhappy with this measure, as it did not directly benefit them. In 1937 the Asian merchants declared a boycott on clove sales, threatening the islands' economy with collapse. The British resident stepped in to work out a compromise so that trade could get under way once more, but this demonstrated the considerable power that Asian merchants had over the economy. Despite government efforts, prosperity would not in fact return to the clove industry until the war.

In Zanzibar, as in the mainland territories, the interwar years produced little in the way of economic initiatives. Although new cash crops were introduced and some attempts at diversification were inaugurated by colonial officials, no change was made in the dependent, export oriented economies that had taken shape before World War I. This was as true for the settler farmers of Kenya as for the African producers of Uganda. When the Great Depression caused very serious difficulties for most of East Africa's export industries, local and imperial authorities responded at first with retrenchment in government spending and then with efforts to spur greater production for export. They were unwilling to attempt any sharp break with past practices which might damage imperial interests.

A substantial political change, on the other hand, may be seen in the British takeover of German East Africa. Particularly under Cameron, the British altered the administrative patterns established by the Germans in the territory now called Tanganyika. Yet the change was not as great as it might have seemed, for the pattern of authoritarian rule through African communicators continued much as in the German period.

In all three mainland territories the colonial state attempted to broaden the scope of African political participation at the local rather than the national level. This was in fact a response to the emergence of African interest in local affairs. After World War I a new African elite of competing modernizers, or to use the term favored by some writers, petty bourgeoisie, emerged to challenge the dominant position of the administration-appointed chiefs. Members of this local elite typically possessed some Western education and (at least in Uganda and Tanganyika) in many cases were involved in cash crop agriculture. As a means of mutual assistance in local political struggles, they often formed associations. These associations represented the interests of only a small and relatively affluent portion of the rural population rather than the interests of the African population at large. Their efforts generally were directed not against the imperial system but rather toward better access to the fruits of that system, such as jobs, cash crops, and education.

Calls for the end of colonial rule were seldom heard between the wars. The local political focus of most Africans precluded interest in nationalism. Yet by the end of the 1930s local politics had had uneven results for the African elite. Power to effect meaningful change lay with the central government, and in the post World War II era, Africans who wished to gain a greater voice in politics would look increasingly to the central government.

Suggestions for Further Reading

Bennett, George. *Kenya: A Political History* (London, 1961).

Brett, E. A. *Colonialism and Underdevelopment in East Africa* (London,1973).

Coulson, Andrew. *Tanzania: A Political Economy* (Oxford, 1982).

Harlow, V., and Chilver, E. M., eds. *History of East Africa* Vol. II (Oxford, 1965).

Iliffe, John. *A Modern History of Tanganyika* (Cambridge, 1979).

Ingham, Kenneth. *The Making of Modern Uganda* (London, 1958).

Kitching, Gavin. *Class and Economic Change in Kenya* (New Haven, 1980).

Mamdani, M. *Politics and Class Formation in Uganda* (New York, 1976).

Maxon, Robert M. *Struggle For Kenya: The Loss and Reassertion of Imperial Initiative* (London, 1993).

Ochieng', W. R., ed. *A Modern History of Kenya* (Nairobi, 1989).

Temu, A. J., and Kimambo, I., eds. *A History of Tanzania* (Dar es Salaam, 1969).

Chapter 10

The Rise of Nationalism and Achievement of Independence in East Africa: 1939-1963

THE PERIOD BEGINNING WITH World War II and extending for some twenty years after its conclusion was one of momentous events for all of East Africa. In these years, Britain initiated her most ambitious efforts at colonial development. Many more schools, hospitals, and health centers were opened, and far more extensive attempts were made to spur agricultural production from African farmers than in earlier decades.

Numbers of schools were increased at all levels, but perhaps most significant was the expansion of secondary and university education. Prior to the war, secondary schools in East Africa were few and far between. After 1945, and particularly in the 1950s and 1960s, secondary education expanded rapidly even though it came nowhere near to providing places to all secondary-age pupils. University education became possible in East Africa after the war, with the association of Makerere College with the University of London. Later the Royal Technical College was established in Nairobi as a second post-secondary institution serving all the East African territories, and finally the University College at Dar es Salaam provided a third.

The colonial authorities envisioned a gradual transition to self-government after the war. Most British officials did not expect such a development much before the end of the century. Yet in less than twenty years, political power had been transferred to African hands in the mainland territories as three independent governments took the place of the colonial states. The rapid decolonization of East Africa, as elsewhere on the continent, was the result of three distinct, yet interrelated sets of factors colonial, metropolitan, and international. By far the most influential was the emergence of increasing levels of discontent within the East African colonies themselves and the growth of nationalism as a powerful political force.

In seeking to develop new policies appropriate to the post war era, policy makers in London were forced to take account of all three sets of factors. Officials at the Colonial Office thus sought after 1945 to work towards decolonization, but as a long term goal. There would be no great sense of urgency, but the Colonial Office wished to promote policies that would co-opt and incorporate African political activists as a prelude for creating stable political systems that would eventually be modelled on that of Britain. At the same time, the British sought to promote economic development and welfare in the colonies as new initiatives after the war.

Yet these new policy initiatives never took the form that Colonial Office policy makers had intended. One reason for this was that hostility from colonial governors and European administrators in the field caused London to back off. Even more significant was the fact that in practice the need to promote economic growth and development took on a far greater significance than the promotion of welfare or democratization. This was largely because of Britain's extreme economic difficulties after the war; thus Africa was made to support Britain's attempted economic recovery. Also the concern, particularly on the part of the Kenya and Tanganyika administrations, to preserve what they considered the vital European economic role and to avoid provoking a settler rebellion led to far fewer opportunities for African political advancement being opened up there.

These concerns led the metropolitan and colonial governments to adopt, with varying degrees of enthusiasm, policies in the 1940s and 1950s that were dubbed "multiracialism" or "partnership". Future prosperity, it was argued, depended on the European and Asian populations remaining in East Africa and continuing to play a significant economic role. Preserving political influence through reservation of legislative council seats or artificial equality in representatives formed the practical application of the policy. Nevertheless, multiracialism was basically undemocratic, and it proved a failure as a result of the almost unanimous opposition of the African majority.

In the long term, the colonial emphasis on economic growth and development was far more significant. On the one hand, it brought about an enlargement of the scope and functions of each of East Africa's colonial states. On the other hand, the policies designed to promote rural development instead helped provoke massive discontent and unrest among the rural population.

The desire to promote rapid economic development led directly to what has been termed the "recolonization" or second colonial occupation of East Africa. This led to a great intensification of government activity and a dramatic increase in the numbers of European administrative officers working in East Africa. The colonial states also took a much more direct part in promoting rural development and in the overall management of the economy than ever before. The three mainland states set out in earnest to capture the peasantry through programs that emphasized crop and technological innovation, improved land use and soil conservation techniques, better transportation, and the inauguration of cooperatives as marketing mechanisms. These initiatives had as much, and often more, to do with enhancing state control as they did to foster development. The colonial states also extended their control over the marketing of agricultural produce that they began during the war. Thus the East African governments greatly increased in size and scope and in their role as economic manager and innovator as well as social engineer.

At the same time, the second colonial occupation reemphasized and reinforced the authoritarian nature of colonial rule. The development imperative led directly to a variety of authoritarian practices to force anti-erosion measures, dipping of livestock, and crop innovation on an often unwilling rural population. Such measures were often resented and resisted by rural people, but the state response was to fall back on executive power and to place more authority in the hands of European administrators and African chiefs. The need to force the pace of development by mobilizing and capturing rural peasants took priority over democratization of local or central governments in the 1940s and 1950s.

Hostility and resistance to attempts to capture the peasantry were not the only reasons for discontent among Africans in East Africa. the rural African middle class were also increasingly aggrieved by the direction of government policy. Like the peasantry, they objected to the heavy handed, state directed, development initiatives of the time. Whereas the peasants often wished to get the government off their backs, the middle class desired an enhancement of economic opportunity and greater government patronage. The latter got neither as the colonial states continued to favor Asian traders and followed policies which aimed at obstructing the development of capitalism because of a fear of the dangers seen to result from increasing differentiation in the rural areas. The colonial states slowed somewhat the latter process, but as a consequence, they provoked a clash which saw many of the African petty bourgeoisie take a strongly anti-government line.

After World War II, moreover, hostility to colonial policies and development initiatives was not confined only to the rural areas. Urban labor unrest and strikes before and during World War II expanded after 1945 as industrialization began and urbanization increased. The colonial governments at first attempted to meet these protests by forceful suppression combined with small economic concessions, but, under prodding from London, they turned in the late 1940s and early 1950s to an attempt to control worker protest by allowing the organization of trades unions under state supervision and control. Nevertheless, this attempt to create and control a trade union movement was far from successful. Some became quite militant in their demands, and almost all became vehicles of anti-colonial protest.

A final dissatisfied group in postwar East Africa was constituted by the educated elite. Very small in numbers before 1945, the expansion of secondary and university education resulted in the steady growth in size of this group. Although they were among the beneficiaries of colonial rule, the educated elite found themselves increasingly disenchanted with their position in postwar East Africa. The colonial governments were unwilling to go very far in their attempts to accommodate this group. The doors to political influence, economic advancement, and social equality remained barely open or completely closed. Thus the educated elite assumed a leading role in opposing colonial rule and calling for its end. They did so most effectively as leaders of the new nationalist parties that emerged in each of the East African territories by the end of the 1940s.

Although anti-colonial protest continued to take many of the shapes it had between the wars, such as local political associations and millennial religious movements, the most significant protest form after 1945 was the nationalist party. Such parties represented a different thrust from interwar protest, particularly in their goals and membership. The nationalist parties in the East Africa colonies quickly articulated their major goal as self government and *uhuru* (freedom). In practice, this meant the capture of the colonial state, particularly the central executive, and the assumption of state power by local people. Such goals were normally couched in democratic and liberal phraseology such as "one man one vote" or "majority rule". At first, the nationalist parties represented a relatively narrow membership, largely restricted to the educated elite and members of the petty bourgeoisie. However, the parties gained the support, as the 1950s wore on, of the trade union movement and the rural population. This was the result of the leadership's effective articulation of the grievances of the latter groups; these, more often than not, reflected local and/or economic concerns more than political. Increasingly, nevertheless, the various reasons for discontent, ranging from a desire to plant more cash crops to higher wages, to an easing of the pressure of development programs on the rural poor were submerged by the call for *uhuru* and independence from colonial rule as a means to both greater economic, political, and social opportunity and an easing of state demands.

African nationalism was able to overcome the obstacles of colonial rule and multiracial policy in East Africa as the growing Western-educated elite joined forces with the uneducated masses to build broadly supported political parties calling for self-government. Faced with this situation and the financial burden of ruling by force demonstrated by the Mau Mau rebellion, a much weakened Britain gave way and granted self-government and independence by the early 1960s. This was done with a hope that the East African territories would maintain close economic ties with Britain and that the social and economic structures existing before independence would remain largely intact.

World War II and East Africa

East Africa was not affected nearly as deeply by World War II as by World War I. Fighting took place only in regions adjacent to East Africa, the Italian territories of Somaliland and Ethiopia, and those territories were relatively quickly conquered by Britain, using Kenya as one base of operations, after Italy's entry into the war in 1940. No doubt the most direct effect of the war was to be seen in the numbers of East Africans taken into military service. Most served in the theatres of the war away from the region itself, including Ethiopia, Egypt, Burma, Madagascar, India, and England. For those called into the service this was a broadening and eye-opening experience. They became acquainted with a different class of Europeans, those of the working class, than they had encountered in East Africa. They saw European power challenged and humbled by Japan. They also saw first-hand Indian and Egyptian nationalism. Many of the soldiers who returned home would not easily accept the continued second- or third-class status marked out for them in the colonial hierarchy of East Africa; they would form an important element in the political and trade union protests and mass nationalism after the war.

Another important effect of the war was to increase prosperity and revenue for the East African territories. Agricultural production was spurred during the war by the needs of the British Empire and the loss of sources of such tropical products as sisal and cloves in the East Indies. Food products did especially well, and settler agriculture in Kenya became profitable for the first time. Tanganyika's revenue doubled between 1939 and 1945 as a result of rising prices and production. With the emphasis on increasing agricultural output came improvement in communications in the form of new roads. A prime example was the paving of the Nairobi-Nakuru road through the white highlands with Italian prisoner-of-war labor.

The British government took its first hesitant steps toward development during the war through the passage of the initial Colonial Development and Welfare Acts. This change of policy was intended to put a better facade on colonialism in the face of criticism both during and after the war, and to help the shattered British economy recover. The first of these acts in 1940 provided only a small sum but established the principle that the colonial power should subsidize development. After 1945 greater amounts of money would be made available, and the colonial administrations themselves would be required to draw up development plans.

Also during and after the war, the issue of Closer Union was raised once again, this time because of a need to coordinate defense, manpower allocations, and production of foodstuffs. In 1940 the East African Governors Conference decided to set up an East African Economic Council so that the three territories could be handled as a unit so far as economic matters were concerned. Sir Philip Mitchell, the former governor of Uganda, was tapped as chairman. Mitchell was by now a strong advocate of federation, and it was he who largely drew up the white paper published by the British government in 1945 that advocated a closer association between the three mainland territories.

Mitchell had by this time been appointed governor of Kenya, and from this vantage point he was very instrumental in the creation of the East African High Commission in 1948. Although it was far from a federation, the organization undertook to provide a number of services for the East African countries. These included railways and harbors, posts and telecommunications, currency, scientific research,- and a literature bureau. All these services were controlled by the East African governors and a central legislative assembly representing the three territories.

Moves toward federation apart, undoubtedly the greatest impact of the Second World War on East Africa was that colonialism was weakened and nationalism strengthened. The war and its aftermath greatly reduced the power of Britain and her capacity to rule the colonies. Britain emerged from the war victorious but much weaker than before. Economically, Britain would be in a rather fragile position for the next few decades. The resources she could devote to control of her colonies were not so great as in the past, given the demand for social reform and improvement at home. Also, the propaganda that the British used against

Hitler rebounded on the colonial power in East Africa: educated Africans began to question why they were fighting for democracy and self-determination and against racism in Europe when in their own home areas they had no say in the government which ruled them and racism obviously still existed. Moreover, there was now less support for colonial rule in Britain. With the victory of the Labour Party in the election of 1945, the liquidation of the empire began with India. This would inevitably spread to her African colonies as well.

As noted earlier, African soldiers travelled outside East Africa and acquired a new awareness of their position. Many of them received an academic and political education while in the service, and their experience gave fresh impetus to African politics after the war. The emphasis on educational expansion and economic development also served to stimulate interest in political activity that would lead to nationalism.

In the post-war world, colonialism was an unpopular doctrine, particularly with the new superpowers that emerged after the conflict. Both the United States and the Soviet Union took a generally anti-colonial stand at the United Nations and elsewhere. The United Nations, moreover, took over the administration of the League of Nations' mandated territories, and proved to be a far greater force than the latter in promoting increased African participation in ruling the colonial territories. For these and other reasons, the war and its aftermath was a time when colonial rule began to weaken and African nationalism to forcefully raise its head.

Tanganyika

Tanganyika would be the first of the East African territories to gain her independence. In 1945, however, this prospect seemed a long way off to most colonial officials and the African population. The first priority for the administration was economic improvement. The administration, advised by Europeans and Asians, would retain political control. African political activity was still centered at the local level, although the Tanganyika African Association (TAA) strove to provide a national forum for educated Africans.

Development and the Post-war Economy

The first five years after the war were ones of increasing prosperity for the territory. With demand in Europe great for agricultural produce, the value of Tanganyika's trade trebled between 1946 and 1949. Yet in spite of this, British officials did not view the territory as having as great potential as Uganda and Kenya, nor did foreign investors show the same kind of interest as in the other two.

The post-war years saw an increasing emphasis on planned development of agriculture, involving among other things, a considerable enlargement of the staff of the agriculture department. Many European experts were sent to the rural areas to experiment with crops and promote agricultural change. To effectively increase production of food crops and cash crops, the officials realized, a revolution in agricultural technology was necessary. New and better techniques of cultivation had to be adopted. These involved not just better seed and tools; changes in land tenure, contour plowing, and soil conversation also were pressed on the African population. Not all such development efforts were successful. For example, the "Groundnut Scheme" in the southeast of the colony, an attempt to grow groundnuts on a huge scale through mechanization, failed because of poor planning and lack of understanding of local conditions. The colossal fiasco cost British taxpayers millions of pounds.

The efforts of agricultural officials and the administration to force agricultural change and to speed up the pace of development were often bitterly resented in the local areas. The chiefs, whose powers to speed development and punish laggards were greatly expanded in the 1940s and 1950s, bore the brunt of this hostility, as it was they who levied fines for noncompliance and who forced cultivation in certain areas. Thus, an extremely important outgrowth of the emphasis on rapid development in agriculture was the rise of radical opposition to government policy in the rural areas and the undermining of the authority of chiefs.

Colonial Policy and African Politics after the War

During and after the war, African attention continued to focus primarily on events in the local arena, which was marked by competition between chiefs and young, educated modernizers. The latter were active in local or tribal organizations whose aims were often economic as well as political. After the war, a new factor came into play in the competition for local power and influence—the widespread resentment of the efforts of chiefs and agricultural officials to force the pace of agricultural development. The modernizers often found themselves able to make common cause with the rural populace unhappy with forced development. The rising rural discontent of the 1950s would form an important element in the emergence of mass nationalism.

The TAA also continued to be active during and after the war. Branches were extended all over the territory. This organization represented the as yet small educated elite (mostly civil servants), teachers, town dwellers, and traders. Their interest was not to overthrow the colonial system but rather to obtain a better place within it for themselves. In 1940 the association issued a memorandum calling for more educational opportunities and for African representation in the Legislative Council. Territorial conferences were used as forums for formulating demands. The 1946 conference held at Dar es Salaam undertook a new initiative. While criticizing the concept of European settlement in Tanganyika and the lack of African educational opportunities, it went on to call for the election of Africans to representative councils and the eventual achievement of self-government.

After the war Tanganyika came under the jurisdiction of the United Nations Trusteeship Council, and this had an effect on political developments. The trust agreement now specifically charged Britain with developing Tanganyika toward independence. The council was much more active and could do more to influence events in the territory than could the League Mandates Commission. The council sent visiting missions every three years, and as a result of their visit made recommendations to Britain for constitutional change. The first mission visited the colony in 1948. The TAA placed its views before the representatives, and the mission supported its claim for greater African representation in government. The mission called for the introduction of elections that would seat Africans on the Legislative Council along with Europeans and Asians.

The colonial administration responded by putting forward its own proposals. Two Africans, both chiefs, were appointed, not elected, to the Legislative Council in 1945, and by 1948 two more had been added. These, together with seven European and three Asians, made up the unofficial side of the legislature. In 1948 unofficial members were added to the Executive Council; none of them were Africans.

Partly as a result of the United Nations visiting mission's call for elections, the administration undertook to draw up a plan for advancement toward greater self-government. Soon after he took up the governorship in 1949, Sir Edward Twining appointed a committee to examine the question of constitutional advancement and make recommendations. The committee's report in 1951 emphasized a gradual approach. It proposed an enlarged legislature but with a continued unofficial majority. Twining felt that Tanganyika needed good administration and economic development more than politics. Elections were not specifically provided for, and the committee stated that the unofficial seats should be equally divided between the three racial groups (seven for each). In a step away from Indirect Rule, it was also suggested that multiracial county councils should be created as instruments of local government.

This gave concrete form to the idea of multiracialism that was particularly close to Governor Twining's heart. The equal division of seats would, it was hoped, go far to maintain harmony and cooperation among the races as well as taking advantage of the more extensive education of the European and Asian communities. On a broader level, this policy was an attempt to avoid what were seen as the extremes of white supremacy on the South African model or African majority rule as it was developing in West Africa. Whatever the intentions, multiracialism rested on extremely shaky grounds. Populations of Asians and Europeans were so small in comparison to the African population that no realistic sharing of power would have been feasible. African resistance doomed this attempt to force the sharing of political power.

To further investigate the issue of elections, the government retained the services of Professor W. J. M. MacKenzie of Manchester University in 1953. He supported the idea of equal racial representation, and he suggested elections of unofficial members on a common roll basis. Although electoral qualifications would keep most Africans from voting, he proposed that each constituency should have three members, one from each racial group. Governor Twining accepted this idea, and in 1955 a new Legislative Council came into being with thirty-two officials and thirty unofficials (ten from each racial group). These unofficial members were nominated, however, rather than elected. At the same time the Executive Council was altered by the inclusion of more unofficial members. Members of this body would now be ministers in charge of departments.

TANU and the Triumph of Mass Nationalism

These proposals were not satisfactory to most of the African elite. It was this group which took the lead in organizing opposition and eventually speeding up greatly progress toward self-government. In the process, they used the multiracial electoral system to defeat the policy and attain African dominance over the political structure. The Tanganyika African National Union (TANU) was the vehicle which accomplished this task.

Without question, the leading figure in the struggle was Julius K. Nyerere. Born the son of a Zanaki chief east of Lake Victoria, Nyerere was educated at a Catholic mission school. Later he attended Makerere College, and after teaching at Tabora he gained a place at the University of Edinburgh in 1949. He returned from Scotland in 1952 with a master's degree, the highest degree earned by any African to that time. He took up a position as a teacher and soon resumed an earlier interest in politics, becoming quite deeply involved in the TAA. In 1953 he was elected its president.

Nyerere then had to try to form the TAA into a strictly political party, and in October 1953 he and others decided to form a new party whose aims would be clearly nationalist—to fight for self-government and independence. Once this decision had been taken, Nyerere visited TAA branches around the country to press the idea. At the annual meeting in Dar es Salaam on July 7, 1954 (Saba Saba Day), the TAA was transformed to the TANU. Nyerere became its president at the age of thirty-two.

Nyerere and his colleagues realized that a successful political movement could not be built on the elite alone but must include local political leaders in the rural areas and the masses of uneducated peasants. At the time TANU was formed, a great deal of discontent existed in rural areas all across the country, largely due to the forced rural development policies of the colonial regime and the heavy-handed way the programs were applied by chiefs. TANU was able to capitalize on rural resentment (and fear of land loss) by championing the cause of the rural modernizers and the farmers who wished to be left alone by local officials. A common reason for the growth of support for TANU would be the mobilization of rural outgroups around agricultural grievances.

Two examples can be cited to show how rural discontent led to support for TANU's nationalist call for self-government. The Meru land case was a local issue that drew wide attention to the threat to African lands under colonial rule. In 1951 the government decided to move a number of Meru from their lands to make room for expanding European settlement. The Meru took their case to the courts and the United Nations in unsuccessful attempts to keep their land. They also sought the help of the TAA and later TANU. African farmers began to realize that the government could not be brought to act in favorable ways because it did not represent Africans. The great resentment over the land case led them to take an interest in national politics. People outside the Meru area recognized that the Meru grievances could easily be theirs.

At the same time, to take a second example, local improvement organizations, particularly cooperative societies, were finding themselves increasingly hemmed in by government regulations and control. The leaders of these cooperatives, such as Paul BOmani of the Victoria Federation of Cooperative Unions in Sukuma country, were drawn to TANU as means of more effectively opposing the economic policies of the colonial government. For them, too, TANU seemed a vehicle for expressing their grievances and attaining the solution to their problems—self-government.

It was a measure of Nyerere's astute leadership that he recognized this. He identified a single issue that would appeal to all. This was the call for *uhuru* (self-government). It was a simple goal that could be accepted by all who were discontented with some aspect of colonial policy.

This is not to say that Nyerere and his colleagues were able to build a party free from problems. The very size and diversity of the territory made the job difficult. The colonial administration was hostile, and it was difficult to sustain interest in national politics. Building on the TAA foundation, new branches were formed and supporters enrolled as members. Under Nyerere and General Secretary Oscar Kambona, the party grew in popularity. Although opposed to the multiracial policies of the government, Nyerere declared that TANU would not follow a discriminatory policy toward Europeans and Asians.

The 1954 United Nations visiting mission was quite friendly to TANU. Echoing Nyerere—and much to the unhappiness of the colonial regime—it called on Britain to draw up a timetable for independence to be reached within twenty-five years. Encouraged, TANU sent Nyerere to New York to place the party's case before the world body in 1955. He made a very satisfactory impression, and on his return he resigned from teaching and worked to mobilize the growing political consciousness in Tanganyika.

Governor Twining did not look with favor on TANU. He viewed party leaders as agitators and felt that they did not represent African opinion. TANU's opposition to multiracialism was another cause of dislike. Twining followed a policy of harassing TANU and Nyerere. In 1956 the governor sponsored a rival political organization, the United Tanganyika Party (UTP). It soon became apparent that the UTP, representing paternalistic idealism, lacked the mass support of TANU.

The period 1957-58 was a critical one in the development of TANU's fight for uhuru. Elections were finally decided upon in 1957; these provided for a common roll with educational, property, and income qualifications. Each constituency would elect three members, and the voter was required to cast three votes, one for a candidate of each racial group. There was some feeling that TANU should not participate on this basis, but Nyerere decided that the party enter the election. He was able to carry the membership with him in early 1958, as African voters would form the majority. This was a significant decision: it meant that constitutional progress to self-government would be rapid. Not all members of the party supported the decision, however; some TANU followers broke away to form the African National Congress, which adopted the slogan "Africa for Africans" and suggested that there should be little place for the immigrant communities in the country.

Another roadblock appeared in 1958 when the government prosecuted Nyerere for criminal libel against two administrators over an article in the party newspaper. Nyerere, found guilty, was placed in a difficult position when he was fined with an alternative of jail. He chose to pay the fine as a conciliatory gesture to the government. One reason was probably that Twining had left the territory before the trial and had been replaced by Sir Richard Turnbull. Turnbull invited Nyerere to meet him at Government House even before the end of the trial. The two were to cooperate in moving Tanganyika rapidly toward self-government along a peaceful path.

The Legislative Council elections had been scheduled in two stages: September 1958 and February 1959. TANU nominated its own candidates and indicated which Europeans and Asians it felt were most supportive of African aspirations. In the five constituencies contested in September of 1958, TANU won 67 percent of the votes cast, and the UTP failed to win a single seat. Thus TANU had used the system and won. In response to this overwhelming victory, Turnbull formally scrapped the policy of multiracialism in favor of African predominance. In the second stage of the elections in early 1959, TANU won practically all the seats uncontested. The way was open for TANU control of the country. Five elected members, though not Nyerere, were added to the Council of Ministers.

The triumph of TANU in 1959 coincided with the victory of Harold Macmillan's Conservative Party in Britain later in the year. Following his victory, Macmillan appointed Ian Mcleod as secretary of state for the colonies and launched a push to liquidate British control in her colonies as rapidly as possible in line with his view of the "wind of change." Although TANU did not achieve its aim of self government in 1959, it found the British government more willing to move toward that goal.

A British-appointed committee drew up new constitutional proposals in 1959. It recommended the expansion of the legislature to seventy-one elected members, fifty of which would be open seats. Ten seats would be reserved for Europeans and eleven for Asians. The franchise was extended but did not provide for universal suffrage (literacy and income qualifications were retained). Although calling for "one man, one vote," Nyerere and TANU decided to participate in the elections scheduled for 1960.

The August 1960 elections were won overwhelmingly by TANU. Only thirteen of the seventy-one seats were contested, and TANU won seventy of the seventy-one elected seats. Nyerere was appointed chief minister in October 1960, pledging himself to lead the struggle against ignorance, poverty, and disease. In March 1961 a constitutional conference attended by Macleod in Dar es Salaam reached very quick agreement on the transition to independence. The country attained internal self-government on May 1, with Nyerere becoming prime minister. On December 9, 1961, Tanganyika attained full independence from British rule under her TANU government.

221

The Colonial Economy

As has been noted, the colonial government after World War II placed considerable emphasis on compulsory agricultural development. By the middle of the 1950s, however, this was proving counterproductive, both politically and economically, and colonial authorities took up a new policy recognizing and indeed encouraging differentiation in the rural areas. Resources were concentrated on relatively well-to-do farmers who were willing to utilize modern methods and machines and to hire labor to increase production for market. Peasants who refused to accept modern methods were branded "lazy" and were increasingly ignored. The colonial government thus sought to increase inequality in the rural areas by the selective extension of credit, advice, and rewards, and as a result, small capitalist farmers (termed kulaks by some writers) could be recognized in all parts of the colony by 1961.

As part of this process of encouraging the emergence of a class of small capitalist farmers, producer prices were raised and cooperative marketing arrangements established in the 1950s. The marketing arrangements were particularly significant since production of export crops rose dramatically after the introduction of cooperative societies across the country. Exports of cotton rose two and a half times and coffee by some 40 percent in the second half of the 1950s, but a large part of this surplus came from the minority of capitalist peasant farmers. As Andrew Coulson has argued, the cooperative movement thus helped foster inequality in the rural areas as the capitalist farmers were able to derive the greatest advantages from cooperative society membership.

Increasing production for export and differentiation in rural areas did not immediately translate into opportunities for industrialization. The initial years after World War II witnessed the continuation of Britain's policy of discouraging industrialization in Tanganyika unless it could be seen as an essential part of some agricultural production program. Where industrialization did begin after 1945, it largely took the shape of import substitution focusing on food products and cheap consumer goods. The pace of such industrialization remained slow, however, and dependence on imports of goods from Kenya actually increased. Tanganyika was a major producer of cotton and sisal, but by the end of the 1950s, no factories to manufacture cotton cloth or rope had been started. A slight increase in manufacturing marked the last three years before independence, but independent Tanganyika would be faced with the truly daunting task of trying to create an industrial base in the highly competitive atmosphere of the 1960s and 1970s with little to start from. Independence thus brought freedom from Britain's political control, but it presented the new nation and its leadership with huge challenges in the economic sphere.

Uganda

The pattern of political development in Uganda after World War II would take a quite different shape than in Tanganyika or Kenya. Mass nationalism here was largely retarded by Buganda separatism. From the middle of the 1950s, the most fundamental political problem for nationalists and colonial administrators alike would be how Buganda could be made part of a united and self governing Uganda.

Popular Discontent in Buganda

During and after the war, political activity and discontent in the Kingdom of Buganda, the most populous and wealthy province of the protectorate as well as the most Christian and Western influenced, continued to focus, as during the interwar years, on the political and economic advantages enjoyed by the chiefs. This was essentially a local issue in which the bataka and the younger, educated Ganda who opposed the dominant role enjoyed by the chiefs called for greater democratization of Buganda's institutions. Sharp divisions in Buganda society were revealed by events in the 1940s.

British policy as implemented by Governor Sir Charles Dundas (1940-44) sought to strengthen Indirect Rule. He tended to deprecate any efforts to introduce Western ideas of greater democratization to the administration of Buganda. He felt that the colonial officials should merely be advisors, with the chiefs left to run the administration, and in 1944 the governor took steps to give more power to the chiefs. He took no measures to pressure the Lukiko for reform by way of increasing its elected membership.

Nevertheless, popular unease with the Buganda system dominated by the chiefs continued to be manifested. In 1943 great opposition was provoked by the protectorate government's wish, supported by the kabaka, to obtain land for the extension of Makerere College. Protests from the Bataka Party were widely supported, as it was alleged that this was part of a plot to secure land in Buganda for European settlers. The Lukiko refused to agree to the measure, and it was effected only after a long struggle. Popular discontent broke into the open in 1945. Unrest in Buganda in January and February was followed in September by the murder of the katikiro. These incidents showed that deep economic and political grievances were being voiced by the Bataka Party.

The new Governor, Sir John Hall (1944-51), reversed the policies of Dundas but did not come to grips with the claims of the Bataka Party.

223

The Lukiko was reformed to include indirectly elected members, but chiefs still held a majority in this body. The Bataka Party's demand for greater democratization was not satisfied by this, and in 1949 the party presented a memorandum to the kabaka demanding sixty unofficial (non-chiefs) members of the Lukiko, the popular election of chiefs, and the resignation of the present Buganda government. These were coupled with economic demands which showed a deep unhappiness with the domination of the cotton industry by Asian middlemen. Backed by the recently formed African Farmers Party, the Bataka Party expressed the desire of Africans to gin their own cotton and to control its sale for export. The strong discontent that produced the petition also gave rise to riots and other disturbances in Buganda in April 1949. Leaders of the Bataka and African Farmers parties were arrested and the parties banned as a result.

At the same time that these events were demonstrating hostility to the existing system in Buganda, the Buganda government itself was continuing to exhibit separatist feelings first manifested strongly on the Closer Union issue. After the war, British authorities sought to increase African involvement in the protectorate's central government and Legislative Council. After much persuasion, the kabaka's government agreed to nominate a representative to the council when the first three African members, all from the south of the protectorate, took seats in 1946. In 1949 it was announced that African membership would be increased to eight. Although Buganda would have two representatives, the Lukiko expressed strong reservations. A pervasive anxiety that the kingdom would lose her special status granted in the 1900 Agreement lay behind these reservations, and this did not bode well for future national unity in Uganda.

Unlike in Tanganyika and Kenya, there was no serious issue of European settler control to overcome in Uganda. As early as 1950, the principle was established that African membership in the Legislative Council should equal that of Asians and Europeans combined. Uganda was a predominantly African country, and little seemed to stand in the way of rapid development toward greater African involvement in politics and government. That at least was the view of Sir Andrew Cohen, who took up the governorship in January 1952.

Sir Andrew Cohen and the "Kabaka Crisis"

Sir Andrew Cohen was a different breed of colonial governor than any Uganda had previously seen. He came from the Labour Party in Britain and was by far the most liberal chief administrator ever assigned to any of the British East African territories. He quickly disposed himself to push for rapid economic and political reform. He wished to expand agricultural production and to help the African grower sell his produce through cooperative societies. On the political side, he announced in 1953 a dramatic expansion of the Legislative Council to include twenty-eight unofficial members, fourteen of whom would be Africans. Reforms in local government also were pushed by Cohen with elected councils to be introduced in most districts.

Buganda did not escape the reforming zeal of Governor Cohen. After consultations between the governor and Kabaka Mutesa II, it was agreed that the kabaka would appoint three more ministers to his government, that the Lukiko should approve all ministerial appointments in the future, and that the elected members in the Lukiko would be expanded to sixty out of eighty-nine. The kabaka's government, moreover, was to take control of primary schools, rural health, and agricultural and veterinary services. Although the kabaka and his government accepted these reforms, it was a rather uneasy compromise. They were alarmed by the expansion of the Legislative Council and the implications of Cohen's moving it toward the status of a national legislature.

Nevertheless, the immediate cause of hostility between the Buganda government and the British administration, the so-called "Kabaka Crisis," was an old Buganda fear, the possible establishment of an East African federation. Speaking in London in 1953, the secretary of state for the colonies made reference to the possibility of a federation for East Africa. This caused great disquiet among Ganda leaders. Their opposition to domination by Kenya's settlers was still strong, and there was now the alarming example of the Central African federation which the British government was imposing on an overwhelmingly hostile African population. Protests by the kabaka and the Lukiko soon turned to extreme demands which they felt would safeguard their position. They asked that Buganda be transferred to the Foreign Office, that "partnership" on the Rhodesian model not be introduced, and that Buganda be allowed to attain independence separate from the rest of the protectorate.

Britain gave a pledge that the issue of federation would not be raised as long as the Ganda were hostile, but this was not enough; the crisis moved to the boiling point as the kabaka entered it. A series of meetings were held between Mutesa and Governor Cohen in October 1953, but these failed to bring a solution. Finally, the governor withdrew British support of the kabaka and had Mutesa flown to exile in Britain on November 30.

Rather than end the Ganda unhappiness, the deportation of the kabaka merely heightened their feelings of support for him and against the British. Previously, the kabaka had been little more than a British puppet, but now his position was transformed into that of a national leader whose popularity and support never faltered among the Ganda down to the achievement of independence in 1962. It was hard to carry on ordinary administration in Buganda, as the people demanded Mutesa's return as their leader. All shades of political opinion—chiefs, peasants, the educated, and radicals—supported this cause. Buganda united to call for the return of Mutesa, but unfortunately the implication behind this support was the claim of a special and indeed separate place for Buganda in Uganda. This would be clearly seen in the settlement eventually reached with Britain to end the crisis and in the growing separatism of Buganda in the second half of the 1950s.

In 1954 the Colonial Office appointed Sir Keith Hancock, director of the Institute of Commonwealth Studies, to study the problem and propose a way out of the impasse. After months of talks and study, a new Buganda Agreement was drawn up between Britain and the kabaka's government in 1955. The kabaka became a constitutional monarch and the Lukiko was to control his ministers, subject to the governor's approval. As Buganda agreed to remain within the protectorate, machinery was established for the choice of representatives to the Legislative Council. With acceptance, Mutesa was allowed to return to Buganda, where he was given a tumultuous welcome in October 1955. On the face of it, the agreement weakened the kabaka's position, but in fact Mutesa was a very dominant force in politics upon his return. He now had the right, which the kabaka had essentially lost in 1889, to appoint members of his government. The 1955 Agreement strengthened Buganda's position within Uganda, and this was the cause of a good deal of ill feeling and tension after 1955.

National Politics and Buganda Separatism

The first nationalist party in Uganda was the Uganda National Congress (UNC), formed in 1952 under the leadership of Ignatius Musazi. Representing the Protestant educated elite from Buganda and other parts of Uganda, it called for unity among all Uganda's peoples, self-government, and the placing of Uganda's economic resources in African hands. However, the party did not seek to deny the rights of Asians and Europeans if they joined with the African population as Uganda citizens. In Buganda, however, the Party was greatly disliked by the chiefs, and it received very little support from that quarter.

As in Tanganyika and Kenya, opposition to colonial agricultural policies had emerged in several of Uganda's districts, and the UNC, like the TANU in Tanganyika, sought to capitalize on local discontent as a means of gaining support. The UNC backed, for example, Gishu coffee growers against the government. However, the party was not nearly as successful as its counterpart in Tanganyika, and by the middle of the 1950s, it was not in a very strong position, having failed to build a truly national base.

After 1955 other parties rose to challenge the UNC. The most important of these was the Democratic Party (DP), founded in 1956 as a direct result of the failure of Catholics to gain political influence in the Buganda government. Since the 1890s, Catholics had been a political outgroup in Buganda and most other parts of the protectorate. The party declared its support for all Uganda's people and for eventual self-government, but most of its support came from Catholics who were unwilling to accept second-class status any longer. The leaders of the UNC, on the other hand, were generally Protestant. Thus, political division at the national level was marked by religious differences, hardly a new feature of Uganda politics. In 1958 the Ganda lawyer Benedicto Kiwanuka became DP leader. Opposing Buganda's isolationism, Kiwanuka made efforts to strengthen and broaden the party.

Buganda's rulers showed no interest in these new parties. The kabaka was now the focal point of a very dynamic but insular nationalism. He and the traditionally powerful chiefs in the Lukiko did not form a party of their own. They preferred to use institutions like the Lukiko and the local administration, which they controlled, by capitalizing on the kabaka's name. Buganda representatives in the Legislative Council were withdrawn when it was announced that a speaker was to be appointed in 1958. The Buganda government also refused to take part in the first African elections, slated for 1958.

These first elections were a stimulus to political consciousness and activity all over Uganda, even though Buganda, as well as the Gishu and Nkore, opposed direct elections and did not take part. The franchise was quite broad, allowing more than three-quarters of the men in the territory to vote in October. The UNC won four seats, the DP one, and independent candidates captured four. After the elections several of the independents combined with some of the UNC members to form a new party, the Uganda Peoples Union. The party position in the Legislative Council then stood, after Gishu and Nkore members had joined, at Uganda Peoples Union seven, UNC three, DP one, with one independent.

The new Uganda Peoples Union was largely a Legislative Council party with little firm base in the countryside. It was the first party to be led by a non-Ganda, and it took an anti-Buganda stance. Another split soon hit the UNC with the non-Ganda, led by the member for Lango, Milton Obote, withdrawing. Weakened and unable to make any headway against Ganda traditionalism, the UNC soon disappeared from active politics. This reflected the shifting nature of political loyalties, but it also demonstrated that none of the parties had developed a mass following. They were more weekend "tea groups" for the elite which lacked broad support from the population. At the same time Buganda's isolation was growing.

Late in 1958, Governor Sir Frederick Crawford announced the appointment of a constitutional committee to recommend the form that direct, common roll elections could take for the whole country. These elections were to be held in 1961. The Buganda Lukiko refused to nominate any members for the committee or to submit evidence. Nevertheless, the committee recommended elections based on universal suffrage. It also proposed that the party that won a majority of the council seats should be asked to form a government.

All this seemed to leave aside Buganda, as not even the Ganda nationalists had participated. These, including former UNC leader Musazi, were drawn closer to the conservative Ganda traditionalists. They did succeed in forming the Uganda National Movement (UNM), which gained a following in Buganda, but it had support from the kabaka's government. In 1959 the UNM organized a trade boycott of Asian and European shops which was accompanied by intimidation and violence—a graphic demonstration of anti-Asian feeling at the end of the colonial period. The British arrested the UNM's leaders and banned the movement.

Toward Independence

The years 1960-62 proved crucial in deciding whether or not Uganda would move to self government as a unified nation. By the beginning of 1960 there was no slackening of Ganda separatism. The kabaka led a delegation to London in mid-year to press for a postponement of the elections until proposals for the establishment of a federal relationship between Buganda and the rest of the protectorate had been completed. Later, the rulers of Bunyoro, Toro, and Nkore also called for a postponement, but this was not enough to cause the British to agree. The leaders of the Lukiko ordered the Ganda not to register and vote and demanded seccession for Buganda, going so far as to proclaim its independence as of the first day of 1961. Although such seccession did not, in fact, take place, it showed the way in which the Ganda traditionalists were moving in a desire to protect their powers and privileges from being submerged in a self-governing Uganda. Moreover, they were able to exploit Ganda nationalism to firmly align the masses with their cause by using the appeal of the kabaka.

This left the elections of 1961 to be contested by the DP and the newly formed Uganda Peoples Congress (UPC). The latter represented a union of the Uganda Peoples Union with the Obote UNC group. Obote emerged as the leader of the new party. Local issues rather than national ones dominated the elections, with the position of Buganda especially crucial. As a result of the Lukiko's call for a boycott, only a small percentage of the eligible Ganda voters registered. Those who did vote elected DP candidates in twenty of the twenty-one Buganda seats. Thus buoyed, the DP won forty-three seats to the UPC's thirty-five, even though the latter won some 80,000 more votes. After the DP victory, the governor appointed Kiwanuka leader of government business at the head of a cabinet.

In July 1961 the Uganda Relationships Committee, set up in response to the anxiety of Buganda and other kingdoms over their future relationship to the central government, made its report. The committee recommended a federal relationship for Buganda and semi-federal status for the other kingdoms. The Buganda Lukiko was to be directly elected, but the report called for that body to have the option of choosing representatives to the national assembly by direct or indirect means. The DP protested strongly, as this would obviously make it difficult for the party to win any election, given its great unpopularity with the ruling Ganda elite, should the Lukiko decide not to hold direct elections.

It was left to a constitutional conference held in London later in the year to make a final decision on this and other issues. At the conference, it soon emerged that an important deal had been made between Ganda leaders and their old enemy, the UPC of Obote. As a result of the "marriage" between the traditionalists and nationalists, the UPC agreed to support Buganda's right to decide on direct elections in exchange for support at the national level after the elections. Recognizing the importance of winning the pre-independence elections so as to obtain a firm grip on political power, UPC leaders thus made a deal which helped entrench Buganda's unique political position to the detriment of the future unity of the country.

The politicians returned to Uganda to prepare for self-government and elections. On March 1, 1962, internal self-government was granted, with Kiwanuka becoming the first prime minister. The Lukiko elections in Buganda, however, had already determined that his tenure would be short. Seeking to win the elections to the Lukiko, the Ganda tradition-alists promoted a new movement, Kabaka Yekka (Kabaka Alone), as their vehicle. The appeal of the kabaka was overwhelming; to be against Kabaka Yekka (KY) was to be against Mutesa. The movement had no ideology and its overriding purpose was to defeat the DP and "protect" Buganda interests. As part of the deal, the UPC did not contest these elections, and the outcome was an overwhelming victory for KY, which won sixty-five seats to three for the DP (all in the Lost Counties). The Lukiko thereafter decided to elect Buganda's representatives to the National Assembly, and the DP would, of course, get none.

In the general election of April 1962, the DP desperately tried to stave off defeat while the UPC campaigned confidently, expecting victory. Kiwanuka particularly appealed to Toro, Bunyoro, and Nkore, promising to improve their status and claiming that the UPC had sold the country to the kabaka. The DP won all but two of the seats in the three kingdoms, but it was not enough. The UPC won thirty-seven seats to the DP's twenty-four. This was not an absolute majority, but the twenty-one KY members joined with the UPC to form a ruling coalition under the leadership of Obote in May. This government took Uganda to independence on October 9.

Left unresolved at the time of independence was the important issue of the Lost Counties. Here a largely Nyoro population was still part of Buganda, ruled by Ganda chiefs. With the coming of self-government, the Bunyoro authorities stepped up pressure on Britain for a return of the counties, and there were disturbances there also, including civil disobedience, arson, and attacks on Buganda officials. Buganda claimed that her control of the area was given permanent standing by the 1900 Agreement. British officials were thus thrust on the horns of a dilemma for whatever they did would displease one group or the other. A commission grappled with the problem and recommended that a referendum be held in counties with a Nyoro majority. The individual counties which voted to join Bunyoro would then be transferred back. At the final constitutional conference in June 1962, it was decided that two years should pass before such a vote was held. While letting the British off the hook, this decision left a very volatile and potentially divisive issue for the Obote government to grapple with.

The Colonial Economy

In many ways the post-war years saw the continuation of earlier trends. Uganda's economy continued to be based on peasant agriculture. The major cash crops were grown by African farmers, and one result of this was that Africans in Uganda could claim a much more substantial share of Gross Domestic Product than could Africans in the other East African territories on the eve of independence. Uganda was still extremely dependent on world prices for her primary products, with fluctuations in price normally being felt at most levels of the economy.

The years after 1945, however, did witness some significant changes. Coffee came to surpass cotton as the protectorate's most important export. By 1962, it accounted for roughly half the total value of Uganda's exports. Lower cotton prices and a greater expansion in coffee planting are the main reasons cotton dropped to second in value. Sugar, on the other hand, continued to be a major crop grown largely on plantations. As in Tanganyika, the colonial administration insisted on policies which sought to foster a class of small capitalist farmers. The great emphasis on cooperative societies was certainly a part of this.

The post-war years also witnessed improvements in communications and a start in manufacturing. The railroad was extended north of Lake Kyoga to the Nile and to the west of the protectorate to tap, among other things, the copper mines in that area. Uganda's roads were greatly improved, and by the early 1960s most main road links had been paved. At the time of independence, Uganda's road network was markedly superior to that of her neighbors. The completion of the Owen Falls hydroelectric dam at Jinja opened the way for the growth of manufacturing in that area. In 1952, the Uganda government established the Uganda Development Corporation as a statutory body to promote industrial projects. It could invest in areas where private firms did not or would not take up projects, and undertake part ownership in established companies; by 1962 manufacturing had begun in the field of textiles, cement, beer brewing, and copper smelting.

Kenya

After 1945, Kenya continued to be the major focus of British interest in East Africa because of the presence of the economically and politically dominant European settlers, its strategic importance on the path from Cape to Cairo and on the Indian Ocean, and the increasing scope—far more substantial than in Uganda and Tanganyika—of British investment there. Within little more than seven years after the war, moreover, Britain was faced with the most serious post-conquest rebellion to take place in a British colony in Africa. Pouring men and money into Kenya to defeat the Mau Mau rebellion and to remedy what were perceived as the social and economic problems underlying it, the British government spurred education and agrarian development to a much greater degree than ever before. The movement toward political independence under an African government (although Kenya was the last of the mainland territories to achieve it) took place much more rapidly than could have been imagined in 1945.

The War and the Mitchell Era

Perhaps the most important impacts of the war on Kenya, after the defeat of the Italian forces on her borders, was to be seen in the upsurge of prosperity enjoyed by the settler farmers and the large numbers of Africans who served in the British army outside Kenya. Prices for agricultural produce rose during World War II and remained at an attractive level for at least a half decade after the return of peace. This represented the first really prosperous period for settler agriculturalists, especially grain and mixed farmers. They were as a result very keen to capitalize on what seemed a promising agricultural future in the colony, and the British encouraged further settlement after the war. As prosperity allowed for greater mechanization, the move to push squatters, mostly Kikuyu, off settler lands, begun in the late 1930s, was greatly speeded up, markedly increasing the problem of landlessness among the Kikuyu.

The increase in prosperity that the war and post-war years brought to African farmers was not nearly so great. Substantial emphasis was placed on food crops, such as maize, during the conflict, and cash crops were largely overlooked. Coffee planting, begun in the 1930s in selected African areas, did not expand beyond an experimental stage. Moreover, the strong opposition of settler planters kept some peoples, notably the Kikuyu, from cultivating the crop. Some important steps were taken to improve the marketing of African crops during the war, such as guaranteeing prices in advance, but the need to promote better methods of cultivation so as to cope with problems of soil exhaustion provoked some opposition despite the potential benefit of the conservation techniques.

The war took many young men outside East Africa for military service. These men received both a formal and informal education from the experience. Many improved their literacy, and they saw how people in other parts of the world lived. The myth of European superiority was undermined for many, and not a few returned home with great expectations. Yet the situation they found in Kenya on their return reflected little change from the past. While they might be treated as equals in, for example, Britain, the returning soldiers found themselves treated as less than second class citizens by Kenya whites. Many veterans became strong, sometimes radical, advocates of African political, economic, and social advancement in the post-war years.

Sir Philip Mitchell, who became governor of Kenya in 1944, recognized the need for African advancement. He sought to bring Africans into the administrative system at levels higher than that of chief, and he supported the appointment of Africans as members of the Legislative Council. Eluid Mathu had been made the first such member in 1944. In addition, Mitchell encouraged formation of the Kenya African Study Union in the same year to provide an organization where the views of the educated African elite could be given a forum and a body with which Mathu could consult.

Mitchell sought to advance educated Africans within a framework of multiracialism. He wanted to see the African majority share political control with the settlers but not take over. Intent on not provoking the settlers, he moved slowly, even in pressing his multiracial policy. Events were to show that many Africans, particularly the Kikuyu, were not at all happy with the pace of economic and political change.

The Coming of Mau Mau

After World War II, African discontent in Kenya grew steadily. Like the buildup of steam within a boiler, it required a release to prevent an explosion. Unfortunately, the administration of Sir Philip Mitchell did not provide such a release, and African protest grew and took increasingly radical forms.

The Kikuyu were the Kenya ethnic group most touched by colonial rule—from the loss of land to Christianity and Western education. It was the Kikuyu who were most involved in the unrest and protests of the period 1945-52.

There were many reasons for the rising discontent. Despite Mitchell's plans for advancement, very few educated Africans achieved any kind of influence in government or the economy. An often cited example was Mitchell's treatment of Jomo Kenyatta after the latter's return from Britain in 1946. Although Kenyatta had lived in Britain for more than a decade and had studied at the University of London, Mitchell refused to appoint him to the Legislative Council. British propaganda of the Second World War had attacked racism and stressed equality, but little of this idealism was evident in Kenya. Segregation and the color bar were entrenched in virtually all aspects of life, and the European settlers were particularly contemptuous of educated Africans.

The African petty bourgeoisie also faced especially strong obstacles after World War II. Many were improving farmers who hoped to gain access to high value cash crops while at the same time moving into trade, shop keeping, road transport and construction. Faced with competition from Asian traders, these "proto-capitalists" obtained little assistance from the colonial state which seemed intent, in fact, on holding back or blocking African capitalism. African capitalists found it virtually impossible, for example, to obtain adequate credit. They thus became increasingly aggrieved with colonial policies, and in the 1940s and early 1950s the most numerous among this group were certainly Kikuyu.

If the elite and the petty bourgeoisie felt blocked by the colonial system, there were also causes for discontent in the rural areas and among the masses flocking to the cities, especially Nairobi, after the war. Here it was three groups of Kikuyu which were particularly affected. The Kikuyu had long suffered from land shortage, and the problem became more severe after the war as a result of rising population, the tightening of individual ownership of land by improving farmers in the Kikuyu homeland, and the closing of squatting on European settler farms as an option for landless Kikuyu. This produced a group of landless Kikuyu

233

with little hope of finding economic betterment. Beginning in the late 1930s, moreover, the settlers had been forcing squatters to work as wage laborers, limited their farming activity, and forced them off their land entirely with the backing of the government. This was to produce a potentially radical group of people who were forced into the Kikuyu reserves, where they could get no land, or into Nairobi, where they lived in utter poverty. This urban poor constituted the third disaffected group after World War II.

Government agricultural policies also caused growing unrest in rural areas. Kikuyu farmers were still not allowed to grow coffee and had little or no control over even those crops permitted by the administration. Particularly strong resistance developed against government attempts to enforce land use and soil conservation rules in the Kikuyu inhabited Murang'a district. There peasant households reacted strongly against forced labor in what they called the *mitaro* (ditching) rural revolt in 1947. Another example of rural resistance is provided by the Olenguruone settlement scheme in the Rift Valley in the late 1940s. There Kikuyu left lands that had been allocated to them by the colonial state because they would not accept government direction on the use of the land.

Seething discontent and radicalism also came to the forefront in Nairobi in the post-war period. Wages and living conditions were extremely poor for most Africans. The city government was largely in the hands of Europeans, and Africans had little more than an advisory role. Here the great contrast between the affluence of the Europeans and Asians and the poverty of the Africans was very stark. The movement of landless Kikuyu to the city also created problems as large numbers were underemployed or lacked any job at all. Rising crime rates in Nairobi were symptomatic of deep social and economic problems which were not tackled effectively. In both urban and rural areas an important radical vanguard was made up of army veterans who had served abroad and had their horizons expanded only to find little economic or political opportunity at home.

In the urban areas, particularly Mombasa and Nairobi, trade unionism was a focus of African discontent. Mombasa had experienced a strike in early 1947 which led to the formation of the African Workers Federation. The arrest of the union's leader, Chege Kibachia, led to its demise, but Asian trade unionist and radical Makhan Singh worked to establish a strong workers' movement from 1948. In May 1949, he joined with African workers' leaders to form the East Africa Trade Union Congress at Nairobi, which sought to unite all workers in the colony in an effective union. Fred Kubai was president and Singh was secretary. The union put forward increasingly radical economic and political demands, culminating with the proclamation of a general strike at Nairobi in May 1950.

Kubai and Singh were arrested, and the union was declared an unlawful organization.

The major vehicle for airing African grievances after the war was the Kenya African Union (KAU). Although it attracted some support from all areas of the colony, the KAU was essentially a Kikuyu organization. It was formed in 1945 as successor to the Kenya African Study Union, made up largely of the educated elite and the KCA, which had the support of Kikuyu in the rural and urban areas. Although it was eventually to be divided between radicals and moderates, the KAU at first adopted a gradualist and constitutional approach to African protest. Greater participation of Africans in the government of the colony leading up to eventual self-government was a major goal, together with the elimination of the color bar and a solution to the land problem. In June 1947 Jomo Kenyatta took over as president of the organization, and he remained its leader until the 1952 declaration of emergency. During the latter years of his tenure he was faced with a divided party and forced to perform a balancing act between the moderate group in the KAU (usually Kikuyu chiefs and members of other ethnic groups) and members of the radical group (almost exclusively Kikuyu).

The KAU's constitutional approach bore little fruit in terms of government action to alleviate African discontent. There was some success, however, in achieving a considerable measure of Kikuyu unity. This was done by the use of oaths which had traditionally bound the Kikuyu people and had been used by the KCA to promote unity and commitment. The oathing of Kikuyu in Central Province, the Rift Valley, and Nairobi took place in stages, the form of the oath changing over time. By the beginning of 1949, a new stage of oathing opened with new aims of militancy and even violence.

This was symptomatic of the split in KAU membership. Prior to 1951 the moderate group had been dominant in the party, but in June of that year militants took control of the Nairobi branch of the party. They called for drastic and rapid reform, notably the rapid achievement of self-government, and they were prepared to back their demands with violence if necessary.

A number of the key radicals who won control of the Nairobi branch in June 1951 had previously been active in militant trade unionism. Fred Kubai had been president of the East Africa Trade Union Congress, and after it was banned and he had served a term in jail, he turned his attention to the KAU. Local government workers' union leader Bildad Kaggia, a former soldier, also joined the party. After the elections, these men came to occupy the seats of chairman and secretary, respectively, of the Nairobi branch. Kubai called for independence under African rule in three years. The Nairobi branch was strengthened by oathing more

Kikuyu members, and a buildup of weapons was begun for a possible resort to direct action.

The moderates, including without much doubt Kenyatta, were placed in a difficult position by the emergence of radicalism in the most important branch of the party and by the radicals' attempts to revive and start branches in other parts of the country. The moderates decided to draw up a large petition listing the land grievances of the KAU for presentation to the British Parliament. For many this represented a final effort at a constitutional solution to the land problem. As it turned out, the petition was not even presented to Parliament until 1953, and it achieved little.

With a rise in militancy came, almost inevitably, a rise in violent acts. These were largely spontaneous, expressions of frustration rather than tactics planned by a central coordinating body and least of all by the president of the KAU, Kenyatta. Evidence of oathing and violence increasingly worried European settlers and government from 1950 on. In that year the government banned the "Mau Mau Association." The name Mau Mau has no meaning in the Kikuyu language or any other spoken in Kenya, but it became a catch phrase used by the government to describe anti-European activity. Attacks on chiefs and sub-chiefs continued in the rural areas, as did attacks on livestock on settler farms. Pressure was applied to Kenyatta and the KAU to come out against Mau Mau. This was not very feasible, as Kenyatta was in a difficult position, balancing between moderates and radicals in the KAU. Nevertheless, Europeans interpreted this to mean that he was the organizer of Mau Mau. He did denounce it at a huge meeting at Kiambu in August 1952, but this was too late to convince the administration and settlers.

As 1952 wore on and violent acts continued in Central Province, the Rift Valley, and Nairobi, European settlers became more and more uneasy. Calls were heard for strong action. In addition, government policy seemed to drift, as Sir Philip Mitchell retired early in the year and his successor, Sir Evelyn Baring, did not arrive until September. Shortly after Baring's arrival, one of the most prominent Kikuyu chiefs and a firm supporter of the colonial regime, Chief Waruhiu, was assassinated in broad daylight in Central Province. This act led Baring to declare a State of Emergency, on the almost hysterical advice of his subordinates. On October 20, 1952, the governor ordered the arrest of Kenyatta, Kubai, and Kaggia, together with other KAU leaders.

The Emergency

The declaration of the State of Emergency marked the beginning of what is normally termed the Mau Mau rebellion. After the arrest of KAU leadership, many men took to the forest and began a guerilla war to overthrow colonial rule and drive the settlers from Kenya. They fought in what they called the Land Freedom Army, and they moved into the forests of the Mount Kenya and Aberdare mountains regions. These were close to Kikuyu settlements and were conducive to guerilla tactics. For much of 1953 the rebel forces, usually operating in small groups and not under an overall command, held the initiative against the colony's police and military forces. The rebels achieved a major victory in the successful attack on the Naivasha police station in March of that year.

The colonial administration needed justification for their declaration of emergency. In November 1952, Kenyatta and six others were put on trial at Kapenguria for the criminal offense of managing Mau Mau. In what was essentially a political trial, Kenyatta was found guilty in April 1953 and sentenced to seven years' hard labor. The KAU continued to exist under the presidency of Walter Odede, but in the same year he was detained and the party banned. Thereafter, the government clamped tight controls on political activity; Africans were unable to form any colony-wide political association for several years.

The ban of the KAU and the arrest and conviction of its leaders did not end the rebellion. Governor Baring was forced to call in a substantial number of British troops to deal with the insurgency. It proved a difficult task, requiring the detention and screening of virtually all Kikuyu in the colony, to say nothing of the related Embu and Meru peoples. The Kikuyu were concentrated into villages where they could be more easily protected, thus altering traditional settlement patterns. Those whose loyalty was suspect were detained without trial for lengthy periods. Operation Anvil of April 1954, for example, resulted in the arrest of practically all the Kikuyu in Nairobi. By the end of 1956 the major resistance of the rebels had been broken, and their most important leaders, such as Dedan Kimathi, had been captured.

As the rebellion wore on it assumed many characteristics of a Kikuyu civil war. Some Kikuyu, the so-called loyalists, took up arms for the British. Though fewer in number than the rebels, the loyalists gained great advantages during the emergency. They wielded tremendous and often unchecked power as chiefs and sub-chiefs, and were able to take over the lands of rebels who were either off at war or under detention. Most loyalists were motivated by strong Christian principles, as the resistance movement rejected Western values and Christianity. More-over, most were relatively well educated and well-to-do. They were in large measure, and would certainly become, the have's of Kikuyu society, while those who took to the forests in the Land Freedom Army were largely the have-not's, the landless and uneducated. To fully appreciate the dimensions of the Mau Mau rebellion, it is important to understand this aspect of the conflict as well as the anti-colonial theme.

The British, recognizing that the Kenya resistance was underlain by deep-seated political, economic, and social problems, aimed not just at achieving a military victory but at enacting reforms to remove African discontent. The huge cost to Britain of suppressing Mau Mau convinced the imperial authorities that they could not afford to underwrite continued settler economic and political dominance in Kenya. Within a decade, the settlers' political influence was wiped out. In this sense the Mau Mau rebellion may be seen to have hastened African self-government.

An important part of the British effort to lessen African discontent was the program of economic reforms focusing on rural areas. The Department of Agriculture introduced an ambitious plan, named after its director, R. Swynnerton, which sought a transformation of African agriculture. It provided for government encouragement of land consolidation and the issuance of individual titles to land, something that was foreign to most of Kenya's peoples, though not to the Kikuyu. The plan also made available more central government money for the introduction of cash crops, improvement of extension services, and the provision of credit to African farmers. Cooperatives were greatly encouraged. Thus, first in the Kikuyu lands, where cash crops such as coffee were finally permitted, and later in all of the best agricultural areas of the colony, a rural revolution was launched using the considerable powers available to the administration under the continuing State of Emergency.

Those who benefited from this revolution were largely the conservative elements: chiefs and sub-chiefs, African businessmen, and progressive farmers. Their rise to dominance in the rural areas thus marked the last years of colonial rule and continued into the independence period.

The other thrust of the British reform effort was to encourage greater African political participation at the center. Changes proposed by the British authorities, however, were to be made within the framework of the policy of multiracialism. African education was expanded, and Africans would move toward a parity of political representation with Europeans and Asians rather than toward majority rule. A major step was taken in this direction with the introduction of a new constitution in 1954, which provided for more African members of the Legislative Council and for an African member of the newly formed, multiracial Council of Ministers, though it still left Europeans with more representation on both bodies than Africans. These measures pleased neither politically conscious Africans nor the majority of settlers, who opposed any extension of African political rights.

Toward African Self-Government

Despite these constitutional changes, Africans were not allowed to form any political organizations after the banning of the KAU. Only in mid-1955 were African parties permitted and these could be organized only at the district level. This discouragement of national political activity helped to perpetuate and foster sectionalism and tribalism. With political activity and leadership on a national level forbidden, it was left to a young trade unionist, Tom Mboya, to provide a national forum through the Kenya Federation of Labour founded in 1953. As general secretary, Mboya sought to protect the rights of workers and forged links with British and American trade union bodies, and he emerged as a national spokesman for African political aspirations.

Africans achieved some small political advances under the new constitution, but they remained a minority in the Legislative Council and the Council of Ministers. A second African minister was provided in 1956, and it was announced in 1957 that eight African members were to be elected to the Legislative Council. These first African elections took place in March 1958. Unlike in the European and Asian communities, the African electorate represented only a small percentage of the total population, as voters had to meet educational and property qualifications. In Central Province, where most of the Kikuyu, Embu, and Meru lived, only loyalists could vote. Mboya won the seat for Nairobi. Mathu, the first African appointed to the council, failed to gain election. Among the first group of elected African members was Daniel arap Moi, later to be Kenya's second president.

New constitutional proposals followed the elections, but they sought to perpetuate multiracialism and their impact proved short-lived. All the African elected members refused office under the constitution, demanding an African majority. Their refusal to participate fully in the new constitution probably ensured that it would have a rather short life.

In 1959 pressure built up on all sides for a constitutional conference to plot Kenya's future course. The relative political unity of the settlers in the earlier 1950s had by this time evaporated. Most settlers supported the United Party led by Group Captain Briggs; they called for white supremacy and for segregation in all fields, and opposed the idea of a constitutional conference. A more moderate group, led by the minister of agriculture, Sir Michael Blundell, had formed the New Kenya Party (NKP); they supported the conference and would play an important part in it.

The political atmosphere had been altered by the Hola Camp affair of 1959. The deaths of eleven "hard-core" Mau Mau detainees at Hola Camp and an attempted cover-up of the brutal circumstances of the deaths by the Kenya authorities served to undermine not only the rationale of "rehabilitation" programs but also the continuation of multiracialism in Kenya. Ian Macleod, who became secretary of state for the colonies in 1959, was convinced by the Hola Camp affair that swift change was needed in Kenya.

The constitutional conference held at Lancaster House in London early in 1960 brought about this change. All elected members of the Legislative Council attended. It had already been announced that the white highlands would be opened to all races, thus beginning the exodus of "die-hard" settlers to Zimbabwe and South Africa. No agreement could be reached at the conference, so Macleod imposed a settlement that ensured an African majority in the new council (thirty-three seats). Europeans were to have ten seats reserved for them, chosen on the basis of a common roll election following a primary election for whites only. Asians were to hold eight seats. The Lancaster House Conference thus ended European pretensions to predominance as well as attempts to foster multiracialism as a political ideal in Kenya. Fortunately for Macleod, Blundell's group accepted the new proposals, thereby easing their acceptance in Britain.

By now the ban on African national parties had been lifted, and by the end of 1960, two parties had come into existence. First to be established was the Kenya African National Union (KANU). This party came to represent the two largest ethnic groups, the Kikuyu and the Luo, as well as the Kamba and Gusii. James Gichuru was chosen as its first president after the party was forbidden to choose Kenyatta, now in detention as a security risk after the completion of his sentence. Also prominent were Mboya as general secretary and Oginga Odinga, another Luo, as vice president. One characteristic of the party in this period was rivalry and factionalism between leading personalities, especially Mboya and Odinga. Somewhat later, the Kenya African Democratic Union (KADU) was formed under the leadership of Ronald Ngala, Masinde Muliro, and Moi. It sought to protect the interests of "minority" ethnic groups such as the coastal peoples, the Luyha, and the Kalenjin.

These two parties fought for the African seats in the elections held as a result of the Lancaster House proposals in 1961. Two parties also took the field in competition for the European seats: Blundell's NKP and the more reactionary Kenya Coalition led by Sir Ferdinand Cavendish-Bentinck. The coalition opposed the direction Kenya was moving in, and called, in effect, for the British government to buy out the settler farmers. The coalition won virtually all the primary elections where only Europeans could vote, but in the common roll elections, African voters, more numerous under the broader franchise, gave the victory to NKP candidates in many instances. On the African side the election was dominated by one issue, the release of Kenyatta. Both KANU and KADU called for his release. In what came to be known as the Kenyatta Election, KANU won nineteen seats to eleven for KADU.

Both parties initially refused the call of Governor Sir Patrick Renison, who had succeeded Baring in 1959, to join the new Council of Ministers. They insisted that Kenyatta should be released and come back to politics, but the governor, describing the detainee as a leader "to darkness and death," refused. Eventually KADU agreed to form a government in exchange for the promise of the eventual release of Kenyatta. Their minority position was overcome by combination with the NKP and the use of the governor's power to nominate further members to the council. In August 1961 Kenyatta was released, and after an attempt to get the two parties to unite under his leadership, he became the president of KANU. Further advance toward self-government would be slowed somewhat by differences between KANU and KADU.

These differences were very apparent at the second Lancaster House constitutional conference held in 1962 to plot the course of Kenya's path to self-government. Chaired by the new secretary of state, Reginald Maudling, the conference was faced with a choice between KADU's vision of federalism (*majimbo*) and KANU's unitary approach. Maudling decided on a federal solution despite the opposition of KANU, which obviously represented the majority of Kenyans. Seven regions with entrenched powers were to be established with their own governments, and at the center there was to be a two-house legislature. Before the new constitution would become operative, further details had to be worked out and elections held.

To effect this, a coalition government was formed, led jointly by the two party leaders, Kenyatta and Ngala. Still, deep divisions appeared to separate the parties; KANU accepted the federal system only reluctantly, hoping to win the pre-independence elections and then alter the constitution. Separatist movements in the coastal strip (still technically the property of the sultan of Zanzibar) and in the Somali-inhabited northeast of the country also posed threats to the future stability and unity of Kenya. With uncertainty about the future and a loss of confidence characterizing the attitude of most Europeans and Asians, the colony's future did not seem particularly bright.

Both KANU and KADU campaigned hard for the elections of May 1963. By the time they were held, Malcolm Macdonald, son of a former British prime minister, had replaced Governor Renison, a change necessitated by the former's inability to work with KANU and his particularly unfortunate relations with Kenyatta. In the vote itself KANU emerged as the clear winner in the lower house (73-31), but the party held only a slight majority in the Senate.

241

As a result of the 1963 elections Kenyatta was called upon to form a government to lead Kenya to self-government and independence. Under his prime ministership Kenya became self-governing on June 1, 1963, with full independence set for December. The KANU government, confronted the choice of working with the federal constitution or changing it to a unitary form against the strong opposition of a minority party, faced the further problem of separatism, especially in the North-eastern Region, where the Somali population had boycotted the elections of 1963. Economic problems also presented themselves to the new African government, as political uncertainty among settlers and European investors led to an economic downspin from 1961 to 1963.

The Colonial Economy

In the 1950s, Kenya's agriculture began to experience a remarkable transformation. With the inauguration of the Swynnerton Plan, emphasis switched to stimulating and transforming African agriculture. All over the territory, enclosure and land consolidation campaigns were set in motion which took Kenya a considerable way toward the creation of African farmers who held land on individual tenure. With more and better agricultural services provided to African farmers and great encouragement given to high value crops, such as coffee, pyrethrum, and tea, gross farm output in Kenya began a dramatic expansion which would continue throughout the 1960s. The settler domination of the agricultural economy was on its way to a rapid end.

As production grew, the process of differentiation in the rural areas gained speed. The gap between the richest and poorest African farmers widened, and government policy was to favor the former group in terms of extension services, credit, etc. Land consolidation and registration of titles allowed the wealthy to purchase additional land. Cooperatives, previously utilized only by Europeans, were increasingly set up for marketing African crops, and these also favored the well-to-do farmers.

Urban areas, especially Nairobi and Mombasa experienced a growth of manufacturing activity after 1945. At first largely settler and foreign owned, the import substitution industries provided processed foods and consumer goods for Uganda and Tanganyika markets as well. During the 1950s, Kenya Asian capital, previously concentrated in commerce, began to move to manufacturing. At the same time, direct foreign investment, particularly from Britain, began to find its way into manufacturing. This was true prior to 1963 in such industries as footwear, paints, soaps, and cement. New industries were started and those begun by settlers were absorbed. Nairobi was emerging as a regional center of industry and finance, a role that was solidified in the years after independence.

Zanzibar

In the period after World War II, the Arab population continued to dominate Zanzibar and Pemba politically and, to an extent, economically. This was regarded with favor by the British, and the colonial administration attempted to maintain the situation down to independence in 1963. The British nurtured the Arab elite who owned most of the clove plantations as the natural rulers of Zanzibar.

Evolution of Political Parties

After World War II political parties initially emerged largely along racial lines. Although the Arabs made up a small minority of the total population (less than 10 percent in 1948), the Arab Association took the lead in safeguarding the Arab position. There were also the Indian Association (for Hindus), the Muslim Association (for Asian Muslims), and the Shirazi Association (for Africans claiming descent from the earliest migrants to the islands). Africans from the mainland (descendants of slaves and migrant workers) joined the African Association, formed in 1934. It was the Arab Association which took the lead in the 1950s in demanding the election of Legislative Council members.

In 1954 the British proposed constitutional changes, suggesting that the racial ratio in the Legislative Council should be four Arabs, four Africans, three Asians, and one European. The Arabs eventually made even greater demands for common roll elections on universal adult suffrage, a ministerial system, and an unofficial majority. As the British would not accept these demands, the Arab Association withdrew from the Legislative Council.

The British maintained that constitutional advance would go on despite Arab opposition. The unofficial representatives in the Legislative Council would be raised from eight to twelve. It was later announced that a special commissioner would investigate the method of their choice. His report in 1956 advised that six seats should be filled by common roll elections and six by nomination. Though the Arabs had opposed these proposals, they agreed to end their boycott.

For the elections held in 1957, political activity became more pronounced. The Zanzibar Nationalist Party (ZNP) had been formed in 1955. The party' had its origin in activity by rural African farmers who formed a short-lived, proto-ZNP party which advocated independence under the sultan. The leadership of the Arab Association joined with these rural radicals to form the ZNP. It increasingly attracted rank and-file Arabs as well as the elite, such as Sheikh Ali Muhsin, who came to make up the party's leadership. Using the appeal of Islam and the traditional leadership role of Arabs, it managed to attract support from other communities in Zanzibar town, such as the Shirazi. It was well organized and, perhaps with North African influence, adopted a strongly anti-colonial stance.

Not all Africans (Shirazis and mainlanders) welcomed the ZNP. The Afro-Shirazi Party (ASP) was formed from the African and Shirazi associations as its chief rival. The African and Shirazi leaders merged in 1957 under the leadership of Sheikh Abeid Karume of the African Association. The ASP was less nationalistic and radical than the ZNP.

The 1957 election campaign was marked by rising racial tensions, and the elections themselves resulted in a victory for the ASP with 61 percent of the vote and three seats to 21 percent and no seats for the ZNP. Karume overwhelmingly defeated the ZNP leader, Muhsin.

Toward Independence

There was considerable political awakening after the 1957 elections. One result of increased party rivalry was tension and rivalry between Arabs and Africans. Attempts at reconciliation, such as the formation of the Freedom Committee, did not meet with success. In 1959 it was announced that elected members would be raised to eight (from six), with women being allowed to vote. Both party leaders called for a rapid advance to self-government.

In 1960 the British proposed an increase in membership in both the Executive and Legislative Councils. There would be twenty-two elected members to the Legislative Council, and the leader of the party winning a majority would be chief minister. Both parties sought to mobilize support, and rivalry between them became ever more intense. In mid-1959, however, a new party had been formed. This was the Zanzibar and Pemba Peoples Party (ZPPP) led by Sheikh Mohammed Shamte. It broke away from the ASP and drew support from Shirazi, particularly on Pemba.

The ZPPP wanted to avoid domination by Arabs or mainland Africans. The ZPPP, the ASP, and the ZNP were the main competitors in the January 1961 elections. The ASP, with its more moderate image, won ten seats, the more radical ZNP nine and the ZPPP three. The ZPPP then split, two members joining the ZNP and one the ASP. As this left an even balance of eleven and eleven, no government could be formed. Further elections were therefore held in June 1961. These were marked by severe violence in which almost twenty people died in political and racial clashes. Although an additional seat had been added to avoid a tie, the election produced another deadlock as the ASP and ZNP both won ten seats, and the ZPPP three. The resident called upon ZNP leader Muhsin to form a government, but in a surprise move ZPPP leader Shamte became chief minister in a ZNP-ZPPP coalition government.

The path to self-government finally was open, but severe differences still separated the parties. After a boycott of government the ASP called for new elections, while the ZNP-ZPPP, wishing to retain the influence they had won, pressed for self-government. The British finally acceded to this demand, but it was decided to expand the legislature and hold another election before granting independence. Shamte thus became prime minister in June 1963 with elections scheduled for the following month.

In these elections the governing ZNP-ZPPP alliance emerged victorious. Despite the fact that the two parties polled only some 73,000 votes as opposed to ASP's 87,000, the ZNP gained twelve seats and the ZPPP six. This gave the ZNP-ZPPP alliance a clear parliamentary majority over the ASP, which held thirteen seats. Despite ASP protests that the electoral outcome was unfair, Britain formally granted independence to;a politically, racially, and economically divided Zanzibar in December 1963. The rule of the ZNP-ZPPP coalition was, however, to be very short.

In Zanzibar, as in Kenya and Uganda, the achievement of independence was marked by political divisions reflecting ethnic and sectional disunity. These would have considerable impact in the future. Tanganyika, on the other hand, reached independence much more united behind its TANU government. Although the poorest of the mainland territories in 1961, Tanganyika had been able to convince the colonial authorities to grant self-government earlier than her neighbors and indeed before most British officials would have expected twenty years before.

The twenty years after World War II were thus ones of rapid change. Spurred by the experience of the Mau Mau rebellion and her desire to bend to the "wind of change," Britain gave up political control of East Africa in the early-1960s. In addition to political change, an economic and social transformation was also set in motion during the last two decades of colonial rule. Cash crop agriculture expanded in all three mainland countries, and agricultural production as a whole reached heights seldom approached in the first decades of colonial rule. Government expenditure on education and medical services, to take just two examples, also rose dramatically.

Yet the attainment of political independence presented the new nations with tremendous problems. East Africa had benefited from a most favorable world economic situation during the 1950s and early 1960s as prices for her exports were rising. This was a situation which would not last, and the dependent, underdeveloped economies which the countries inherited on independence presented daunting challenges for the years ahead.

Suggestions for Further Reading

Apter, David. *The Political Kingdom in Uganda* (Princeton, 1967).

Berman, Bruce and John Lonsdale. *Unhappy Valley Book 2* (London, 1992).

Coulson, Andrew. *Tanzania: A Political Economy* (Oxford, 1982).

Iliffe, John. *A Modern History of Tanganyika* (Cambridge, 1979).

Karugire, S. R. *A Political History of Uganda* (Nairobi, 1980).

Kitching, Gavin. *Class and Economic Change in Kenya* (New Haven, 1980).

Low, D. A., and Smith, Alison, eds. *History of East Africa* Vol. III (Oxford, 1976).

Pratt, Cranford. *The Critical Phase in Tanzania, 1945-1968* (London, 1976).

Rosberg, Carl, and Nottingham,J. *The Myth of Mau Mau: Nationalism in Kenya* (New York, 1966).

Temu, A. J., and Kimambo, I. eds. *A History of Tanzania* (Dar es Salaam,1969).

Throup, David. *Economic and Social Origins of Mau Mau* (London, 1988).

Chapter 11

Independent East Africa, 1960s to 1990s

Between December 1961 and December 1963, Tanganyika, Uganda, Kenya, and Zanzibar achieved political independence from Great Britain. Inheriting a roughly similar colonial legacy, the newly independent states faced many similar problems in their first years as free nations. One of the most fundamental was, and continues to be, the issue of speeding and broadening economic development. All enjoyed success in expanding production and social services, but huge difficulties remain in the nations' attempts to eradicate poverty, ignorance, and disease. Politically, the trend of events was toward a one-party state. In two of the countries, however, governments were forcibly overthrown. The post-independence era also witnessed the forging of closer ties between the East African states through the formation of the East African Community, but its life proved to be relatively short.

Independence and Dependency

Although the East African nations theoretically gained control of their own destiny at independence, self-government and majority rule did not end rather heavy dependence on Britain. In some ways this dependence was increased, and it is difficult not to believe that the colonial power expected this dependency to keep her former colonies closely aligned to her, both politically and economically. It was expected, first of all, that the political and administrative structure bequeathed by the British would serve the new nations for a considerable time. The countries would be governed by a non-partisan civil service using the administrative structures created to facilitate colonial rule, while national politics would be dominated by a parliamentary system based on the Westminster model. However, the East African nations, especially Zanzibar, quickly made significant constitutional and administrative changes away from the systems inherited from Britain.

Given the lack of trained local manpower to staff high-level technical and administrative positions, a crucial kind of dependency involved skilled manpower. It was recognized that the governments would have to employ European civil servants and experts for a long time to come. Reliance on foreign-born or non-African, local-born advisors was a potential hindrance to independence. The potential for rapidly training Africans to take over civil service positions depended on the educational system left by Britain. This system emphasized academic rather than technical education, and the schools were not well equipped to produce large numbers of trained men and women. Moreover, most teachers at the higher levels were Europeans.

The East African nations sought to overcome this type of dependency through crash training programs and an expansion of educational facilities. Secondary and university education was significantly expanded, even though the institutions providing such training have not come near to catering for the majority of the populations. Large numbers of students were sent abroad, notably to the United States, for education and training that would equip them to run the governments of their countries. Africanization programs were instituted in all the countries to put Africans into jobs held by non-Africans, but the pace of this process was never fast enough to please all citizens. After more than thirty years of independence, the East African countries have largely Africanized government services, but in certain skilled professions, such as medicine, Africans have yet to take over completely.

The greatest dependency was in the economic field. All the East African countries were closely tied to Britain as members of the sterling area, their prime overseas market and the source of almost all development funds. Britain, for its part, hoped to retain a large share of the East African market for her exports. The states had inherited a basically capitalist economic structure in which non-Africans played a major role. Agricultural development along lines begun in the final years of colonial rule seemed the only route for the new nations to follow. In the rural areas this generally meant a continued attempt to help the so-called "progressive" farmer and to facilitate the emergence of a class of well-to-do peasant farmers who would produce crops for exports and subsistence. Any attempt to completely break this dependence, it was argued by colonial officials, would likely prove harmful.

Nevertheless, the three countries did attempt to alter and break the pattern of economic dependence on Britain. Markets and export crops were diversified. Industry was encouraged, particularly for import substitution, on a much greater scale than during colonial times. Development aid was obtained from the United Nations, the so-called Western bloc, Russia and its allies, and China. All the new nations moved to what they termed socialism. This provided a greater degree of state control and ownership of industry and the means of production than previously, as well as more social welfare services.

Despite considerable efforts, economic dependency has proved extremely difficult for the East African countries to break. Although no longer so dependent on Britain, they are still dependent on the developed world for markets and sources of capital. Their major money earners remain agricultural produce dependent on world markets over which the producer countries often have little control. Multinational companies also have come to dominate some areas of marketing and manufacturing of goods in East Africa, thus introducing another element of dependency. Money provided for projects by the developed countries has usually not been without strings. Tourism, the major new source of foreign exchange to emerge after independence, is of course dependent on overseas visitors.

The relationship of the independent East African nations with Britain was complicated by the presence of the European and Asian minorities. Britain initially hoped the position of these non-Africans would remain much as it had been under the colonial regime and encouraged both groups to take citizenship in the new states, a suggestion which was received with little enthusiasm. Eventually Britain had to offer the option of British citizenship. In Kenya many Europeans had their farms bought out with money provided by Britain, and most of these former settlers left East Africa. Asians throughout East Africa felt they faced an uncertain future; many were losing their jobs and businesses to Africans, who saw the Asians as obstacles to their own progress. The majority of Asians therefore elected to take British citizenship. Britain, having extended citizenship to the East African Asians, was reluctant to admit them in large numbers, and British governments in the 1960s and 1970s attempted to negotiate quota arrangements with the East African states to allow for a gradual relocation of Asians.

Attempts to Achieve Closer Cooperation in East Africa

With the achievement of political self-government, attempts to bring about a federation or Closer Union were revived. These had foundered during the colonial period as a result of fears in Uganda and Tanganyika that Kenya's settlers would assume a dominant role in the affairs of the other East African territories. This was no longer a possibility, and popular sentiment began to swing in favor of federation. In 1961 the East African Common Services Organization came into being to provide the common services for the East African territories that the East African High Commission had previously provided, as well as to promote a free trade area for East Africa. Over the next three years chances seemed good that the organization might form the basis of an East African federation. In mid-1963 Nyerere, Obote, and Kenyatta met in Nairobi and pledged to work for the political federation of East Africa. Uganda, however, held back, and the drive toward union did not reach fruition.

Kenya's dominant position in East Africa, largely a colonial legacy, was one problem standing in the way of closer economic cooperation. Kenya had the lion's share of manufacturing and was exporting far more goods within the organization than the other countries. Nairobi was the financial center of the region. In 1964 the Kampala Agreement was drawn up as a means for the three countries to deal with the situation in which Kenya seemed to be gaining disproportionate advantage from the operation of the common market under the Common Services Organization. The agreement was intended to redress the balance of interterritorial trade and to promote the siting of new industries away from Kenya. It also provided for a quota system in interterritorial trade.

Despite this cooperation, the three countries soon abandoned their common currency, and each instituted its own money. Despite such tendencies toward economic divergence, the three countries attempted to reach some more conclusive agreement on common services, economic cooperation, and greater political unity. In June 1967 the Treaty for East African Cooperation was signed in Kampala by the three East African presidents. The Common Services Organization was replaced by the East African Community, whose headquarters was to be in Arusha in northern Tanzania. The common market and services were maintained, while measures were introduced to promote a more equitable distribution of benefits between the partners. A notable provision allowed Tanzania and Uganda to tax, under certain circumstances, imports of goods manufactured in Kenya in order to protect their own industries. Another measure established an East African Development Bank to channel more investment to Uganda and Tanzania. Headquarters of several of the corporations established to provide services, such as harbors (Tanzania) and posts and telegraphs (Kampala), also were moved from Kenya.

The East African Community proved unable to overcome some significant divisive factors. The community's existence involved a degree of sacrifice and compromise by all of the states, but this could be taken only so far. Each partner state followed its own fiscal and development planning strategy, and as time passed these strategies became more divergent. Lacking joint policies in crucial areas, the community inevitably ran afoul of the differing aims and perceptions of the members. Tanzania followed an increasingly socialist economic policy after 1967, stressing self-reliance. Kenya, while officially following a policy of African socialism, adhered to what was perceived, certainly in Tanzania, as a capitalist development strategy. These diverging approaches, accompanied by ideological differences, produced strains between the leadership of the two countries.

A second divisive factor was the persistence of the trade imbalance. Industry in Kenya continued to develop more rapidly than in the other two states. Kenya also continued to export far more goods to Uganda and Tanzania than they did to her. By the mid-1970s those countries formed about one-third of Kenya's export market. Kenya's leaders were increasingly unwilling to make sacrifices to hold back her economic progress; the other two states saw Kenya as prospering at their expense.

After January 1971 the three presidents did not meet as a group to discuss community problems and prospects. A coup had overthrown the government of President Obote of Uganda and established a military dictatorship. President Nyerere steadfastly opposed this development. He offered Obote a haven in Tanzania and refused to meet in any official capacity with the dictator, Idi Amin. In such conditions, the community could not function in the fashion that had been intended.

As a result of these and other factors, the community collapsed in early 1977. Services broke down, and they were assumed by each of the countries as national (e.g., Tanzania Airways, Kenya Railways) rather than regional entities. Tanzania closed her border with Kenya at the time of the collapse, and relations were strained for a number of months. The move toward regional cooperation and a possible federation suffered a large, perhaps insurmountable setback. After years of negotiations, agreement on the division of the community's assets and liabilities was finally reached in 1983. In November of that year the Tanzania-Kenya border was reopened. Over the next decade, the three East African nations strove to promote increased understanding and improved economic relations, but there was no serious attempt to reestablish the Community.

Tanzania

Formed as a result of the 1964 union of Zanzibar and Tanganyika, the United Republic of Tanzania has in many ways travelled the furthest from the colonial system of the East African countries in its three decades of freedom. New administrative and political structures have been forged, breaking decisively with the dependency arrangements that had existed at independence. Tanzania has also gone far toward establishing a socialist economy in the period since 1961.

Establishment of a Republic

Tanganyika became independent in December 1961, with Julius Nyerere as prime minister. By any standard of economic measurement, Tanganyika was the poorest of the East African countries. The new nation was heavily dependent on Britain for development aid and plans, for trained manpower, and in the political and administrative structure she inherited. Most high-ranking positions in the civil service were held by non-Africans, a situation which provoked calls for increased Africanization from the ranks of the ruling party, TANU.

In January 1962 Nyerere startled many by resigning the prime ministership in favor of Rashidi Kawawa. To build up popular support for TANU, Nyerere wanted to renew his relationship with the rank and file of the party and to find ways to involve them more closely in the development of the country. He thus sought, in contrast to the post-independence experience in Kenya and Uganda, to prepare the party to serve as an effective force in mobilizing the population. Nyerere's decision to resign and to work with the party and people had another important impact. As Cranford Pratt has argued, it marked the end of Nyerere's acceptance of dependency and a neocolonial relationship. Hereafter, Tanganyika would increasingly move away from the governmental and developmental models imposed on the country by Britain.

This move away from the system left by the British can be seen during the prime ministership of Kawawa. The pace of Africanization of leading government posts was greatly accelerated. The character of administration was fundamentally altered with the appointment in 1962 of regional and area commissioners to replace the provincial and district commissioners of the colonial days. These administrators were TANU members, and a number were members of Parliament. Thus, the British tradition of a nonpartisan civil service was quickly broken. Kawawa's government also moved to bring the trade unions, a potential source of troublesome opposition, under closer supervision and control. Finally, it was decided to move away from the British-model parliamentary system and substitute an executive presidency.

At the end of 1962, a republican constitution was introduced which provided for a strong presidency. Nyerere returned to the center of politics to seek this office. His opponent was Z. Mtemvu of the African National Congress. Nyerere won by 1,127,978 votes to 21,276. Although only some 25 percent of the potential voters had cast ballots, the supremacy of TANU was once again clearly demonstrated. Party and government at all levels were hereafter closely linked.

Tanganyika to Tanzania

Zanzibar achieved independence some two years after Tanganyika. The new government, still headed by the sultan and under the control of the ZNP-ZPPP coalition, proved to be short-lived. It had a majority of seats in the legislature but a minority of the popular vote in the pre-independence elections. To the ASP and the new and more radical Umma Party, this was a most unsatisfactory situation and a continuation of Arab domination.

In January 1964 a revolution, carried off by the self-styled Field Marshall John Okello, toppled the government, sending the sultan into exile. Okello handed over power to a Revolutionary Council under the leadership of ASP chief Sheikh Karume, and the man who overthrew the ZNP-ZPPP government was soon expelled by the new regime. Revenge was also taken against those Arabs who did not flee the islands. Although claiming to represent the people, Karume made no attempt to seek a popular mandate by elections. The ASP leader moved rapidly to establish a state controlled economy. The clove industry was nationalized, as were most other businesses. Large estates were expropriated and some were distributed to peasants.

Shortly after the revolution, President Nyerere proposed a union of the islands with his nation. Karume agreed, and the United Republic of Tanzania was formed in April 1964. Nyerere was president and Karume was first vice president. The political and economic integration of the two entities into a single state did not occur rapidly; for more than a decade the ASP exercised authority on Zanzibar and Pemba in a much less democratic fashion and with far less concern for human rights than did TANU on the mainland. Zanzibar also enjoyed much closer ties with the East European nations, notably East Germany, than did the mainland. Only in 1977 would the two parties, TANU and ASP, unite to form a single entity.

The One-Party State

TANU's triumph in the pre-independence elections and in the presidential ballot of 1962 meant that for most purposes Tanganyika was a one-party state. This trend was not altered by the union with Zanzibar, for TANU remained supreme on the mainland. To many within TANU, therefore, the establishment of a one-party state in law would only recognize the de facto situation. Moreover, it was stressed that an opposition party was a luxury the country could not afford in its drive for rapid development and the eradication of ignorance and disease.

Not only was the government dominated by TANU. The trade unions had been brought under government control, and dissidents could be dealt with through the powers of preventive detention given to the president. Shortly after the Zanzibar revolution, there had been a mutiny in the army caused by demands for better conditions and an end to command by British officers. The mutiny was suppressed with British help. The army was disbanded, and a new peoples' army eventually recruited. By 1965 TANU was in an unchallengeable position.

President Nyerere appointed a commission to recommend to his government how a one-party state could be introduced in Tanzania. Out of the commission's recommendations came the constitution of 1965, which reflected the mixture of democratic and authoritarian tendencies that marked the thinking of party leaders. TANU was made the only legal party. Any party member could stand for election to the National Assembly, but he or she would have to be nominated by local party members, and the National Executive Committee of TANU made the final decision on the two candidates to stand in a constituency. The National Assembly was given power to select additional members of that body, as was the president. Regional commissioners and members of the Zanzibar Revolutionary Council (a non-elected body) also were members of the assembly.

The first parliamentary election under this constitution took place on the mainland in October 1965. More than twenty-five sitting members chose not to seek reelection. Thirteen were rejected by local district party branches, and a further seventeen members of Parliament (MPs) were defeated in the election itself. This turnover was a reflection of both the democracy of the one-party system and the desire of the masses for change. In general, the National Assembly in Tanzania has not played a leading role in policy making. The presidential election in 1965 and in subsequent polls took a different form. Only a single candidate, in this case, Nyerere, presented himself to the electorate. Voters were required to vote yes or no.

Socialism and Self-reliance: the Arusha Declaration

One result of the continued difficulties associated with moving away from a dependency relationship with Britain and the West and attempting to develop a new nation on an equitable basis was the move toward socialism. Though the country's annual economic growth rate was more than 4 percent from 1960 to 1968, the rural peasant gained precious little benefit. The urban worker fared much better, as the gap between rural and urban incomes widened after independence. Class differences also continued to develop in both urban and rural areas. The communal values of the traditional African way of life were being eroded. Because

President Nyerere wished to avoid the emergence of a governing class of wealthy property owners and businessmen, he decided to move toward a socialistic system for Tanzania. He made the transition to socialism his central concern not so much because of a surging demand from the masses but in response to his own vision of Tanzania's future. Nyerere's vision of socialism was to prove popular with his countrymen.

Nyerere was also concerned about his country's overreliance on foreign aid. Not only was foreign aid less than hoped for and attached to strings, but Nyerere was greatly distressed by the African policies of such nations as Britain and the United States. Overreliance on foreign aid, Nyerere felt, was inhibiting Tanzania's development, and he became convinced of the need to promote self-reliance.

Nyerere's Arusha Declaration of 1967, a blueprint for socialism in the country, called on Tanzanians to concentrate their energies on what they could do with their own resources. Nyerere stressed that socialism had been a part of the African social and economic system in the past; he was not attempting to import European Marxism. The declaration forbade TANU leaders and high civil servants any association with capitalist practices. They could not hold shares or become directors in private companies. They could not receive more than one salary, own rental property, or employ others to work for them. Rapid nationalization followed the declaration, as all private banks were taken over, along with major food processors, insurance companies, and the major export and import companies. Nyerere also identified several manufacturing firms in which the government would take a majority shareholding, and indicated the state's intention to take a major role in the sisal industry. Eventually (1972-73) estates and settler farms were taken over by the state, as was property—particularly rental—in cities and towns. In 1976 the state in effect nationalized cooperative societies, setting up government corporations, such as the National Milling Corporation for food crops, to market agricultural produce. It was a measure of the president's stature and the respect he commanded that he was able to get his policy accepted by the party and nation with little opposition.

Building a Socialist Tanzania

For Tanzania, as for many Third World countries, the period since 1967 has not been an easy one economically. The generally buoyant and rising prices for the country's exports in the 1960s were succeeded in the 1970s by fluctuating and even falling prices. Poor rainfall in the 1970s also produced drought conditions and food shortages. Moreover, the steady rise in petroleum prices put severe strains on the economy. During this period, Tanzania continued to diversify her trade patterns. Increasing exports found their way not only to Britain but to the European

255

Economic Community, China, and the United States. After 1975 trade with Mozambique expanded greatly.

The decade following the Arusha Declaration also demonstrated Nyerere's continuing commitment to socialism and self-reliance. In 1971 he issued new leadership guidelines (*mwongozo*) that stressed adherence to socialist principles in leadership behavior for the party and government. There has also been a changing emphasis in education. Rather than stressing academic education and preparation for college, a system which focuses on agricultural education at the primary level has been established. The government sought to introduce a policy of universal primary education by the end of 1977, and a considerable measure of success has been achieved. Emphasis has also been placed on adult education, and significant progress has been achieved in reducing illiteracy. In contrast, academic secondary and university education have not been greatly encouraged. Indeed, since 1975 a potential student must have been employed for at least two years before being admitted to the University of Dar es Salaam.

One of the most important ways in which Nyerere attempted to build socialism was the establishment of ujamaa (socialist) villages where communal values and efforts are encouraged. Soon after independence, village settlement schemes had been introduced and new villages created as an answer to land shortage and production problems in the rural areas. However, these efforts had not been particularly successful. After the Arusha Declaration, it was decided that communal effort in production and marketing should be emphasized. In addition, services, such as health and education, could more easily be provided with rural populations concentrated in villages. The process of moving rural peoples into villages did not proceed very rapidly until the end of 1973, when the government decided to greatly speed up the creation of ujamaa villages. Villagization increased tremendously over the next two years as the authorities resorted to force to move peasants into the villages.

This success brought in its wake some severe problems. Many villages were established long before effective water supplies and social services could be provided. Even more significant, the use of force to speed villagization appears to have had a negative effect on agricultural production. Planting and harvesting of crops declined, and this, combined with severe drought in many parts of the country in 1974-75, left Tanzania short of food supplies. Many foreign observers believed that the villagization program was pushed too quickly and forcefully, and it is perhaps still too early to say whether the creation of socialist villages as centers of rural population will be successful.

Another economic sector which has not been as successful as hoped after the Arusha Declaration has been state-run industry. New industries have been created, and many have been shifted away from concentration in Dar es Salaam. By most standards, however, the performance of Tanzanian industry has not been good. Production per worker has not risen significantly, and the proportion of Gross Domestic Product created by industry has risen only slightly since the 1960s. The main cause for the difficulties of industry appears to be political: despite considerable investment of state funds, poor management and lack of incentives have held back industrial expansion.

The 1970s on the whole were not an easy time for Tanzania economically. Coulson maintains, in fact, that rural producers, urban workers, and upper income earners were all worse off at the end of the 1970s than they had been at the beginning. There were also shortages of food and consumer goods. However, the government could claim success in literacy, primary education, and the extension of medical services.

A similar mixture of success and difficulties has characterized one of the major development projects undertaken in the post-independence period, the Tazara Railway. Even before 1967 the need for another outlet for landlocked Zambia was seen as a necessity. Only China, however, was willing to undertake the building of a railway to link Dar es Salaam with the Zambian copper belt. China's largest aid project in Africa was begun in 1970 and completed (1,770 kilometers) late in 1975. The railroad has the potential of opening up southern Tanzania for agricultural expansion and the exploitation of valuable minerals, such as coal, found there in large amounts. Port congestion and problems with rolling stock, however, have hampered efficiency on the line.

A significant political success of the 1970s was the union of the country's two political parties. Since 1964 TANU had been supreme on the mainland and ASP on Zanzibar. Although united in government on a theoretical level, the two parties remained separate entities. After the death of Sheikh Karume in 1972, however, his successor, Aboud Jumbe, eventually agreed to a merging of the two parties. In early 1977 the ASP and TANU merged to form Chama cha Mapinduzi (Revolutionary Party), or CCM, under Nyerere's chairmanship. Amid rising opposition to the union on Zanzibar, Jumbe resigned in January 1984, and was replaced by Ali Hassan Mwinyi. In the same year Nyerere announced that he would not again be a candidate for the presidency.

To the surprise of some observers, the CCM chose Mwinyi as Nyerere's successor. The latter stepped down in November 1985, one of the few African leaders to leave office voluntarily. The new president announced no change from past policies as he sought to deal with the difficult economic problems facing his country.

Since 1979 poor weather conditions have caused agricultural problems for some parts of the country. In 1980 and 1981 Tanzania had to import food. The war with Uganda also proved a tremendous drain on funds. At an estimated cost of a million dollars a day, it crippled Tanzania's efforts to rebound from the economic slump of the latter 1970s. Tanzania's export earnings, moreover, have not kept pace with the country's import costs. Prices of Tanzania's major exports have not risen significantly, and production of sisal fell during the late 1970s.

Potentially significant changes in policy were announced in the 1980s to meet the worsening situation in food production. The amount of food crops purchased by the state marketing authority had steadily declined since 1978. So in May 1982, legislation was introduced to reestablish rural cooperatives as a means to stimulate production. In addition, a larger share of the development budget was allocated to agriculture. It is still too early to assess the long-term impact of these changes in policy.

Although the government has promoted self-reliance, Tanzania was one of the largest recipients of foreign aid in Africa. The 1980s have brought a lessening of such aid, further complicating the country's economic difficulties.

Retreat from Ujamaa

From the mid-1980s, Tanzania began to gradually move away from the political and economic structures established during the first twenty-five years of independence. This change was the result of external and internal pressures. Continued poor economic performance in both the agricultural and industrial sectors together with political mismanagement and corruption caused new President Mwinyi to examine alternative strategies. He was also faced with pressure for a change in economic policies from the International Monetary Fund (IMF) and the World Bank that was hard to resist, given the Tanzanian economy's dependence on external financial aid. Despite opposition from former President Nyerere, the government would begin, after 1986, to implement many of the structural adjustment policies advocated by the international donor organizations and nations. These included cutting government expenditure, devaluing the currency, cutting subsidies to parastatals, encouraging local and foreign investment, and encouraging private enterprise. The measures undertaken in pursuit of these policies, particularly the latter, moved Tanzania perceptibly away from socialism and self reliance. Although some progress had been accomplished by the early 1990s in reducing inflation and spurring the growth of gross domestic product, the Tanzanian economy approached the end of the century facing huge difficulties and an uncertain future.

Just as in the economic sphere, there has been gradual but very significant changes in Tanzanian politics. The period since 1990 has seen President Mwinyi more firmly establish his authority. Nyerere remained as chair of the CCM following his retirement from the presidency, but in 1990 he gave up that position. President Mwinyi was elected as party chair and thus gained greater influence in the party and government. His dominance was affirmed in the general and presidential elections of 1990. Nevertheless, the latter year marked the emergence of increasingly strong calls from within and outside Tanzania for an end to the one-party state and the adoption of what came to be known as multi-partyism. This demand was hardly unique to Tanzania as it was characteristic of changes occurring in many other African countries. As the debate spread among the public, former president Nyerere spoke out in favor of a consideration for multi-partyism. Following the appointment of a commission to study the issue in 1991, CCM endorsed the switch to political pluralism in February 1992. Legislation allowing the formation of opposition parties followed. CCM would no longer have the political field entirely to itself, but its control over the government and political patronage meant that it would remain in a strong position.

Foreign Affairs

Since independence Tanzania has sought to follow a policy of non-alignment. Nyerere charted a course between the Eastern and Western blocs, and his high principles and moral integrity won him respect from the leaders of both. Nyerere's principles are perhaps best seen in the context of the southern African problem. He stood for African majority rule in Zimbabwe, Mozambique, Angola, Namibia, and South Africa. Since the early 1960s Tanzania has been the headquarters for most of the liberation movements operating in southern Africa. The successful takeover by Frelimo in Mozambique owed much to Tanzania's support and sacrifices in the long war against Portugal. As head of the Front Line States giving support to the Patriotic Front in Zimbabwe and SWAPO in Namibia, Nyerere championed wars of liberation against racism and oppression. Yet he always stood for a respect for human rights and a nonracial policy as the only solution for southern Africa.

Within East Africa itself, the overthrow of President Milton Obote of Uganda in January 1971 created some difficult diplomatic problems for Tanzania. Nyerere refused to recognize the military regime of Idi Amin, and he gave Obote asylum in Tanzania. This led to tension between the two states. In late 1972 a force of pro-Obote exiles invaded Uganda from Tanzania. They were quickly defeated, and Amin launched air attacks on Tanzanian towns south of the border. This conflict finally ended with the help of mediation by the Somali Republic, but relations were never cordial. In late 1978 Amin's forces launched a brutal attack on Tanzanian territory west of Lake Victoria. Nyerere mobilized the Tanzanian armed forces, drove off the attackers, and invaded Uganda. The success of the

Tanzanian invasion caused Amin to flee and his regime to collapse, but it also proved costly to Tanzania.

Tanzanian soldiers remained in Uganda for some three years following Amin's downfall. Their presence was seen by some observers as being a key factor in Obote's return to power at the end of 1980. This certainly led to a great improvement in relations between the two countries, and eventually relations with Kenya, strained since the breakup of the East African Community in 1977, improved as well.

The 1980s found Tanzania and its leader still playing a leading role in African affairs. Indeed, President Nyerere had become, prior to his retirement from office, an eloquent and respected spokesman, not only for Africa, but for the Third World as a whole. The collapse of the Soviet Union at the start of the 1990s and the moves toward democratization in South Africa, on the other hand, had the effect of reducing Tanzania's impact and standing in international affairs.

Uganda

Uganda's history since independence has been characterized by far more political strife than that of the other East African nations. The problem of Buganda separatism remained at independence. Prime Minister Obote's attempts to conciliate Buganda and provide stability for the whole country by politics based on reconciliation leadership and brokerage between powerful local leaders proved futile. Obote fell back upon the army for support in crushing Buganda and making himself president under a new republican constitution. His attempts to unite the country and to shift to a system of mass mobilization politically through the introduction of a Common Man's Charter came to naught. Dependent upon, but unable to effectively control, the army, Obote was overthrown by the army commander, General Idi Amin.

Cooperation and Conflict with Buganda

Uganda's government at the time of independence in 1962 consisted of a coalition between Prime Minister Obote's UPC and the KY, representing the kabaka and Buganda traditionalists. Four cabinet posts were given to KY members of the National Assembly, and Buganda enjoyed federal status in the new state. Obote went further to conciliate the kingdom by taking a wife from Buganda and making the kabaka president when Uganda became a republic in 1963. Although the position of president was largely ceremonial and most executive powers remained with the prime minister and cabinet, the appointment of Mutesa as president of Uganda was a significant step. It marked the high point in UPC-KY cooperation.

Cooperation between the two parties was undoubtedly doomed to be of short duration, as there was just too much potential for discord. As it turned out, Obote and the UPC broke decisively with the Buganda authorities over the issue of the Lost Counties. The Bunyoro demand for the return of these territories, which had been added to Buganda at the turn of the century, had been voiced strongly at the end of the colonial era, but the British had deferred the matter for decision by referendum after independence. Kabaka Mutesa and the KY were opposed to the holding of any such vote, but Obote went ahead with the exercise in November 1964. Residents of the counties were given the choice of remaining under Buganda, returning to Bunyoro, or coming under the administration of the central government as a separate district; the largely Bunyoro electorate voted overwhelmingly in favor of a return to Bunyoro by 13,600 to 3,500 (only about 100 favored administration by the central government).

The kabaka and the traditionalists (usually referred to by Obote supporters as feudalists) who ruled Buganda were very unhappy with the outcome. Some 9,000 Ganda who had moved into the counties since 1962 had not been allowed to vote. The KY had already withdrawn from Obote's coalition government, and Mutesa now took court action to try to block the transfer of the counties to Bunyoro. Despite the withdrawal of KY support, Obote was not in a difficult position politically since a number of DP and KY members of Parliament had by the end of 1964 crossed the floor to join the UPC. Among those who crossed to the UPC was the DP parliamentary leader, Basil Batarangaya, subsequently to serve as a minister under Obote (at the end of 1964 the UPC had sixty-seven seats, KY fourteen and the DP ten).

One other event of the first years of independence deserves mention. This was the army mutiny of early 1964. This mutiny, like others in Kenya and Tanganyika, was inspired by demands for better pay and terms of service and for control by African officers. Unlike the other two countries, however, Uganda did not court martial and dismiss members of the army as a result. Their demands were largely met. One of those who benefited considerably by moving up rapidly in the command structure thereafter was Idi Amin, one of the first African officers.

Political Turmoil and the Kabaka's Downfall

Obote's strong political position at the end of 1964 was short-lived. He soon found himself not only faced with the intransigent hostility of Kabaka Mutesa and the Buganda government, but also threatened by a split within his party in which his leadership was challenged. The UPC was split over matters of policy, personality, and sectionalism. At the party's conference in 1964, John Kakonge, who was close to Obote, was defeated for the post of general secretary by a cabinet minister from Nkore, Grace Ibingira. Ibingira became a rallying figure for those, particularly from the south of Uganda, not altogether satisfied with Obote's leadership, and by the end of 1965 he had the support of about one-third of the cabinet.

In early 1966 Obote's leadership was presented with a severe challenge in the form of accusations of theft and corruption against the army's second-in-command, Idi Amin. These allegations, made in Parliament, also charged Obote and two other ministers with corruption relating to money, ivory, and gold that was obtained as a result of dealings with forces opposed to the central government of Zaire. A call for an investigation and Amin's suspension was passed by Parliament with only a single dissenting vote.

Obote was not in Kampala when the motion was debated and passed. Having assured himself of grass roots support in the north and, more importantly, of the backing of Amin and the army, Obote returned to the capital, and two weeks later at a cabinet meeting he arrested Ibingira and four other ministers. They were placed in detention without trial, and Obote announced that the constitution was suspended. The kabaka was accused of having sought help from a foreign power and was removed as president. Amin was promoted to army commander. Having dealt with his opponents, Obote completed what amounted to an official "coup" in April. He convened the National Assembly and produced a new republican constitution. Buganda lost its federal status and all its special privileges (e.g., the right to choose all members of Parliament from Buganda). An executive presidency with wide powers was established, and Obote assumed the position.

The Buganda Lukiko quickly met and rejected the new constitution. In May it passed a resolution calling upon the central government to withdraw from Buganda. Obote declared a state of emergency, and on May 24 he ordered the army under Amin to attack the kabaka's palace on Mengo Hill. Mutesa escaped, but Buganda's resistance was broken by force of arms. The kingdom was thereafter divided up into four districts. Buganda separatism had been crushed, but the price was heavy. Buganda's hatred of Obote and his government did not abate, and Obote was forced to rely on military power, rather than the popular will as expressed in elections, to stay in a dominant position.

Uganda's New Republic

In 1967 a new constitution was introduced by Obote. All four kingdoms were formally abolished. After some discussion the Uganda parliament agreed to the new constitution, which gave considerable powers to the president. He could even legislate without parliamentary consent in certain conditions.

Obote continued in power as president under the 1967 constitution. He had overwhelming support in Parliament (eighty-three seats to six for the DP in 1968), and the continuing state of emergency allowed for control of Buganda. The new constitution won support in Parliament, as it meant continuation of the salary and privileges of membership without the prospect of facing elections in the immediate future. Obote also enjoyed the backing of the army under Amin. Indeed, Professor Mazrui has described this period of Obote's rule as an alliance between the intelligentsia (i.e., well-educated politicians) and the army (mostly possessing little formal education).

Nevertheless, Obote evidently realized that he needed to buttress his position by appealing to the masses. In so doing, he obviously was influenced by the Arusha Declaration and the Tanzanian experience. It may well have been that Obote wished to shift to the politics of mass mobilization with an appeal to the rural masses. Whatever the reason, Obote attempted to move to the left in his policies beginning in 1969.

This move toward socialism was begun by the publication of the Common Man's Charter, a sort of Uganda Arusha Declaration. The charter however, was addressed more to the events of 1966, attacking tribalism and feudalism, than to socialism, about which the charter was rather vague. It promised an extension of a social security scheme and formation of new agricultural cooperatives, and made general reference to possible nationalization. At the UPC conference in December 1969, Obote attempted to gain support for his move to the left. Following a successful address to party delegates, he was wounded in an assassination attempt. Obote soon recovered, but the assassination attempt appears to have spurred him to move more quickly in implementing the Common Man's Charter while at the same time moving strongly against those perceived to be enemies. Under a state of emergency, many, including former DP leader Kiwanuka, were detained.

A series of measures were announced in the first half of 1970 which appeared to move Uganda to the left. All parties other than the UPC were banned, making Uganda in effect a one-party state. A complicated electoral system was put forward which had as its prime goals the promotion of national rather than tribal or sectional interests (a successful candidate would have to stand in constituencies outside his home area) and, just as important, the continuation of Obote in power. Uganda had not had a national election since 1962. Measures also were announced to hold down salary increases and financial benefits for civil servants. A somewhat controversial proposal required everyone to do a period of "national service" upon graduation from primary school unless they were proceeding to secondary school. Nationalization plans were announced on Labour Day (May 1). The state would assume 100 percent control of all import and export trade, and a majority share in banks, insurance companies, and the Kilembe copper mines. The full impact of these measures had not become apparent, however, by the time the Obote regime ended.

Obote's Fall and the Amin Dictatorship

Obote's fall from power and forced exile from Uganda had less to do with his move toward socialism than with his relations with the army. Dependent upon military force for his continued stay in power after 1966, Obote continued the military-intelligentsia alliance down to 1970, allowing continued privileges to accrue to the soldiers. No one benefited more than Idi Amin, who, though he had virtually no formal education, had risen from the rank of colonel to major general within three years and had been given virtual control of the country's armed forces. In this position Amin strengthened his hand by promoting officers friendly to him and recruiting mercenaries from former Anyanya guerillas in the southern Sudan. He also greatly overspent the military budget allotments. In late 1970 Obote did begin to move to establish control over the army, but it proved to be too late.

It is clear that Obote was concerned about military overspending and the growth of Amin's power. He demanded from Amin an accounting of funds spent by the army before he left to attend the Commonwealth Conference in Singapore in January 1971. Amin was also suspected of being responsible for the brutal murder of Brigadier Okoya, an officer who had been openly critical of Amin's conduct at the time of the 1969 attempt on Obote's life. It was to avoid possible prosecution and/or removal from his military position, as well as to gratify a taste for power and luxury, that Amin led a military takeover of the Uganda government while Obote was in Singapore.

Amin's takeover was greeted with happiness in many quarters, notably in Buganda. Political detainees, including Kiwanuka and Obote's former ministers, were released. The body of Kabaka Mutesa, who had died an exile in Britain, was returned to Uganda for burial. Amin promised an eventual return to civilian rule, but it is doubtful if he ever intended to relinquish power to an elected regime. Amin's first appointments showed a desire to place highly qualified persons in positions of responsibility, but he soon adopted a dictatorial style, taking the title Life President.

Amin's dictatorship combined brutal force, scapegoatism, and a public cult of personality that glorified the ruler. Amin's dictatorship was soaked in blood. Beginning with Obote's Langi people and the Acholi, who were very numerous in the army, Amin's regime killed thousands of Ugandans.

Intellectuals and politicians disappeared, victims of the notorious State Research Bureau, which had license to eliminate Amin's opponents. Among those who perished was Kiwanuka, who had been made chief justice by Amin. Near the end of his reign of terror Amin did not even shrink from ordering the murder of Uganda's Anglican Archbishop Luwum.

Amin's main scapegoats were the Israelis, whom he expelled from the country, and Uganda's Asian population. Amin was popular with many Arab leaders, such as Colonel Qaddafi of Libya, who saw the Uganda dictator as a fellow Muslim leader of an Islamic nation. These leaders helped Amin to obtain funds to prop up his regime, in which spending for the army and the benefit of the soldiers took precedence over any kind of development projects, which virtually ceased. The expulsion of all Asians, including Uganda citizens, in 1972 initially proved popular with Ugandans, but it contributed to the economic disasters that marked the years of Amin's rule. Exports declined and came almost to a halt, and essential commodities were in short supply. Although Amin declared an economic war and seized a number of foreign firms, Uganda's economy sunk from bad to worse.

Amin's attempts to turn the attention of Ugandans to a foreign enemy in late 1978 proved disastrous. His invasion of Tanzania was repulsed, and the Tanzanian army invaded Uganda itself. Amin's army proved virtually useless, he fled the country, and in April 1979 his murderous regime collapsed.

Post-Amin Uganda

In March 1979, shortly before the dictator's fall, various Uganda exiles had met in Moshi, Tanzania, to form a temporary administration to succeed Amin. Once Tanzanian forces had chased Amin and his army out of Uganda, a legislature was established, and Yusuf Lule, former head of Makerere College, assumed office as president.

The new government sought to restore order and stability to Uganda's troubled economy and administrative system. Political bickering and rivalry followed the establishment of the new administration, however. President Lule was forced out of office in June 1979 with the approval of the government of Tanzania, which kept a large number of troops in the country. Lule's replacement as president, Godfrey Binaisa, also enjoyed a short period in office as he was removed by the new Uganda army in May 1980. A Military Commission was established under the leadership of P. MuWanga, a strong supporter of former President Obote.

The Military Commission organized elections which were set for December 1980. Obote had by this time returned to Uganda to lead the UPC. The party's main opposition came from the reborn DP under P.

Ssemegomere. A third party in the field was the Uganda Patriotic Movement (UPM) led by the young radical Yoweri Museveni.

With MuWanga orchestrating the elections, the UPC won a majority of twenty seats in the new National Assembly, and Obote resumed the presidency. Obote also held the posts of minister of finance and minister of foreign affairs. MuWanga was made vice president and minister of defense. The DP and the UPM complained of electoral fraud, but with the election victory and the obvious support of the army, Obote had made an unprecedented political comeback.

His comeback did not bring a quick end to Uganda's problems. Huge inflation, shortages of domestic and imported goods, and insufficient exports set a daunting task for the new administration. With aid from the World Bank, the International Monetary Fund, and Western countries, some progress was made in attacking the country's economic ills during the second Obote presidency. Producer prices were raised as much as fivefold, and exports resumed. In 1981 and 1982, for example, Uganda met her quota for coffee exports. In the latter year, the Obote government allowed for maize exports to Tanzania.

Less progress was made in righting the country's political ills. Civil disorder was the order of the day since early 1981. Under Obote, as under the Amin dictatorship, detentions, torture, and killings characterized an essentially unstable and violent political situation. Claiming that Obote had rigged the elections, Museveni proclaimed a guerilla war of resistance to overthrow him by force. Museveni's National Resistance Army (NRA) was one of several groups using armed force to bring this about. The NRA gained support in Buganda, still hostile to Obote, Nkore, and other portions of the south of the country. The new Uganda army, made up of relatively untrained troops loyal to individual commanders of their own ethnic group, responded to anti-government violence with brutality of its own.

It was the army which brought an end to the second Obote presidency in August 1985. Unable to quell the NRA's anti-government campaign, the army began to split along ethnic lines into hostile factions. One ethnic leader, General Tito Okello, used the support of his fellow Acholi, the dominant group in the army, to force Obote into exile. This, however, did not bring an end to problems with the NRA. Despite Kenyan attempts to bring about peace, the NRA waged war on the Okello regime. In January 1986 the NRA defeated Okello's forces and drove him from Kampala. The NRA established a new government with Museveni as president. NRA forces gained control of other major towns in the following two months, but it would take much longer to establish the new government's authority in the rural areas, especially in the north.

Although new President Museveni proclaimed national reconciliation as one of his government's top priorities, various groups opposed his takeover, in many cases forcefully. Thus the government was engaged in various types of military and security operations aimed at dissident groups from 1987 through 1991. One of the most serious challenges to the NRA government came from the religious/political movement led by Alice Lakwena. Attracting strong support for her anti-government message, particularly from the most disadvantaged amongst the people in the north and east of the country (especially Acholi), Lakwena's protest movement was eventually crushed with the loss of several thousand lives. By the end of 1991, the government had solidified its control, and though violent dissident activity had not been completely eliminated, the security situation in the country as a whole was much improved from what it had been a decade earlier.

Upon assuming power, Museveni created a National Resistance Council, with both military and civilian membership, to serve as an advisory legislative body. He included in his cabinet members of diverse political parties and interest groups, but political party activity was prohibited as Museveni contended that the nation needed time for recovery from dictatorship and war before democratic elections could be held. While the return to democracy was initially set for the end of 1989, the government, prior to the end of that year, prolonged its term of office until 1995, stating that it needed more time to prepare a new constitution and organize elections. It continued to rule through the National Resistance Council, the institution of Resistance Committees organized from village to district level, and, most fundamentally, through the same military force that brought it to power. Thus while having contact with grass roots politics, the Museveni government, unlike Tanzania and Kenya in the early 1990s, resisted moves towards multi-party elections and increased democratization. For Uganda the early 1990s was thus characterized by a political structure that was hegemonic, authoritarian, and reflected a top-down approach to political control and mobilization.

In addition to serious security and political difficulties, Museveni faced daunting economic problems and prospects at the time of his take over. The economy had been devastated by the Amin years, and it had never really gotten back on its feet under the second Obote regime, despite assistance from the IMF and World Bank. The national economy was virtually bankrupt with inflation running at astronomically high levels, exports unable to generate sufficient revenue for national development, shortages of essential goods, empty shops, and a large share of government expenditure directed towards military purposes. In these circumstances, Museveni was forced, after 1987, to accept the structural adjustment policies advocated by the IMF in return for essential economic aid, abandoning many of his long held socialist principles in the process. Even with such international aid, economic recovery and reconstruction has been slow given the destructive policies of the past and the dependent nature of the economy itself. In the short term, inflation had been brought down by 1992, private foreign investment increased, tourism revived, food production improved, and consumer goods were more widely available than five years earlier. In the long term, however, Uganda's economy faces difficult prospects as the century draws to a close.

Foreign Affairs

In the first years of Uganda's independence, Obote was more concerned with domestic than international affairs (an exception was the situation in the Congo), but after the establishment of his republic in 1966-67, he became more active in African affairs. Although still tightly tied to Britain economically, Uganda became closely linked with Tanzania and Zambia on the issues of continued white rule in southern Africa and the Nigerian civil war. This was the result of Obote's intimate personal ties with Presidents Nyerere and Kaunda. Uganda played a leading part in attempting to find a settlement of the Nigerian conflict. Obote was increasingly outspoken in his criticism of British policy toward South Africa under Prime Minister Edward Heath. It was primarily to voice his concern over a British decision to sell arms to South Africa that he attended the Commonwealth Conference at Singapore. While there, he was, to the relief of some in Britain, overthrown.

Amin's first foreign policy pronouncements were highly neo-colonial. However, as he failed to obtain the money and arms he desired from Britain, he became radical in his statements. He strongly supported the Palestine Liberation Organization and the Arab states, especially Libya, and he vIrulently attacked Israel. The self-proclaimed field marshal also called for military action to overthrow racism in southern Africa. His continual mocking of British power proved popular in some quarters, but Britain and the United States eventually cut diplomatic ties with Amin's regime. He was able to obtain considerable supplies of military hardware from Russia, but Amin refused to toe the Soviet line in all foreign policy issues. Amin's greatest diplomatic triumph came with the holding of the Organization of African unity summit conference of 1975 in Kampala. Amin was elected chairman of the organization for the succeeding year despite the protests of Zambia and Tanzania.

Despite this diplomatic success, Amin's international standing was never very high because of the murderous nature of his regime. When faced with invasion in early 1979, his appeals to the OAU and the

United Nations drew no response. Only Colonel Qaddafi sent assistance to the beleaguered dictator, and it was not enough to prop up his regime.

With the inauguration of the second Obote presidency. Uganda, faced with immense economic and internal problems, kept a relatively low profile in foreign affairs. Museveni, on the other hand, sought to play a more active role in regional and continental affairs. In pursuit of this, he took a leading role in the OAU as well. Regionally, Museveni's Uganda has enjoyed good relations with Tanzania, but relations with Kenya and Rwanda, in particular, have often been strained. In the case of the latter Museveni's admiration for Libya and its leader, Gaddafi, caused Kenyan leaders concern, and since 1987 both nations have accused the other of harboring anti-government dissidents. The resulting tension never reached the level of hostility that characterized the period of the Amin dictatorship, however. In the case of Rwanda, the presence of a substantial number of Rwandan refugees in Uganda and an invasion launched from the latter in late 1990 caused tension with Uganda's southwestern neighbor as well. In the final analysis, however, domestic affairs have been, and will likely continue to be, the main interest of Uganda's rulers.

Kenya

Despite what some observers felt was a considerable potential for political turbulence and ethnic rivalry, Kenya experienced a relatively stable post-independence period characterized by impressive economic growth under the firm, charismatic leadership of Jomo Kenyatta. Even after Kenyatta's death, Kenya moved smoothly through the constitutionally prescribed transition to a new president.

In many ways, most particularly economically, Kenya maintained the closest ties of the East African nations with Britain. Kenya has been one of the largest recipients of British aid in Africa. The administrative system inherited from colonial rule has been retained with little change, except that it was manned by Africans. With considerable British aid, Kenya has been able to effect a smooth transfer of the white highlands to African farmers. This transfer, the successful Africanization of the public service, and the integration of schools and public facilities stands, when contrasted to the turmoil that has characterized southern Africa in the 1960s and 1970s, as one of independent Kenya's outstanding achievements.

KANU and the Unitary State

Kenya achieved independence with a constitution providing for a federal system, but the party in control of government, KANU, stood strongly for a unitary system. KADU leaders pressed for the continuation of federalism, and they commanded enough support in both houses of Parliament to block any constitutional amendments. As 1964 wore on, however, numerous KADU members of both houses crossed the floor to join the ruling party. By the end of the year KANU was in a position to shape a new republican constitution, and the KADU leadership in November voluntarily dissolved their party and joined KANU in the interest of national unity. A republican constitution which provided for a unitary state was inaugurated on the first anniversary of independence. Thus, Kenya became in effect a one-party state. The final vestige of federalism was scrapped in 1967 with the merging of the Senate into the House of Representatives to form a unicameral legislature. It has been usual to see the former KADU leaders coming into KANU as strengthening the moderates, such as Mboya, within the party.

Kenyatta was elected president of the new republic with considerable executive powers. Oginga Odinga, the Luo leader, was chosen vice president. Long a rival of Mboya, Odinga had established himself as the leading spokesman of those within the party who favored a more radical and socialist policy for Kenya. One of the KADU leaders, Daniel arap Moi, was brought into the cabinet as minister of home affairs. Mboya was placed in charge of economic planning.

The moderate emphasis of the Kenyatta government became clear in 1964 and subsequently. Little departure was made from the administrative structure left behind by the British other than to put Africans into key positions. KANU was largely disdained as a vehicle for mobilization and control, and the provincial administration was used instead. In 1965 the government published its economic blueprint under the name African Socialism. The policy outlined was quite moderate, reflecting the thinking of Mboya and Mwai Kibaki, later to become minister of finance. State ownership and control was not emphasized to the exclusion of private enterprise and investment. Foreign investment was encouraged. Kenya's definition of African Socialism has in practice been very different from that of Tanzania, as many elements of capitalism have continued to play a large role in the Kenya economy. The policy was favored by the emerging African middle class, a group consisting of the land owners (whom colonial land consolidation and agricultural practices helped to create), businessmen, and entrepreneurs. The middle class grew in strength and influence during the 1960s and 1970s.

Political problems, constitution making, and economic policies were not the only concerns of the new Kenya government. By far the most serious threat to the stability of the new nation came from the guerilla war waged by Somali dissidents in the Northeastern Province. The population of the province was almost entirely made up of Somalis, a considerable number of whom favored seccession from Kenya and union with the Somali Republic. The Kenyatta government refused to countenance such a loss of territory, and shortly after independence Somalis inside and outside the province launched attacks on government installations and servants there. These guerillas, called shifta (bandits) by the Kenya authorities, were actively supported by the neighboring state. A large portion of Kenya's armed forces was involved in military action in the dry and barren northeast of the country until a peace agreement was finally worked out with the Somali Republic in 1967. The province would remain part of Kenya.

What could have been a severe problem involving the European settlers and the white highlands was largely avoided through assistance from Britain. Kenyatta urged all residents of Kenya to forget the past and work together; his own willingness to forget the harsh treatment he had received at the hands of the Europeans provided an example. He made *Harambee* (let us pull together) the national motto, encouraging hard work and national unity. Britain provided funds to buy out the farms of settlers who wished to leave after independence so that the land could be broken into smaller portions and provided for Africans as a way to address the strong hunger for additional land felt by the African population. The process was gradual, but over the first decade and a half of independence, some two million acres had been resettled. Loan funds also were made available to Africans who wished to purchase European farms intact. Initially advanced to Kenya in the form of loans, the millions of pounds made available by Britain to enable the purchase of settler farms and estates had by the end of the 1970s largely been written off. The majority of settlers left Kenya after independence, but a number, such as Sir Michael Blundell and Lord Delamere (son of the former political leader), became Kenya citizens and continued to play a role in the country's agriculture and industry.

Likewise, the Asian population of Kenya continued to play an even more sizeable role in Kenya's economy after independence. Many, however, were caught on the horns of a dilemma over citizenship. A good number, probably a majority, of Asians opted for British citizenship. Kenya introduced new immigration and work permit rules in 1967 which were designed to speed up Africanization of the public and private sectors of the economy. This led to non-citizen Asians being refused work and trading permits. Many Asians therefore wished to go to Britain, but they found the British government not eager to receive them. Stricter controls on entry into Britain were introduced, and many Asians were caught in a sort of a vice. Those who chose Kenya citizenship have not suffered any open discrimination. Although Africans have moved into wholesale distribution, Asians continue to play a large role in retail trade and in manufacturing.

Two-Party Politics: the KPU

Though KANU was Kenya's only political party after 1964, divisions within the party eventually led to a split in the ranks. The leading figure in the split was Oginga Odinga, vice president of Kenya, who held the same position in KANU. Odinga stood for a more socialist orientation for Kenya economically and for closer ties with the socialist bloc. This was not the view of the president and a majority of the cabinet, and Odinga was increasingly left out of the limelight in public affairs. Added to this was continued political rivalry between himself and Mboya. Odinga's unhappiness culminated in March 1966 at the KANU party conference when the KANU constitution was changed to do away with the position of vice president. Instead, a vice president would be chosen from each of Kenya's provinces; Odinga was not elected to any of those positions. In mid-April Odinga resigned as Kenya's vice president and from KANU, complaining that the government's guiding star had become personal gain, not the welfare of the masses. Less than two weeks later, he announced the formation of a new party, the Kenya Peoples Union (KPU).

Other KANU members resigned to join Odinga's KPU, including a cabinet minister and two assistant ministers. Most who joined the KPU were drawn by ethnic solidarity (i.e., they were Luos) or because they agreed with Odinga's contention that the government was ignoring the masses and favoring the rich. In all, twenty-nine representatives and senators resigned from KANU to join KPU. The government, with Mboya taking a leading role, responded by passing, a constitutional amendment which required those who changed their party allegiance to resign from Parliament and seek a new mandate from the electorate. This amendment led to the Little General Election of 1966.

The government used its considerable resources and influence to ensure KANU success, and in the end the KPU drew the bulk of its support from the Luo-inhabited districts. Though Odinga was returned with a comfortable margin, only three seats (of nine) were won by KPU outside the Luo areas. Although Odinga claimed to have great support from the poor masses, the elections left KPU in a relatively weak position. It could also be contended that the KPU was the party of a single ethnic group. In reality, however, Odinga and the KPU did not enjoy the full support of the Luo community. Kenya's second largest ethnic group split between those loyal to Odinga and the supporters of Mboya who remained with KANU. One other important consequence of the formation of the KPU and the resignation of Odinga was the appointment of Moi, former chairman of KADU and a member of the Kalenjin in ethnic group, as vice president. He succeeded to the post in 1967, and he combined the position with that of minister of home affairs for the next eleven years.

The KANU government maintained its dominance over the next few years. Any threats to its position were dealt with by a combination of political maneuvering and the use of the powers of the administrative apparatus. Means were found, for example, of disqualifying all KPU candidates for municipal elections in 1968 because of the improper completion of nomination papers. The assassination of Tom Mboya in July 1969, however, aroused strong feelings. Mboya's death led to uncertainty in many quarters, especially among Luos. Disturbances which left several people dead occurred when President Kenyatta came to open a new hospital at Kisumu, in the heart of Luo-inhabited territory, in October 1969. Almost immediately thereafter, Odinga and other KPU leaders were taken into preventive detention and the party was banned. Odinga remained in detention without trial until 1971.

The government combined suppression of the KPU with an exercise in popular democracy. Following the arrest of the KPU leaders, elections were set for December. Only one party was allowed, and of course no KPU members could stand. Nevertheless, the elections were freely carried out, with numerous candidates for almost every seat. President Kenyatta was returned to power unopposed, but two-thirds of the sitting members, including several ministers, were thrown out by the electorate.

Kenya in the 1970s

Kenya politics in the 1970s was dominated by a single party, though Kenya was not a one-party state by law. President Kenyatta continued to be the dominant political force, but advancing age kept him from taking an active part in day-to-day politics. He more than ever became a "patriarchal" leader or father figure for the nation. Known to Kenyans as *mzee* (old man), he normally intervened in politics when his ministerial colleagues proved unequal to a crisis or when some politicians were quarrelling among themselves. As the years went by, criticism was not normally directed at him.

The question of succession to Kenyatta took on increasing interest in the 1970s, culminating in 1976 with a suggestion, supported by several influential ministers and politicians, that the constitution should be amended to bar the vice president from succeeding on the death of the president. This was interpreted as an attempt to keep Moi from becoming the chief executive and as reflecting conflicting political ambitions within the ruling party. The president and the attorney general, Charles Njonjo, eventually intervened to force the proposal to be dropped.

As the 1970s began, Kenya's economy continued to expand and production levels of most crops rose. Tea and sugar production increased greatly. Coffee production also expanded, and the crop remained the country's leading export. Once very much the monopoly of the settlers, coffee was now grown in greater quantity on small African holdings than on large estates. By the 1970s the introduction of individual ownership and title deeds had made great changes in land tenure in most parts of the country. Tourism was increasingly exploited as a source of revenue in the 1960s and 1970s. Many new hotels were built, and tourism grew to become second only to coffee as the country's leading foreign exchange earner.

Like agriculture, industry in Kenya presents a picture of a mixed economy. Government, cooperatives, and private enterprise all have a place. A large proportion of cash crops are marketed through cooperative societies, which greatly increased in numbers after independence. Commerce and industry are largely in private hands. Taking advantage of the head start gained during the colonial period in industrial plant, financial institutions, and transportation, Kenya's industry has continued to lead East Africa. Many multinational companies have constructed plants and begun operations in Kenya. The government of Kenya takes shares in most such enterprises, but management normally remains in non-African hands.

While the 1960s had witnessed satisfactory economic growth, this slowed somewhat in the 1970s. A variety of factors, including poor harvests, falling world prices, and the tremendous rise in petroleum prices, slowed the rate of economic growth and development. Only the boom in coffee prices in 1976-77 proved an exception to this trend. As in the 1960s, Kenya's extremely high birthrate negated to some degree the strides made in development.

Not all districts in Kenya have benefited from agricultural and industrial development to the same degree. The northern, primarily pastoral Nilotic and Cushitic-speaking peoples have, for example, been little touched by development schemes. Even within the most highly developed agricultural districts, distinctions based on wealth have continued and indeed enlarged. Government development policy has tended to focus on the successful yeOman farmer rather than on the subsistence cultivator. This has tended to perpetuate and promote class divisions in some rural areas.

One result of Kenya's economic policies has thus been the emergence of an economic elite in both the rural and urban areas. The urban elite is undoubtedly the most influential group in the country. Owning much land in rural and urban areas, this group is Western educated and very powerful in the government bureaucracy. Moreover, it has been the government's policy in Kenya, unlike in Tanzania, to allow civil servants to engage in business in addition to their government responsibilities.

Despite a diversification of markets, Kenya has continued to maintain close economic ties with Britain. Britain is Kenya's major export market and the country from which the most imports come. Britain is also a major source of foreign aid; many have seen in this close relationship a neocolonial situation. In this view, Britain and British companies have continued to wield great influence in Kenya to the detriment of the latter. Whether the link with Britain and her allies is regarded in a negative or positive light often depends on the political persuasion of the observer.

The political situation in the early 1970s was not marked by interparty rivalry. The 1974 elections provided a continuation of the situation observed at the previous polls. A substantial number of candidates sought the mandate of the voters to enter Parliament. Only Odinga and most other former KPU members were banned from standing by KANU. Once again a sizable portion of the sitting members were turned out by the electorate. Personalities and the perception of which individuals might best promote development in the areas they sought to represent seem to have counted most heavily with the electorate.

After 1974, the political scene was clouded with some uncertainty and what was perceived by some observers as a tightening of government control. Unease was expressed at alleged Kikuyu domination in government, the prominence of a relatively small, wealthy elite in places of power, and the expansion of corruption. In this atmosphere one of the leading critics of government policy, J. M. Kariuki, was murdered in 1975. It was widely believed that some government leaders were implicated in the killing, and the government blocked an effective investigation of Kariuki's murder by Parliament. In subsequent years, a number of members of Parliament who criticized the government were placed in detention by order of the president. This had the effect of quietening dissent.

The death of President Kenyatta in August 1978 brought some significant changes in the political atmosphere. Despite many dire predictions by foreign observers, Vice President Moi smoothly assumed the reins of power. Although he maintained that he was following the *nyayo* (footsteps) of the deceased leader, the new president relaxed the political atmosphere considerably by releasing all political detainees and taking steps to stamp out corruption. These and other moves made President Moi exceedingly popular with the Kenya public.

275

The Moi Presidency

President Moi was elected unopposed for a full term in late 1979 at the same time as a new Parliament was chosen. These elections were notable, among other things, for the election of a European and an Asian candidate to seats previously held by Africans for the first time in independent Kenya. Mwai Kibaki, a Kikuyu, was appointed vice president while continuing as minister of finance.

Moi's years in office have not been easy ones for Kenya economically. Export earnings have not expanded as rapidly as in earlier years, and petroleum imports have caused a serious drain on foreign exchange. Kenya entered the 1980s facing shortages of some foodstuffs, thanks to poor harvests and unwise planning. Severe drought compounded these problems in 1983 and 1984, forcing Kenya to import food.

Economic difficulties combined with allegations of corruption and disputes involving leading political personalities, notably between Kibaki and Njonjo, who had in 1980 resigned as attorney general to enter the cabinet as an elected MP, led to growing criticism and uncertainty in the country. The government's agreement to grant military facilities in the country to the United States was unpopular in some quarters. Moi's administration responded in the first half of 1982 with measures directed at strengthening its position and silencing dissent. Parliament passed legislation making Kenya a one-party state. Odinga, previously welcomed back into the fold by Moi, was now expelled by KANU, and a number of politicians and academics regarded as being sympathetic to Marxist ideas were detained without trial.

In this atmosphere of rising political tension, Air Force personnel attempted to stage a coup d'etat on August 1, 1982. With the support of some university students, they seized, for a time, control of the Voice of Kenya (the government-owned broadcasting center), Nairobi airport, and the city's main post office. Corruption and restrictions on freedom were given as reasons for seeking the forceful overthrow of the government, but the Kenya army soon crushed the attempted coup. Some 150 lost their lives, and looting caused extensive property damage in Nairobi. The Air Force was disbanded and hundreds of enlisted men jailed, while the University of Nairobi was shut for an extended period. President Moi thus resolutely restored order and sought to buttress his authority by isolating those about whose loyalty he felt doubtful. One prominent figure who fell into this category was Charles Njonjo. Njonjo was dropped from the cabinet in May 1983, and he resigned his seat in parliament the following month. Widely attacked as a political traitor, Njonjo had his affairs subjected to a judicial enquiry on the orders of the president that lasted through most of 1984. The enquiry produced evidence of illegal actions. Njonjo was eventually pardoned by the president, but his political influence seemed at an end.

In addition to isolating Njonjo, Moi called fresh elections to validate his leadership. He and Kibaki were returned to office, but about 40 percent of the members of Parliament, including five ministers, lost their seats. Only about 48 percent of the electorate voted in the September 1983 election, some 20 percent less than in 1979. President Moi was left in a somewhat stronger position, and over the next five years he launched several initiatives aimed at broadening and solidifying his control over Kenya's political structure by greatly expanding the powers of the executive branch. Constitutional amendments were enacted to remove security of tenure for the attorney general, the controller and auditor- general, high court judges, and the chair of the Public Service Commission thus giving the president the right to dismiss those holding these offices at will. For the 1988 elections, legislation was introduced to provide for queue voting in the one party elections. This provided for an initial stage in the electoral process where supporters would queue behind a photo of their favored candidate in open meetings, and it was strongly advocated by Moi and other KANU leaders as being more "democratic" than the secret ballot. Those who received 70 per cent of the vote at the queue stage would be declared elected to parliament without having to participate in the secret ballot contest. This system was first used for the parliamentary elections of March 1988 which were marked, as even President Moi was later to admit, by massive electoral fraud and rigging of results.

These innovations had the effect of greatly expanding the power of the executive at the expense of the legislative and judicial branches of government. While overwhelmingly approved by the single party parliament, they did provoke opposition. The constitutional and electoral changes were forcefully criticized by clergymen, most notably several Anglican bishops, and by the Law Society of Kenya. Clandestine dissidence in the shape of the "Mwakenya" movement emerged in the mid-1980s; several individuals were sentenced to terms of imprisonment for membership in this organization which was said to advocate the violent overthrow of the government. From 1987 the government was faced with increasing international criticism of its human rights record, particularly with regard to a lack of democracy, detention without trial, and torture by police and security forces. Deteriorating economic conditions in the second half of the decade provided another reason for internal discontent.

Until the end of 1989, the position of KANU and Moi appeared unchallengeable. Following the 1988 elections, Kibaki was dropped as vice president though he remained in the cabinet while others previously

277

politically prominent, such as Kenneth Matiba, were dropped from the cabinet and booted out of the party. Nevertheless, 1989-90 witnessed a rising tide of discontent with the authoritarian nature of the Moi regime. Most prominent was the demand for political pluralism or an end to the one-party state. This was voiced by church leaders, politicians such as Matiba and Charles Rubia, and increasingly by the Kenyan public. The detention of Matiba and Rubia did little to quell the demands for multi-partyism; political protest combined with heightening economic difficulties to cause the July 1990 riots in Nairobi. The February 1990 murder of Kenya's Foreign Minister, Robert Ouko, and the government's inability to arrest those responsible further eroded the regime's credibility with the public. With increased international pressure for political reform also playing a part, the government was forced to alter some of the changes made in the 1980s. At the end of 1990 it was agreed to drop queue voting and return to the original system of secret ballot elections and to restore security of tenure to those offices from which it had been previously removed.

These changes did little to quiet the increasing demand for a greater measure of democracy. At the top of the list of demands to promote the latter was an end to the one-party state. Growing internal discontent combined with increasing pressure for political pluralism from Kenya's major international donors to force the Moi regime to accede to the demands for the legalization of additional political parties at the end of 1991. This was followed by the formation of several opposition parties, most notably the Forum for the Restoration of Democracy (FORD) and the Democratic Party (DP). The latter was launched by Kibaki following his resignation from KANU in December 1991. The year of 1992 thus witnessed a multi-party era as several political groupings prepared for presidential and parliamentary elections which were held in December 1992. Prior to the poll, however, FORD split into two parties, FORD-Asili led by Matiba and FORD-Kenya led by Odinga. Moi thus faced three major, and several minor, rivals in the presidential elections, and he emerged victorious, despite receiving slightly more that 36% of the total votes cast. KANU also won a majority in the new parliament over the divided opposition parties.

Foreign Affairs

Following the achievement of independence, Kenya officially followed a neutralist or non-aligned policy. In practice, Kenya has followed a pro-Western orientation in her foreign policy. Kenya has maintained close ties with Britain and, increasingly in the 1970s and 1980s, with the United States, and those countries have been the source of the bulk of Kenya's foreign aid and military hardware. Relations with the Soviet

Union have generally been correct but cool since the mid-1960s, the Russians were suspected in some quarters of providing backing to Odinga and the KPU. In general, Kenya did not follow a very activist foreign policy. During the time of his presidency, Jomo Kenyatta seldom left Kenya on trips related to foreign affairs.

Perhaps the most important factor in Kenya foreign affairs in the 1960s was the shifta war in the northeastern part of the country. Seeking allies in the struggle against the Somali-backed rebels, Kenya was drawn naturally to Ethiopia, another country against which the Somali Republic entertained territorial claims. Close ties were forged between the two nations, and these have survived the fall of the imperial regime in Ethiopia and its replacement by a radical Marxist one in the 1970s. Despite widely differing ideologies, Kenya and Ethiopia have remained closely allied in opposition to Somali claims on their territories. The shifta conflict was finally brought to an end in 1967 thanks to the mediation of other African leaders, notably President Kaunda of Zambia. Kenya nevertheless has remained suspicious of Somali ambitions on her territory.

In the 1960s and 1970s Kenya played a low-key role in African affairs compared to Tanzania and Uganda. On those occasions when President Kenyatta became involved in attempts to solve African problems and conflicts, such as the Congo civil war in 1964 and the Angolan civil war in 1976, Kenya's mediation did not prove successful. Although sharing a similar history of white domination with Zimbabwe and Namibia, Kenya was not in the forefront as a member of the frontline states.

By the middle of the 1970s, moreover, Kenya seemed considerably isolated in East Africa. Relations with the Somali Republic have never been cordial, and after 1975 relations with the Amin regime soured considerably. President Amin made claims on western Kenya, and the Israeli planes which carried out the rescue of hostages at Entebbe in mid-1976 were allowed to stop in Nairobi. The breakup of the East African Community soured relations with Tanzania, which closed its border with Kenya. This isolation, however, has given way to better understanding in the 1980s. The fall of Amin played a part in this, and President Moi has been able to establish much more harmonious relations with his neighbors than at any time in the 1970s. The late 1983 agreement to reopen the Tanzania-Kenya border and establish formal diplomatic relations between the countries stands testimony to this fact.

Under Moi's presidency Kenya has taken a much larger role in African and world affairs. He has attempted to travel widely abroad, making known Kenya's position on issues of continental and global importance. He has spoken out particularly on the southern African situation. In

1981 he was chosen chairman of the Organization of African Unity following Kenya's hosting of the annual meeting.

The 1980s also witnessed Moi's government taking an increasingly pro-Western line in foreign relations, as Kenya looked more and more to the United States, rather than Britain, for military and financial aid. Kenya joined the American-led boycott of the 1980 Moscow Olympics, and the United States was granted military facilities, notably at Mombasa. It is probably not too much to say that Kenya was the least nonaligned of the three East African countries in the early 1980s. Kenya's close ties with such powers as the United States were increasingly strained, on the other hand in the late 1980s and early 1990s. The cold war had ended, and criticism of Kenya's political system and human rights record led to a deterioration in relations.

In the years since independence the East African countries moved in different directions to address the political and economic problems they faced at the time of the formal break with British rule. In a sense, however, none of them has been able to break really decisively with a colonial legacy which left them very much dependent on the developed world. Tanzania has departed most from her colonial past and Kenya the least, but both have been forced to live with the difficulty of altering effectively the economic patterns created by some six decades of colonial rule. External markets and sources of development aid remained powerful factors in determining their destiny. Kenya and Tanzania developed one-party political systems of different types. But both nations experienced relative political stability thanks to the leadership of their widely respected first presidents, Jomo Kenyatta and Julius Nyerere. In their different ways these two men, and especially Nyerere, put their stamp on their nations after independence. Each nation developed a measure of unity admirable by African standards as well as a reasonably viable political culture.

Uganda's post-independence history presents, by contrast, a picture of political turmoil growing out of the problems of the colonial era, notably Buganda's separatism, religious rivalry in politics, and the Lost Counties. The political expediency of the early 1960s which brought the UPC and KY together was short-lived and ineffective. As might have been expected, such expediency, which marked, in Dr. Karugire's words, "a triumph of hope over experience," proved painfully unequal to the challenges of nationhood. Uganda has still to establish a viable political culture and unity of the sort that has come to typify Kenya and Tanzania. Although at the time of independence Uganda's economy was the strongest and best balanced between agriculture and industry of the East African nations, subsequent events have shattered it. Still, the potential for economic viability remains if a popularly accepted government is able to establish order.

Suggestions for Further Reading

Coulson, Andrew. *Tanzania: A Political Economy* (Oxford, 1982).

Gertzel, Cherry J. *The Politics of Independent Kenya* (Nairobi, 1970).

Karugire, S. R. *A Political History of Uganda* (Nairobi, 1980).

Kitching, Gavin. *Class and Economic Change in Kenya* (New Haven, 1980).

Kyemba, Henry. *State of Blood* (London, 1977).

Leys, Colin. *Underdevelopment in Kenya* (Nairobi, 1974).

Mazrui, Ali. *Soldiers and Kinsmen in Uganda* (Beverly Hills, 1975).

Pratt, Cranford. *The Critical Phase in Tanzania* (Cambridge, 1976).

Selected Bibliography

Alpers, Edward. *Ivory and Slaves: Changing Pattern of International Trade in East Central Africa to the Later Nineteenth Century.* London, 1975.

Apter, David E. *The Political Kingdom in Uganda.* London, 1961.

Atieno-Odhiambo, E. A. *Siasa: Politics and Nationalism in East Africa, 1905-1939.* Nairobi, 1981.

Barnett, D. L., and Njama, Karari. *Mau Mau From Within.* London, 1966.

Bates, Robert. *Beyond the Miracle of the Market.* Cambridge, 1989.

Beattie, J. H. M. *Bunyoro: An African Kingdom.* New York, 1960.

Bennett, George. *Kenya: A Political History.* Nairobi, 1963.

Berman, Bruce. *Control and Crisis in Colonial Kenya.* London, 1991.

Berman, Bruce and John Lonsdale. *Unhappy Valley.* London, 1992.

Bishop, W. W., and Clark, J. D., eds. *Background to Evolution in Africa.* Chicago, 1967.

Brett, E. A. *Colonialism and Underdevelopment in East Africa.* London, 1973.

Buell, Leslie. *The Native Problem in Africa.* 2 vols. New York, 1928.

Bunker, Stephen G. *Peasants Against the State.* Urbana and Chicago, 1987.

Chittick, H. N., and Rotberg, Robert I., eds. *East Africa and the Orient.* New York, 1975.

Clark, J. D. *The Prehistory of Africa.* London, 1970.

Clayton, Anthony, and Savage, Donald. *Government and Labour in Kenya, 1895-1963.* London, 1974.

Cliffe, Lionel, and Saul, John, eds. *Socialism in Tanzania.* Dar es Salaam, 1973.

Clough, Marshall S. *Fighting Two Sides: Kenyan Chiefs and Politicans, 1895-1949.* Niwot, Col., 1990.

Cohen, D. W. and E. S. Atieno Odhiambo. *Siaya.* London, 1989.

Cohen, D. W. *The Historical Tradition of Busoga, Mukama and Kintu.* Oxford, 1972.

Cole, S. *The Prehistory of East Africa.* London, 1963.

Cooper, Frederick. *From Slaves to Squatters.* New Haven, 1980.

———. *Plantation Slavery on the East Coast of Africa.* New Haven, 1977.

Coulson, Andrew. *Tanzania: A Political Economy.* Oxford, 1982.

Dilley, M. R. *British Policy in Kenya Colony.* 2nd ed. London, 1966.

Dunbar, A. R. *A History of Bunyoro-Kitara.* Nairobi, 1965.

Ehret, Christopher. *Ethiopians and East Africans.* Nairobi, 1974.

———. *Southern Nilotic History.* Evanston, 1971.

Ehret, Christopher, and Posnansky, Merrick, eds. *The Archaeological and Linguistic Reconstruction of African History.* Berkeley, 1982.

Eliot, Sir Charles. *The East Africa Protectorate.* London, 1905.

Elkan, Walter. *The Economic Development of Uganda.* London, 1961.

———. *Migrants and Proletarians: Urban Labour in the Economic Development of Uganda.* London, 1961.

Fallers, L. A. *Bantu Bureaucracy.* Cambridge, 1956.

Fearn, Hugh. *An African Economy.* London, 1961.

Feierman, Steven. *The Shambaa Kingdom.* Madison, 1974.

Ford, V. C. R. *The Trade of Lake Victoria.* Kampala, 1955.

Freeman-Grenville, G. S. P. *The East African Coast: Select Documents From the First to the Earlier Nineteenth Century.* Oxford, 1962.

Freund, Bill. *The Making of Contemporary Africa.* Bloomington, 1984.

Furedi, Frank. *The Mau Mau War in Perspective.* London, 1990.

Galbraith, John S. *Mackinnon and East Africa, 1878-1895: A Study in the 'New Imperialism.'* Cambridge, 1972.

Garlake, P. S. *The Early Islamic Architecture of the East African Coast.* Natrobi, 1966.

Gertzel, C. J. *The Politics of Independent Kenya.* Nairobi, 1970.

Goldsworthy, David. *Tom Mboya: The Man Kenya Wanted to Forget.* Nairobi, 1982.

Gray, Richard, ed. *Cambridge History of Africa.* Vol. 4. Cambridge, 1977.

Gray, Sir John. *History of Zanzibar for the Middle Ages to 1856.* London, 1962.

Greenberg, Joseph H. *The Languages of Africa.* The Hague, 1963.

Hansen, Holger Bernt and Michael Twaddle, eds. *Uganda Now.* London, 1988.

Harlow, V. C., and Chilver, E. M., eds. *History of East Africa.* Vol.2. Oxford, 1965.

Hill, M. F. *Permanent Way*. Nairobi, 1961.

Hollingsworth, L. W. *Zanzibar Under the Foreign Office, 1890-1913*. London, 1953.

Huxley, Elspeth, and Perham, Margery. *Race and Politics in Kenya*. 2nd ed. London, 1956.

Huxley, Elspeth. *White Man's Country*. 2 vols. New York, 1968.

Iliffe, John. *A Modern History of Tanganika*. Cambridge, 1979.

———. *Tanganyika Under German Rule, 1905-1912*. Nairobi, 1969.

Ingham, Kenneth. *A History of East Africa*. London, 1962.

———. *The Making of Modern Uganda*. London, 1958.

Jackson, Sir Frederick. *Early Days in East Africa*. London,1930.

Johnston, H. H. *The Uganda Protectorate*. 2 vols. London, 1902.

Jorgenson, Jan J. *Uganda: A Modern History*. London, 1981.

Kaggia, Bildad. *The Roots of Freedom*. Nairobi, 1975.

Kaniki, Martin, ed. *Tanzania Under Colonial Rule*. London, 1980.

Kanogo, Tabitha. *Squatters and the Roots of Mau Mau, 1905-63*. London, 1987.

Karugire, S. R. *A History of the Kingdom of Nkore in Western Uganda to 1896*. Oxford, 1971.

———. *A Political History of Uganda*. Nairobi, 1980.

Kenyatta, Jomo. *Facing Mount Kenya*. London, 1938.

Ki-Zerbo, J., ed. *General History of Africa*. Vol. 1. Berkeley, 1981.

Kimambo, I. N. *A Political History of the Pare*. Nairobi, 1969.

Kimambo, I. N., and Temu, A. J., eds. *A History of Tanzania*. Nairobi, 1969.

Kimambo, Isaria N. *Penetration and Protest in Tanzania: The Impact of the World Economy on the Pare, 1860-1960*. London, 1991.

Kirkman, J. S. *Men and Monuments on the East African Coast*. London, 1964.

Kitching, Gavin. *Class and Economic Change in Kenya*. New Haven, 1980.

Kiwanuka, S. S. *A History of Buganda From the Foundation of the Kingdom to 1900*. London, 1971.

Kyemba, H. *State of Blood*. London, 1977.

Lamb, Geoff. *Peasant Politics*. London, 1974.

Lamphear, John. *The Traditional History of the Jie*. Oxford, 1976.

Leakey, Richard, and Lewin, Roger. *Origins*. New York, 1977.

Leys, Colin. *Underdevelopment in Kenya.* London, 1975.

Leys, Norman. *Kenya.* 4th ed. London, 1968.

Lofchie, M. *Zanzibar: Background to Revolution.* Princeton, 1965.

Low, D. A. *Buganda in Modern History.* Berkeley, 1971.

————. *Religion and Society in Buganda, 1875-1900.* Kampala, 1957.

Low, D. A., and Pratt, R. C. *Buganda and British Overrule, 1900-1953.* London, 1960.

Low, D. A., and Smith, A., eds. *History of East Africa.* Vol.3. Oxford, 1976.

Mair, L. P. *Primitive Government.* London, 1962.

Mamdami, Mahmood. *Imperialism and Fascism in Uganda.* Nairobi, 1983.

————. *Politics and Class Formation in Uganda.* London, 1976.

Martin, David. *General Amin.* London, 1974.

Matson, A. T. *Nandi Resistance to British Rule, 1890-1906.* Nairobi, 1972.

Maxon, R. M. *John Ainsworth and the Making of Kenya.* Washington, 1980.

Maxon, Robert M. *Conflict and Accommodation in Western Kenya, the Gusii and the British, 1907-1963.* London, 1989.

Maxon, Robert M., *Struggle for Kenya: The Loss and Reassertion of Imperial Initiative.* London, 1993.

————. *Struggle for Kenya: the Loss and Reassertion of Imperial Initiative.* London, 1993.

Mazrui, Ali. *Soldiers and Kinsmen in Uganda.* Beverly Hills, 1975.

Middleton, John. *The Kikuyu and Kamba of Kenya.* London, 1953.

Mitchell, P. *African Afterthoughts.* London, 1954.

Morton, Fred. *Children of Ham.* Boulder, 1990.

Moyse-Bartlett, H. *The King's African Rifles.* Aldershot, 1956.

Mungeam, G. H. *British Rule in Kenya, 1895-1912.* Oxford, 1966.

Munro, J. Forbes. *Colonial Rule and the Kamba.* Oxford, 1975.

Muriuki, Godfrey. *A History of the Kikuyu, 1500-1900.* Nairobi, 1974.

Murray-Brown, Jeremy. *Kenyatta.* London, 1972.

Mwaniki, H. S. K. *The Living History of Embu and Mbeere.* Nairobi, 1985.

Mwansasu, Bismarck, and Pratt, Cranford, eds. *Towards Socialism in Tanzania.* Dar es Salaam, 1979.

Niane, D. T., ed. *General History of Africa.* Vol. 4. Berkeley, 1984.

Nottingham, John, and Rosberg, Carl. *The Myth of Mau Mau: Nationalism in Kenya.* New York, 1966.

Nurse, Derrick, and Spear, Thomas. *The Swahili.* Philadelphia, 1985.

Nyakatura, J. W. *The Anatomy of an African Kingdom.* New York, 1973

Nyerere, Julius. *Freedom and Unity.* Oxford, 1967.

———. *Freedom and Socialism.* Oxford, 1968.

Ochieng', W. R. *A Pre-Colonial History of the Gusii of Western Kenya, C. A. D. 1500-1914.* Nairobi, 1974.

Ochieng', W. R., ed. *A Modern History of Kenya.* Nairobi, 1989.

Ochieng', William R. and Robert M. Maxon, eds. *An Economic History of Kenya.* Nairobi, 1992.

Ochieng', William R., ed. *Themes in Kenyan History* (Nairobi, 1990).

Odinga, Oginga. *Not Yet Uhuru.* London, 1967.

Ogot, B. A. *History of the Southern Luo.* Nairobi, 1967.

———, ed. *Kenya Before 1900.* Nairobi, 1976.

———. *Zamani.* New ed. Nairobi, 1974.

Oliver, Roland, and Fagan, B. *Africa in the Iron Age.* Cambridge, 1975.

Oliver, Roland, and Mathew, Gervase, eds. *History of East Africa.* Vol. 1. Oxford, 1963.

Oliver, Roland. *The Missionary Factor in East Africa.* London, 1952.

———. *Sir Harry Johnston and the Scramble for Africa.* London, 1957.

Oliver, Roland, ed. *Cambridge History of Africa.* Vol. 3. Cambridge, 1977.

Perham, Margery. *Lugard: The Years of Adventure.* London, 1956.

Phillipson, D. W. *The Later Prehistory of Eastern and Southern Africa.* New York, 1977.

Polome, Edgar, and Hill, C. P., eds. *Language in Tanzania.* Oxford, 1982.

Pratt, Cranford. *The Critical Phase in Tanzania, 1945-8.* Cambridge, 1976.

Prins, A. H. J. *The Swahili Speaking Peoples of Zanzibar and the East African Coast.* London, 1961.

Richards, A. I., ed. *East African Chiefs.* London, 1960.

Roberts, A. D., ed. *Tanzania Before 1900.* Nairobi, 1968.

Robinson, R. E., Gallagher, J., and Denny, A. *Africa and the Victorians.* London, 1961.

Ross, William McGregor. *Kenya From Within.* 2nd ed. London, 1968.

Rotberg, Robert, and Mazrui, Ali, eds. *Protest and Power in Black Africa.* New York, 1970.

Rotberg, Robert, ed. *Imperialism, Colonialism and Hunger: East and Central Africa.* Lexington, 1983.

Sandbrook, R. *Proletarians and African Capitalism: The Kenyan Case, 1960-72.* Cambridge, 1975.

Schmidt, Peter. *Historical Archaeology.* Westport, 1979.

Shiviji, Issa. *Class Struggles in Tanzania.* New York, 1976.

Sorrenson, M. P. K. *Land Reform in Kikluyu Country.* Nairobi, 1967.

——. *Origins of European Settlement in Kenya.* Nairobi, 1968.

Southall, A. W. *Alur Society.* Cambridge, 1956.

Spear, Thomas. *Kenya's Past.* London, 1981.

Spear, Thomas. *The Kaya Complex.* Nairobi, 1978.

Steinhart, E. *Conflict and Collaboration: The Kingdoms of Western Uganda, 1890-1907.* Princeton, 1977.

Stichter, Sharon. *Migrant Labour in Kenya: Capitalism and African Response.* London, 1982.

Strandes, J. *The Portuguese Period in East Africa.* Nairobi, 1961.

Sutton, J. E. G. *The Archaeology of the Western Highlands of Kenya.* Nairobi, 1973.

Swainson, Nicola. *The Development of Corporate Capitalism in Kenya, 1918-77.* London, 1980.

Thomas, H. B., and Scott, R. *Uganda.* Oxford, 1935.

Throup, David. *Economic and Social Origins of Mau Mau.* London, 1988.

Tignor, Robert. *The Colonial Transformation of Kenya.* Princeton, 1976.

van Zwanenberg, R. M. A. *Colonial Capitalism and Labour in Kenya, 1919-1939.* Nairobi, 1975.

van Zwanenberg, R. M. A., with King, Anne. *An Economic History of Kenya and Uganda, 1800-1970.* Atlantic Highlands, 1975.

Wasserman, Gary. *Politics of Decolonization: Kenya Europeans and the Land Issue.* Cambridge, 1976.

Welboum, F. B. *East African Rebels.* London, 1961.

Were, G. S. *A History of the Abaluyia of Western Kenya.* Nairobi,1967.

White, Luise. *The Comforts of Home.* Chicago, 1990.

Whiteley, W. H. *Swahili: The Rise of a National Language.* London, 1969.

Wilson, Monica. *Good Company: A Study of Nyakusa Age Villages.* Oxford, 1951.

Wolff, Richard. *The Economics of Colonialism.* New Haven, 1974.

Wright, M. *Buganda in the Heroic Age*. Nairobi, 1971.

Wrigley, C. C. *Crops and Wealth in Uganda*. Kampala, 1959.

Yeager, Rodger. *Tanzania: An African Experiment*.2nd Ed. Boulder, 1989.

Glossary of African Terms

abarusura—a standing army, partly made up of mercenaries, established by Mukama Kabarega of Bunyoro-Kitara.

ahoi—tenants-at-will among the Kikuyu.

bakungu—the most powerful chiefs who ruled the largest territories in Bunyoro-Kitara and Nkore.

bataka—traditional clan heads in Buganda who controlled land allocation and were influential in local affairs before the rise of a powerful monarchy

batangole—the lesser chiefs who ruled smaller areas in Bunyoro-Kitara and Nkore.

busulu—traditional labor obligation owed to chiefs in Buganda which was commuted to cash after the inauguration of colonial rule.

euvujo—traditional tribute in produce paid to chiefs in Buganda which was commuted to cash after the inauguration of colonial rule.

gombolola—sub-counties in Buganda.

jago—village chiefs among the Acholi.

kabaka—title of the king of Buganda.

katikiro—chief minister of Buganda.

kipande—Swahili word meaning piece. It came to be used for the registration certificate which all African males were required to carry in Kenya after 1919.

liwali—title given to those appointed by Omani rulers to govern the East African city-states on their behalf.

maji—Swahili word for water.

mbari—sub-clan among the Kikuyu.

moran—young man belonging to the "warrior" age grade among the Maasai.

mugabe—title of the king of Nkore (Ankole).

mukama—title of the kings of Bunyoro-Kitara and Toro.

muramati—locally prominent individual who played a leading role in councils of elders among the Kikuyu.

mwongozo—guidelines for political leaders in Tanzania which were issued in 1971.

ntemi—name given to the relatively small chieftaincies and the chiefs who ruled them in western and central Tanzania.

nyika—Swahili word for desolate wilderness. It is used to refer to the dry hinterland separating the East African coast from the interior plateau, especially in Kenya.

oloiboni—traditional religious leader among the Maasai.

omwami—locally prominent individual who played a leading role in councils of elders among the Luhya.

orkoiyot—Nandi religious and political leadership position which became institutionalized during the nineteenth century.

pororiet—local semi-autonomous unit of government among the Nandi. It was governed by a council of elders.

ruga ruga—name given to roving bands of outlaws and soldiers of fortune in nineteenth-century Tanzania.

ruoth—title of the chief among the Luo of Kenya.

rwot—title for king among the Acholi.

saza—county in Buganda.

shifta—literally means bandit. It was used to refer to Somali separatists in Kenya after 1963 who fought to unite Northeastern Province to the Somali Republic. Thelatha Taifa, Tisa

Taifa—the three tribes and the nine tribes; the traditional divisions of the Swahili population of Mombasa.

uhuru—Swahili word for freedom. It was used by nationalist politicians as a slogan calling for independence from colonial rule.

witong—war leaders who emerged among the Langi in the nineteenth century.

Index